# TRAIL
## OF THE
# LOST

# TRAIL
## OF THE
# LOST

THE RELENTLESS SEARCH
TO BRING HOME THE MISSING HIKERS
OF THE PACIFIC CREST TRAIL

# ANDREA LANKFORD

hachette
BOOKS
*New York*

Hachette Books
Hachette Book Group
1290 Avenue of the Americas
New York, NY 10104
HachetteBooks.com
Twitter.com/HachetteBooks
Instagram.com/HachetteBooks

First Edition: August 2023

Published by Hachette Books, an imprint of Hachette Book Group, Inc. The
Hachette Books name and logo are trademarks of Hachette Book Group, Inc.

The Hachette Speakers Bureau provides a wide range of authors for
speaking events. To find out more, go to hachettespeakersbureau.com or
email HachetteSpeakers@hbgusa.com.

Books by Hachette Books may be purchased in bulk for business,
educational, or promotional use. For information, please contact your
local bookseller or Hachette Book Group Special Markets Department at:
special.markets@hbgusa.com.

The publisher is not responsible for websites (or their content) that are not
owned by the publisher.

Library of Congress Control Number: 2023937975

ISBNs: 9780306831959 (hardcover); 9780306831973 (ebook)

Printed in the United States of America

LSC-C

Printing 4, 2023

# Contents

## PART THREE: FACT AND THEORY

## PART FOUR: WITNESS AND CLUE

# Author's Note

**D**URING THE FOUR YEARS I JOINED FORCES WITH A GROUP OF AMATEUR SEARCHERS looking for three hikers missing along the Pacific Crest Trail, I accumulated over sixty hours of recorded interviews. My files include hundreds of handwritten notes, case reports, news articles, emails, texts, screenshots, and photographs. Quoted dialogue and excerpts of written communications are verbatim, but I've occasionally made minor edits to improve the grammar, and a few statements have been compressed for narrative efficiency. Interior thoughts have been fact-checked with the attributed source. When speculating about things that remain unproven, I forewarn the reader with words such as "I imagine," "perhaps," or "most likely."

In addition to these narrative choices, I've made a few alterations and additions to help guide the reader along their own journey through the book. A few sources asked for their names to be withheld to protect them from online harassment. I have left several others unidentified for the same reason. In terms of geographic reference points, I've included the PCT mileages from the *Pacific Crest Trail Data Book*, fifth edition, published by the Wilderness Press in 2013. The Pacific mountain range known as "the Cascades" spans from California's Mount Lassen to the Fraser River in British

Columbia. In this text, the geographical term "North Cascades" refers to the section within Washington State.

An early trigger warning: this narrative includes reporting on suicide, including a case involving a person who received mental health treatment after attempting to take his own life. If you or someone you love is exhibiting warning signs, help is available and there is hope for recovery. Call the National Suicide Prevention Lifeline at 1-800-273-TALK (8255) and/or seek help from a medical or mental health professional.

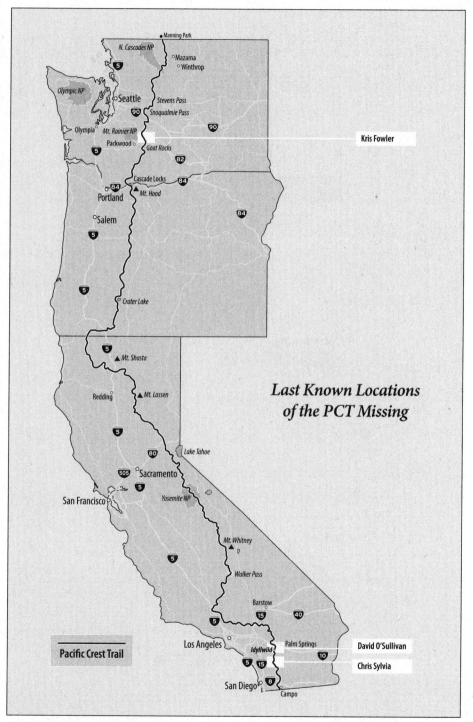

Kris Fowler

Last Known Locations
of the PCT Missing

David O'Sullivan

Chris Sylvia

Pacific Crest Trail

PCT Overview Map. Map by Joe David.

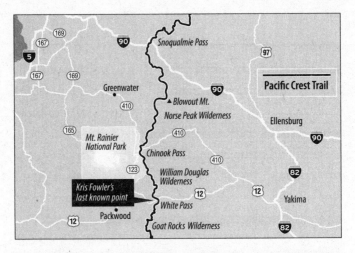

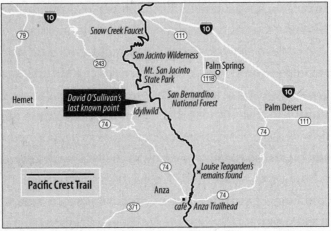

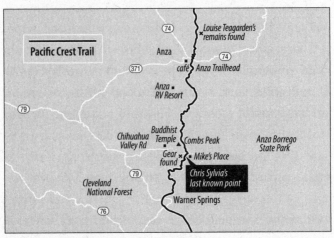

Case Maps of Points Last Seen. Map by Joe David.

# *Introduction*

To GET INSIDE THE HEAD OF THE MISSING YOUNG MAN I'D SET OUT TO FIND, I SAT IN the driver's seat of his abandoned vehicle and studied the interior. Fast-food detritus, dirty clothes, and empty cigarette cartons littered the seats and floorboards. The upholstery was stained. The windows were greasy. I'm a tad fastidious, but in this context, I considered Gabriel Parker's messy habits to be a good thing. Perhaps, like fairy tale children with their breadcrumbs, my lost hiker had left evidence behind in his wake.

It was October 1995. Parker's car was parked at a trailhead near the Grand Canyon's North Rim. I was a thirty-one-year-old supervisory park ranger for the National Park Service (NPS) with a distinguished graduate diploma from the Federal Law Enforcement academy in my file and an impressive number of search and rescue (SAR) missions padding my résumé. Before coming to Arizona, I'd worked in Yosemite Valley, California, one of the busiest search and rescue districts in the world. When it came to locating overdue hikers and plucking them from nature's danger zones, I considered myself experienced.

The tourists paid me no mind as they exited their own cars and hurried toward the cliffs in search of the best view of the sunset before nightfall turned the canyon's orange-reds to purple-black. I spotted a cheap day pack left behind in the back seat and inventoried the contents. When I unzipped an exterior pocket and saw it was filled with crushed cigarettes, I was charmed by the conscientiousness but also disappointed. Parker treated his car like a trash can, but when hiking, he made Woodsy Owl proud. There would not be a trail of discarded cigarette butts leading us to this missing hiker. On the dashboard, positioned in a manner to keep the driver company, sat a beanbag frog with googly eyes. It looked handmade, perhaps a gift from someone who cared about Parker. I made eye contact with the frog. It smiled back at me with a weary grin sewn into its face.

According to the initial report, Gabriel Parker had left his home in Olympia, Washington, on September 15. He was twenty, unemployed, and living in a friend's apartment. "I've got to stand on my own two feet," he said to his roommate before driving away. By the time a park ranger in Arizona noticed Parker's car gathering dust in the trailhead parking lot, it was almost Halloween.

As the operations chief, I was in charge of coordinating and leading the physical search effort to find Parker in collaboration with the planning officer, who, per protocol, took a more cerebral role in helping me delineate and prioritize search areas. Working under the presumption that our subject most likely parked his car and went hiking, the search team focused on the paths that spoked out from Parker's vehicle. During our nightly recap meetings, we discussed all the clues and tips that searchers and investigators brought in and adjusted our search strategy accordingly. One day, for example, a ranger informed me that a cadaver dog had alerted near a cliff top. The next morning, I directed him to scout the bottom of the four-hundred-foot wall of limestone from a helicopter.

He found nothing.

Back inside the command post, I updated the missing man's dad and explained the search process displayed on our maps. We even flew him over the search area in the park helicopter to show him how difficult it can be to find a person lost in a massive park of steep canyons and forested plateaus. A professional searcher should remain impartial and objective during a mission, but once you meet the family, it's nearly impossible to *not* become emotionally invested in reuniting the missing with their loved ones. Over the course of this particular operation, I'd become fond of both Parker and his father, Doug, who showed me the photos that he'd framed from Parker's high school graduation. That night, in my journal, I wrote: *The boy's smile is so genuine. I can't help but like him.*

On day seven, it was time to wind down the search effort. Soon, I would have to hand over the operation to local rangers who would respond to any new leads but discontinue active searching while I returned home to resume my normal duties on the canyon's South Rim. When I informed Parker's father about this impending change in leadership, his body slumped. He knew this meant the NPS would soon call off the search. He also suspected this meant I thought his son was dead.

"It's okay to stop searching." I placed my hand toward him on the conference table, trying to bridge the distance between us. "You've done your best. You've been a good father. Your son would be proud of how hard you've worked to find him."

Doug looked away. His voice cracked, releasing a feeble sob. "I don't know what else to do."

I didn't know what else to do either. I believed we had done all we could at that point. And Parker wasn't the only visitor we needed to consider. The Grand Canyon is a busy and dangerous park. The rangers are understaffed and overworked. Every day we kept searching for Parker was another day we were taking limited resources away from rescuing others who could be saved.

When I left, the helicopter ferrying me to the other side of a mile-wide canyon was juggling calls—a cardiac emergency in the village and a gunshot wound to the head near a campground. I climbed into the front seat and nodded to a canine team sitting in the back.

The dog had been discharged from the incident just as I had, and his handler looked as glum as I felt. We were in the air, halfway across the canyon's abyss, when the planning officer called me over the radio. Through the earphones in my flight helmet, I heard him say, "Doug [the father] wants to thank you for all your hard work."

The helmet's dark visor concealed my regret. I hadn't found Parker. I had, in a sense, given up. I did not deserve to be thanked.

Parker's case taunted me like a critic. If only I had been more competent and caring, if only I had done my due diligence, if only I'd directed my rangers to search one more cliff bottom—maybe then we would have found him. This is the searcher's burden, and the weight is heaviest when the subject remains lost. It's hard enough for a professional searcher tasked with solving the case; if the searcher is a parent of the missing, well, then the strain becomes unbearable.

Eventually, many months later, we did find Parker. By accident. Two maintenance workers surveying a remote pipeline ran across Parker's body at the base of a three-hundred-foot escarpment of iron-stained limestone known as the Redwall. A small amount of cannabis was tucked among his belongings. There was no note, but my colleagues concluded that the young man must have hiked down the trail to an isolated precipice and jumped. He was likely dead before we started looking for him.

When another ranger filled me in on these details, I thought about what little I knew of Parker, from Doug's proud graduation photos to the smiling frog left behind in his car. I didn't want to believe Parker had been suicidal. Instead, I suspected that the twenty-year-old had sat on a ledge and smoked a joint. Then, as he got up to leave, he lost his balance. "He was stoned while taking in the beauty of the Grand Canyon," I explained. "He would have hit the ground before he knew what happened to him."

The other ranger looked at me as if I'd gone soft.

But that's my theory. And I'm sticking to it.

Three years later, the responsibilities I had shouldered as a first responder for an underfunded agency outweighed the benefits. In 1999, I left the NPS. Stressed and sad by my decision to abandon a profession that once felt like a calling, I first sought solace by hiking the Appalachian Trail. Then I wrote a few books, returned to school, and became a registered nurse. But twelve years as a park ranger was enough to forever tarnish my love of the great outdoors.

I know what really happens behind the scenery. Too many times, I came across menacing individuals in the woods who were doing things they shouldn't be doing. Too many times, I witnessed what nature's wrath can inflict upon a human body. Despite the ever-growing sprawl of civilization and the advent of smartphones, the American wilderness is still vast and treacherous. There are dozens of ways to die out there, hundreds of parks and forests to get lost in, and a million places that can easily conceal a corpse. I'm never shocked when someone disappears from a trail. But when our rescue teams can't track down a body—despite all the bloodhounds, ground searchers, and technology—it still bugs the *hell* out of me.

As a former park ranger well acquainted with nature's temper tantrums, I'm often approached by filmmakers mining for a story or journalists looking for a quote about our national parks—especially when a park visitor dies or goes missing. In early 2017, producers developing a television series about lost hikers asked me to conduct some research for possible episodes. One that stood out to me was an odd case involving a young man named Chris Sylvia who had vanished from the renowned Pacific Crest Trail (PCT) in California. The subject—twenty-eight, unemployed, and living in a friend's apartment—reminded me instantly of Gabriel Parker. In February 2015, hikers had discovered Chris Sylvia's gear discarded alongside the trail, but even after fifty professional searchers—some with dogs, some from the air—searched the area for five days, they found no sign of the missing hiker.

Even so, the lost hiker's gear *had* been found and that intrigued me. When I advised the television producers that the Sylvia case was unique, compelling, and logistically practical (from Los Angeles, you could drive to his last known point in less than three hours), a production assistant contacted Chris's family and asked them if they'd participate in interviews for the show. A few months later, however, the episode about Chris was dropped. The producers moved on to other projects, but I couldn't let it go.

An unsolved case is a loose end that begs us to snip it. When I first heard about Chris Sylvia in 2017, it had been nearly two decades since I'd left the NPS, and I was entrenched in my second career as a nurse, crucial work that consumed a great deal of my time and energy. But a compassionate impulse compelled me to call Chris's mother, ask for her blessing to conduct a pro bono investigation in my spare time, and promise to get her some answers.

Right off the bat, I learned something disturbing. Chris Sylvia was the first of three thru-hikers (someone attempting to "hike through" the entire route in one year) who had recently vanished from the PCT. In October 2016, Kris "Sherpa" Fowler, thirty-four, had also gone missing the day after he entered Washington's North Cascades, a more northern stretch of the trail. Then, six months later, a twenty-five-year-old from Ireland, David O'Sullivan, hiked into California's San Jacinto Mountains on April 7, 2017, and was never seen again. Three missing hikers. All unmarried young men. One each year. Three years in a row. From the same footpath. And numerous searches for all three of them had failed. This cluster of unsolved disappearances on the PCT struck me as uncanny and unprecedented. Were the cases somehow connected?

The PCT travels 2,650 miles from Mexico to Canada and the people who hike it face a constellation of perils. From a statistical perspective, you could argue that hiking the PCT is safer than driving to work, but in the last forty years, as of December 2022, sixteen thru-hikers have died while trekking the PCT, and I consider that a significant number. The most ruthless assassin on this trail is water in its various forms; four thru-hikers have plummeted to their deaths after slipping off an icy slope, two drowned while crossing a bloated stream, and one hiker succumbed to high-altitude pulmonary edema (an accumulation of fluid in the lungs triggered by a too rapid ascent in altitude). On the flip side, a lack of water was an accomplice in the three deaths by heat stroke. Two hikers fell off steep sections of the trail. A car hit another pair of hikers who were walking along a road, killing them both. The remaining two were victims of a falling tree and hypothermia (assumed). As devastating as these cases may be, at least we know what killed these hikers—because their bodies were found.

At first, I surmised that Chris Sylvia, Kris Fowler, and David O'Sullivan—I call them "the PCT Missing"—must have joined the long list of nature's casualties, but the fact that their bodies hadn't been recovered nagged at me. After all, Mother Nature is not the only killer lurking along our trails. In addition to the lions, snakes, and bears inhabiting the PCT, there are liars, con artists, and thieves. The trail has also been the stomping ground of at least one kidnapper, a rapist or two, dozens of ill-tempered cannabis farmers, some homicidal maniacs, and a cult.

What happened to the PCT Missing? Where are they? And why can't anyone find their bodies? In 2017, I embarked on a lengthy quest to answer these and other questions. During my investigation, I met others who were likewise hell-bent on solving this puzzle. I soon partnered up with a dedicated group of amateur searchers—working with them as much as writing about them—and, before long, we became trusted collaborators and friends. We also became obsessed, each in our own way, until our dogged pursuit for answers jeopardized our livelihoods, our mental stamina, and our health.

Our little search party messed up plenty along the way, but we also accomplished more than I expected. Today, our maps are marked up with convoluted webs connecting dozens of tantalizing leads—cell phone pings, discarded gear, wrecked cars, dubious sightings, novels with underlined passages, bleached bones, and a bloody sock. Because of these volunteers, three families learned what happened to their missing loved ones. Also, because of these volunteers, my left ankle needed one titanium plate and five screws.

What follows is a true story of determination, generosity, and hope—both false and real. It is also a cautionary tale. On the trail of the lost, you may not find what you're searching for, but you will find more than you seek.

# TRAIL
## OF THE
# LOST

# PART ONE
# POINTS LAST SEEN

CHAPTER 1

# An Antidote to
# the Ills of Civilization

M AGNIFICENT IDEAS OFTEN ARISE IN THE PLACES THAT WE LEAST EXPECT, AND THE Pacific Crest Trail is no exception. The first mention of developing a wilderness footpath across the mountainous crest of the Pacific Coast states occurred nearly a hundred years ago—in a basement—where, on or about January 13, 1926, teaching supervisor Catherine Montgomery had to endure a sales pitch from Joseph Hazard, a famed mountaineer who sold textbooks.

Thanks to the diligent research of PCT hiker Barney "Scout" Mann, we know this fateful meeting happened in an underground office on the campus of what is now Western Washington University in Bellingham, Washington, inside a room that I imagine had no windows. Montgomery, a lover of the outdoors and self-described "tramper," was the type of woman who would rather be hiking a trail or bagging a peak than listening to Hazard's speech. But choosing the right textbooks for the school year was among Miss Montgomery's duties as a founding faculty member, so the Canadian-born American waited patiently for the mountain-climbing salesman to finish his spiel before getting to the business that was foremost on her mind.

"Do you know what I have been thinking about, Mr. Hazard, for the last twenty minutes?"

"I had hoped you were considering the merits of my presentation of certain English texts for adoption!"

"Oh that! Before your call I had considered them the best....I still do! But why do not you mountaineers do something big for Western America?"

"Just what did you have in mind, Miss Montgomery?"

"A high trail winding down the heights of our western mountains with mile markers and shelter huts—like these pictures I'll show you of the 'Long Trail of the Appalachians'—from the Canadian border to the Mexican Boundary Line!"

Joseph Hazard documented this pivotal conversation in his book *Pacific Crest Trails*, published in 1946. The "Long Trail of the Appalachians" refers to a magazine article Montgomery had been reading about a marvelous trek being developed in the East called the Appalachian Trail. The way Montgomery saw it, the American West deserved its own long-distance footpath, and, incidentally, Hazard agreed. That night, he shared the teacher's thoughts with members of the Mount Baker Club (a recreational group of mountaineering enthusiasts) and the seed was planted. But for Montgomery's idea to flourish, the PCT needed someone to bear the torch—a tireless crusader with romantic notions, political connections, free time, and lots of money—to guide the project, and that person was Clinton C. Clarke.

Hiking clubs up and down the West Coast had toyed with the concept for years before it sparked an obsession inside Clarke's brain, compelling the Boy Scout leader to design a footpath "along the summit divides of the mountain ranges" in California, Oregon, and Washington. At the time, in 1932, the United States was suffering through the Great Depression and Clarke was fifty-nine years old. The Harvard grad's youthful days of rambling up High Sierra passes with a pack on his back and a spoon in his cap were over, but, thanks to family money, he could huddle over maps inside his posh hotel room in Pasadena, California, while piecing together long segments of existing trails to create a spectacular route that would "traverse the best scenic areas" while maintaining "an absolute wilderness character." To achieve this ambitious goal, Clarke needed help corralling a cat herd of government bureaucracies, influential partners, wealthy benefactors, and private landowners. He circled the wagons by forming the Pacific Crest Trail System Conference, an organization uniting numerous government agencies and sympathetic groups, including the Boy Scouts of America, the Sierra Club, and the YMCA. For decades, Clarke cajoled, pressured, and publicized—spending his own money to print twelve thousand promotional pamphlets and producing a set of maps of the proposed trail that, when laid out on the floor, was sixty-five feet long.

Montgomery's lofty idea and Clarke's fevered passion didn't become a reality, on paper, until the National Trail Systems Act of 1968 designated two routes, the Appalachian Trail (AT) and the Pacific Crest Trail, as the United States' first national scenic trails. Fast-forward fifty years and, today, out of thousands of trails, the PCT (2,650 miles) and the AT (2,200 miles) are arguably the most revered long-distance footpaths in the United States, if not the world.

Neither of the PCT's earliest champions ever saw the fruits of their shared dream come to pass. And as far as we know, the pair never met in person. But one can hope Montgomery and Clarke enjoyed a hike together in the hereafter, because the two departed this earth during the same year, within months of one another, in 1957.

Thirteen years after Montgomery and Clarke died, and two years after the PCT became official in 1968, Eric Ryback, an

eighteen-year-old with a "relentless drive to follow routes unknown
to other men," set out to trek the entire PCT in one continuous journey. Seeking "accomplishment, adventure, solitude, [and] freedom,"
Ryback carried an eighty-pound pack and chose to walk the route
southbound from Canada to Mexico, starting on June 10, 1970. The
eighteen-year-old was experienced for his age—he had already
completed the AT the year before—when he entered the wilderness longing "for the isolation and purity of nature," but icy slopes,
cutting winds, unruly wildfires, and knee-slicing rocks battered
Ryback's innocence "into cunning," his trust "into watchfulness
and suspicion," and his "misanthropic yearnings... [were] exposed
as foolish and untenable." No doubt, by the end of Ryback's "struggle for survival," the trail had taught the young man a thing or two.
"I had lost innocence," he concluded as he neared the Southern Terminus at the Mexican border, "but I had found respect—respect
for myself, respect for nature, respect for humanity." A year later,
in 1971, he published a book about his achievement, the earliest
recorded thru-hike of the Pacific Crest Trail. *The High Adventure of
Eric Ryback* sold over three hundred thousand copies, making the
first PCT memoir a bestseller.

Despite the success of Ryback's book, the PCT continued to play
second fiddle to the AT, its shorter, but more celebrated, sister in the
East for decades. That is, until recently. Today, the Pacific Crest Trail
Association (PCTA) estimates that over a million people (including
day hikers, backpackers, horse packers, hunters, and fishermen)
visit the PCT every year. Some attribute the sudden increase in the
PCT's popularity to what they call "the *Wild* effect"—a reference to
Cheryl Strayed's memoir, *Wild: From Lost to Found on the Pacific Crest
Trail*, which was published in 2012. Like Ryback's swashbuckling
account, Strayed's moving story of a flawed, grieving young woman
seeking spiritual and personal growth on the PCT hit a nerve with
readers around the world. Since the release of the movie based on
*Wild* in 2014, PCT thru-hike attempts have quadrupled, forcing the

need for a permit system to manage the number of hikers on the trail. According to statistics collected by the PCTA, 1,879 people requested a permit to thru-hike the PCT in 2013. Six years later, in 2019, the association issued a whopping 7,888 permits. "There are a lot of Strayeds out there" is how one veteran thru-hiker described the situation, referring to the influx of broken souls with no outdoor experience seeking redemption on the PCT.

The way *Wild* inspired a whole new demographic of dilettantes to thru-hike the PCT still irks some veteran enthusiasts, but I suspect Facebook, Instagram, and YouTube are equally responsible for the expanding range of personalities responding to the trail's siren call. The naïveté displayed online by these wannabe thru-hikers at the start of the hiking season is often so earnest, it's painful. Lots of newbie questions. Lots of angst over transportation, gear, and mail drops. Plenty of misplaced fears. Before March, their five-month adventure to hike across three large states is a mere fantasy populated with idealistic notions and unrealistic goals. And yet, no matter how long an aspiring thru-hiker studies the guidebooks, no matter how many times they pack and repack their gear, the reality of a PCT thru-hike will surprise them *every time*. That's why a substantial percentage of thru-hikers fail and fail quickly. Hundreds quit within the first week. Dozens on the first day. Most of them suffer an injury at some point. And occasionally, someone even dies or goes missing.

The internet's tentacle reach into hiker culture would astonish the likes of Montgomery and Clarke. And I imagine, they—alongside their fellow twentieth-century conservationists—would feel an uneasy mixture of satisfaction and dismay to see the sheer number of humans one now encounters in the backcountry. The growing hordes of novice (and occasionally uncouth) hikers flooding the wilderness have disenchanted a few modern trail enthusiasts as well.

"There used to be only hikers on the trail," one of them lamented to me in 2019. "Now, it's all of humanity."

A Scripps College art student, Jenn Livermore, explored this friction in her senior thesis, "The Pacific Crest Trail: A History of America's Relationship with Western Wilderness." According to Livermore, Clinton Clarke originally envisioned the PCT as "an antidote to the ills of an overly refined and civilized modern world"; his Depression-era writings make it clear that he was not designing a playground for the "soft and flabby" or the "casual camper and hiker": Clarke was creating a 2,600-mile path for the "true wilderness lover," a primitive route where a man like Ryback could test his mettle against the landscape, a winding trek through forty-four wilderness areas and eleven mountain ranges, a self-reliant odyssey on foot that eschewed the trappings of civilized conveniences. Clarke's "untrammeled by man" wilderness ethos also set the course for how the PCT would be built and managed. On this western trail, adventure seekers could experience nature in its rawest form. The few rugged comforts hikers appreciated on the AT, such as three-sided huts for shelter and frequent trail blazes to mark the way, would not be a part of the PCT experience.

Clarke's ascetic dream for the PCT continues to guide trail management policies on public lands in the West to this day, but modern hikers tend to be a more relaxed, open-minded, and encouraging breed. "A far cry from Clarke's exclusive vision," Livermore writes in her insightful thesis, "there is a new 'everyone can do it' mentality about hiking the trail." The memoir *Wild* and the reaction to it represent this shift in attitude. Strayed's "experience was not so much about a desire to experience pristine wilderness," Livermore muses, "as it was a personal quest for self-reflection."

These changing values, along with increasing use levels, magnify the pressure on agencies like the NPS and the United States Forest Service (USFS) as they attempt to protect the public while also preserving the natural environment. The inherent conflict between these mandates is compounded by a "mountains without handrails" credo subscribed to by wilderness managers and the rose-colored glasses many hopeful hikers appear to be looking through; the trail is now seen as less a test and more a cure, and Strayed's lack of hiking prowess when she embarked on her thru-hike is viewed as inspiring as opposed to foolhardy. *If a struggling young woman with no backpacking experience can thru-hike the PCT,* some of her readers seem to conclude, *so can I.*

Alas, beginner's optimism can take us only so far. Less than 12 percent of wannabe thru-hikers will successfully trek the PCT's entire length in one go. Even Strayed fell short of this goal. Although her overall feat is impressive, Strayed hiked less than half of it, skipping the High Sierra and making it only as far as the Oregon border with Washington. Regardless of your experience level, committing five to six months of your life to hike 2,650 miles involves sacrifices that most can't fulfill. Family and friends must be left behind. Careers have to be put on hold. Money is spent that "should" go to investments considered more "sensible." Routine comforts like running water, comfy beds, and shelter from the elements are given up. On top of all these impediments, add injuries, fatigue, and homesickness to the long list of things eroding one's dedication to completing the trail.

Ultimately, it's an arduous journey requiring strength and fortitude, and, although gender ratios are leveling, most thru-hikers have been men. Yet, the first person known to have disappeared while hiking along the PCT corridor was not.

Born in 1920, Louise Teagarden was a nonconforming nature lover who preferred long tramps in the desert over party dresses. In 1949, she moved from the Los Angeles area to Ribbonwood, California— a pit stop along Highway 74, west of Palm Springs, and about five road miles east of the PCT. This remote corner of Southern California suited Teagarden, whose "solo walkabouts" had long been a source of anxiety for her family.

Ten years later, at the age of thirty-nine, Teagarden was reeling from a series of tough breaks. Her girlfriend (an amateur archaeologist) had moved away, her father and sister had died, and Teagarden's ailing mother needed her daughter's help. That winter, on December 17, 1959, Teagarden told a friend she was driving to Hemet, California, to do some Christmas shopping. We'll never know if she actually drove to Hemet or if "the shopping trip" was a ruse, because Louise Teagarden never came home.

Growing uneasy, a friend went searching for Teagarden and discovered her car parked on a remote dirt road near an access path leading to what is now the PCT—about four miles north, as the crow flies, of the Anza Trailhead, where Chris Sylvia later began his hike. The friend noticed that Teagarden had emptied the radiator and placed the cap on the driver's seat. This act, a wise practice before the use of antifreeze, implied Teagarden planned to return to her car. At first, few were concerned. Teagarden, who was described by some as "moody," often spent weeks alone in the wilderness. But then the weeks turned into months, and the months turned into years.

"When Auntie Louise disappeared, it was hush-hush," Teagarden's niece told a reporter years afterward. "Nobody in the family wanted to talk about it," and before long, people forgot about the missing tomboy with the long dark braids.

Three decades later, in 1991, hikers exploring a shallow cave about two miles from the PCT stumbled upon a human skeleton inside a sleeping bag—a skeleton the authorities suspected could belong to the missing Teagarden. Upon closer inspection, the bones showed no signs of trauma, which furthered the theory that it could be Teagarden, who was athletic and knew the area so well she had drawn her own maps. The coroner also noted that the deceased's teeth were stained in a manner suggesting the person had been foraging on seeds prior to her death, mirroring the diets of local indigenous people centuries prior.

Because her closest relatives were deceased, authorities identified the remains by comparing a known sample of Teagarden's handwriting to notes left behind on papers that were lying about the campsite; it was a match. A calendar with crossed-out dates suggested she had died on February 20, 1960—four days after her fortieth birthday and two months after she was last seen alive.

In 2009, Ann Japenga wrote an article about Teagarden's story called "Lost and Found," which was published in *The Sierra Club*. After investigating the case thoroughly, the writer from Palm Springs speculated that the missing hiker may have been heartbroken after her girlfriend moved away and dreading the responsibility of caring for her dying mother. But Japenga believes Louise Teagarden wasn't "running away; she was going toward something." Toward solitude. Toward independence. Toward the beauty of the backcountry.

"The last things she would have seen before she died were stone pools full of snowmelt and dense thickets of cholla cactus wearing halos in the low winter light," Japenga muses. Even so, "no one knows what her last days were like. Maybe she was freezing, fevered, or depressed. She may have regretted many things about her life but going to the mountains was probably not one of them."

Louise Teagarden may have been the first of the trail's casualties, but she wasn't the last. Over the next fifty-five years, thousands of aspiring thru-hikers would attempt the PCT. A few of them went missing for hours or days, and one wasn't found for months, but eventually, all of these ill-fated adventurers were tracked down and their cases were closed.

That is, until 2015, when Chris Sylvia disappeared.

# CHAPTER 2

# Without Compass:
# The Case of Chris Sylvia

## MISSING PERSON
## Christopher Stephen Sylvia

| MISSING SINCE: | 02/16/2015 | SEX: | Male |
|---|---|---|---|
| DOB: | 12/12/1986 | RACE: | White |
| HEIGHT: | 5' 9" | EYES: | Hazel |
| WEIGHT: | 155 lbs. | HAIR: | Brown |
| CLOTHING: | Camouflage pants, poly shirts and brown and black hiking boots | | |
| DENTAL X-RAYS AVAILABLE: | Yes | | |

Christopher Sylvia was last seen on February 16, 2015.

## Contact

| AGENCY: | San Diego County Sheriff's Department |
|---|---|
| PHONE NUMBER: | |
| CASE NUMBER: | 15109721 |

*In February 2015, twenty-eight-year-old Chris Sylvia disappeared near PCT mile 127. Public domain via the California Department of Justice.*

**A**CCEPT.
Learn.
Let go.

Wise advice from three palm-sized Chinese symbols tattooed on the left side of Chris Sylvia's torso. Unfortunately, accepting, learning, and letting go are always easier said than done, and when you're twenty-eight, broke, unemployed, practically homeless, and nursing a heart twice broken, it can seem damn near impossible.

In early 2015, Chris was living with his longtime friend, Min Kim, in Vista, California. Min and Chris were like brothers; they grew up together near Baltimore, Maryland, and were best friends in high school. They had coached each other through sad times and often traveled together. Artistic types, they also both painted.

Min, a cook, went to California first, with Chris following in his footsteps and moving into the same apartment not long after. When Chris first arrived, Min helped him get a job at the same restaurant, but he soon lost it. The two shared their apartment with a third roommate, a cute blonde woman named Elizabeth Henle. On the rebound after breaking up with his long-term girlfriend in Maryland, Chris fell for Elizabeth, but like the job, the new romance didn't last long. Unemployed and twice rejected, Chris partied away his disappointments, while a harried Min worked even harder to pay the rent on time. With Chris caught between one roommate who didn't want him the way he wanted her and another who resented having to support him financially, the tension in their apartment grew thick.

By early 2015, Min thought Chris should split for a while and give everyone some much needed space. Go for a solo hike of the PCT, he suggested. Soak in some desert silence. Get your head straightened out.

The PCT is lonely in February, and Chris preferred to backpack with friends, but Min's advice made sense. Winters were mild in Southern California. On February 12—the day Chris first stepped foot on the PCT at the Anza Trailhead and headed south toward the Mexican border—the weather was perfect.

Min loaned Chris some gear and gave him something to read. Chris—who hated computers and didn't own a cell phone—stuffed the book in his pack, along with a fifth of vodka and a flip-style cell phone he'd borrowed from Elizabeth. In exchange for the phone, Chris left her his "lucky" compass. "Don't think you're keeping it," he wrote in a flirtatious note to Elizabeth, "because I'm coming back for it."

At the trailhead, the parting of best friends was routine, their plans for reuniting loose. The section Chris intended to hike first was 152 miles long and would take a couple of weeks to complete. If all went well, when Chris reached the Mexican border at Campo, he might do what thru-hikers call "a yo-yo" by turning around and hiking in the opposite direction—north—all the way to Canada.

But things didn't go well. Or maybe Chris just got lonely. The twenty-six-mile section between Highway 74 and Chihuahua Valley Road travels through a stark, high-desert landscape with lots of prickly plants but few water sources and, as far as we know, Chris encountered no one while hiking it. On February 16, only four days into what was supposed to be at least a two-week trip, he called Min asking to be picked up and brought home. At the start of their conversation, Chris was upbeat, even though he'd made a big change in plans. "Dude, I've got so many stories to tell you. I've found this awesome temple! Pick me up there, tomorrow."

Min was not pleased. For starters, Chris had called early in the morning while he was getting ready for work. Plus, the drive from Vista to the PCT would take several hours. Min had to pull a shift the same evening that Chris wanted a ride home. *He's been on the trail for only four days*, Min thought, *and now he's expecting me to drop everything and pick him up?*

The tone of their brief conversation went south, like brothers annoyed with one another's antics. In the end, Min reluctantly agreed. "Fine, I'll pick you up."

In return, Chris let Min know he did not appreciate his attitude.

As promised, the next morning, Min arrived at the Buddhist monastery. The temple was cool and a little spooky at the same time. But the place was also deserted, and Chris was completely AWOL. Min waited several hours before he had to go if he was going to make it back in time for his shift. He assumed Chris was still angry from their phone call and, in an ultimate "fuck you, man," move, decided to continue hiking south per the original plan.

Still, something about the whole thing left Min feeling uneasy. A week later, when Min had not heard from Chris and all of his calls to the flip phone remained unanswered, he called the authorities and reported his friend missing.

# CHAPTER 3

# The Things They Carry

THE SOUTHERN CALIFORNIA STRETCH OF THE PCT THAT SITS BETWEEN WARNER Springs and the Anza Trailhead runs forty-one desolate miles between two rural highways, State Routes 79 and 74. Despite the long views of barren ridges, the meanderings through fields of strange boulders, and the occasional funky cactus, this isn't the most scenic section, but it was a convenient place for a trail hopeful named Eric Trockman, who lived in nearby Temecula, to test out his equipment for three days before he began his PCT thru-hike for real.

On February 20, 2015, four days after the contentious call between Chris and Min, Trockman hiked north from Warner Springs. Eighteen miles later, his calves feeling sore, he came across something "a little peculiar." Another hiker's stuff—a yellow and silver ground pad, a blue sleeping bag, a backpack, a tarp, and a pair of trekking poles—was lying next to the trail, as if the owner might return at any moment. Trockman assumed the hiker must be out looking for water or going to the bathroom or trying to find cell service. But, in case there was more to it than that, he snapped a picture of the gear with his phone. The photo recorded the time and date of this fateful encounter: February 20, 2015, at 2:15 p.m.

After he got home, Trockman logged online and clicked his way to PCT Class of 2015, a Facebook group of about three thousand members that consisted of that year's thru-hikers (and their fans). Trockman had posted a handful of tips in the past (even advising fellow hikers that "Loose stuff in the pack is annoying, get more Ziplocs/stuff sacks"), but he learned as much from the group as he shared with them. On the twenty-fifth, however, Trockman read an unsettling post that reminded him of the abandoned gear he'd seen a few days earlier. A 2015 PCT hiker had gone missing. The lost man was twenty-eight, the same age as Trockman, and he'd disappeared from the same section Eric had hiked—except Chris Sylvia had walked it in the opposite direction. Trockman shared his photo of the abandoned gear in the Facebook thread and provided his name and phone number to search and rescue, but no one interviewed him about what he'd seen until I called two years later.

When I first spoke to Trockman over the phone, he told me he felt guilty about this. Perhaps he should have made more of a fuss when he first saw Chris Sylvia's belongings.

"Hikers find weird stuff all the time!" I reassured him. "You took a picture. That's more than I might have done, and I'm a former law enforcement officer."

A few weeks before I called Trockman, I came across a Reddit post published in February 2017 by Chris Sylvia's oldest sibling. Still haunted by the TV series episode on Sylvia that never aired, I'd kept tabs on the case and was saddened to see that little progress— if any—had been made in finding the lost hiker. "This month my brother will have been missing for two years" is how Joshua Sylvia introduced a thread he had created on the second anniversary of his brother's disappearance. In an attempt to stir up interest in the case, Joshua made himself available to answer any questions a would-be sleuth might have. "Hopefully the chance of him being a John Doe isn't too high. I was able to track down his dental records. And DNA was taken from our mom."

I winced. *That's so heartbreaking.* Then, as I scrolled through the entire thread, I came across this comment:

"I was contacted not long ago about a pilot that is being put together for A&E about missing hikers," Sylvia's brother informed the Redditors. "If all goes according to plan, my mother and I should be getting flown to California this summer."

Reading this stirred something in me. Joshua had misplaced his hope for resolution on Hollywood attention, but because I'd been involved in the project's early development, I knew the television producers had since moved on. I surmised that no one had informed the family of this outcome, so a few days later, I contacted Joshua to let him know the show wasn't happening. Then I called his mother, Nancy Warman, who thanked me for taking an interest in her son's disappearance, and I made that promise to get her some answers.

Six weeks later, on November 6, 2017, I was at the Paradise Valley Café near Anza, California, waiting for Eric Trockman to join me for breakfast. He arrived looking every bit the part of a veteran PCT thru-hiker—wearing modern khaki attire, a neatly trimmed beard, and an agreeable disposition. After a brief greeting, I cut to the chase ("I want to know more about the gear!") and shoved my coffee out of the way so I could spread out a topographical map on the table between us. Then I pointed to the Anza Trailhead on State Route 74, one mile east of us. From there, I moved my finger southbound along a dashed line representing the PCT. When I hit Chihuahua Valley Road, I stopped. "Is this where you found it?"

"Yes," Trockman confirmed. "About a four-minute walk south of that road."

After I finished my brandied French toast, we left the Paradise Valley Café and headed to the spot where Trockman last saw Chris Sylvia's gear. Once we were in the vicinity, we consulted a color copy of the photo he'd taken that I'd printed out and brought along until we located a unique rock verifying the exact location. Across the trail, I noticed a small cross constructed from reclaimed wood and rusty nails. The unnamed rustic memorial had since collapsed. I picked it up and hammered it back into the ground with a stone.

Our experience as thru-hikers led Trockman and me to the same conclusion. The Sylvia gear site was not a camping spot. With its lack of shade, rocky surface, and awkward angle, it wasn't even a tempting location for a long break. What the site *did* offer, however, was an advantageous view of Chihuahua Valley Road. You could watch a vehicle coming from a mile or more away and have time to trot back to the trail before the car passed. Even so, this hitchhiking method would test one's patience. We only saw one other car on that road the entire time we were there.

We climbed a hill behind the gear site to check for cell service. To our east, the Anza-Borrego Desert stretched out below the PCT, which meandered high above ridges covered with shrubs typical of California chaparral, a semiarid landscape of chamise and manzanita that grow thick and scratchy but rarely higher than your head. At the top, we could see for miles in every direction. The PCT was identifiable as was Chihuahua Valley Road and other landmarks.

Unable to find cell service, we reconnected with the trail and hiked south. A five-minute walk from the gear site brought us to a handmade sign welcoming hikers to a hostel known as Mike's Place. Years ago, Mike Herrera bought a patch of land on an isolated ridge east of the PCT and built himself a man-cave getaway. A big fan of the trail and its hikers, Herrera invited the travelers to fill up their canteens from a water tank on his property. He also encouraged them to camp on his homesite. This act of charity had earned Mike the title of "trail angel"—a generous person who supports a thru-hiker's journey in various ways, such as by giving them free rides, food, or lodging. Up to a hundred backpackers visited his hostel each day during peak hiking season. To handle the demand,

Herrera had hired caretakers to live at his compound. His hospitality was genuine, but his hostel had a mixed reputation, causing some to avoid it. As one hiker told me, "I don't stop at Mike's; it's too much of a party atmosphere."

At the sign, we turned off the PCT and continued to the compound past the metal water tank. Red plastic cups in the bushes hinted at the vibe—part desert rat, part rowdy frat house. On the back patio of the ranch-style home, the caretaker, a guy in his thirties with a shaved head and a bushy goatee, catered to three young women thru-hiking south. When Eric and I joined them, the caretaker greeted us. "What brings the two of you here?"

It was apparent by our gear—or lack thereof—that we weren't thru-hiking.

"I'm looking into the case of the young man who went missing from the trail near here," I answered. "Do you know anything about it?"

"And what do *you* know about it?" The caretaker's hostility made me flinch.

"I'm working with the family, and I know his gear was found less than a ten-minute walk from here..."

"He didn't make it here."

The abrupt certainty of this statement made me apprehensive. To soften the tension, I introduced myself and mentioned Chris Sylvia's family would be grateful for any help he could provide. The caretaker identified himself as Josh McCoy. When I asked to see the 2015 trail register (a logbook in which hikers write the dates they passed through a particular site), McCoy got up from his plastic chair, pulled a dusty composition notebook from an outdoor shelf, and handed it to me.

"This register begins in April," I said, flipping through the pages. "I need to see the one from February and March."

"Are any pages torn out of it?" Again, McCoy's tone seemed to be accusing me of something.

*Damn, this guy is as suspicious of me as I am of him.* "No, it's intact. There must be an earlier one."

McCoy denied there were any more trail registers for 2015.

I doubted this, but prying information out of McCoy was like shucking oysters with a nail file. Everything came out in sharp bits. Apparently, Chris's toiletries had not been in the pack. Mountain lions had been heard howling right around the same time he'd disappeared. Search and Rescue had based their operations at Mike's Place. The scent dogs had searched everywhere. McCoy himself had checked every nook and cranny, but the only thing he'd found was a blue denim jacket with a fake wool liner.

I made note of his description of the jacket, but I believed McCoy had more info to give. "You must know this area better than anyone," I said. "Do you have a theory?"

"Hmm…" Obviously, a scenario came to mind, but before he could utter it, McCoy pressed his lips together, effectively clamping his mouth shut. With body language so startlingly closed off, this guy seemed increasingly dubious.

At that same moment, some new visitors arrived, and McCoy left us alone on the porch to greet them. While Trockman distracted the female thru-hikers with small talk, I walked over to where McCoy had retrieved the trail register, pulled out all the notebooks, and scanned the dates. *I knew it!* There was a register with entries dated in late February and early March 2015. I snapped pictures of those pages with my cell phone and quietly returned the notebooks to the shelf.

We left soon after.

On the drive back to Trockman's car, I asked him what he thought about my exchange with the caretaker.

I'd been too direct in my questioning, he said, "but that guy was definitely hiding something."

Back at my rental cabin in Warner Springs, I mulled over the day's events. Perhaps McCoy had sensed the authoritative park ranger that would forever be a part of me. That's what the encounter with him had felt like—all those times I'd stood in front of some sketchy-looking dude who would rather chew nails than talk to a woman in uniform. But on the trail, perhaps more than anywhere, appearances can be deceiving.

There's a term seasoned trail experts use—"hiker trash"—that refers to how the uninitiated often confuse weather-beaten, disheveled, skinny-as-a-rail thru-hikers with more worrisome types like ne'er-do-wells, escaped convicts, and meth addicts. It's a taxonomic challenge, not unlike separating a poisonous mushroom from a batch of edible ones, but as experienced hikers will tell you, tiny details can help you distinguish friend from foe on the trail. Here's a hint: pay close attention to the things they carry.

Needing an unbiased sounding board for my theories, I called my husband, a former Secret Service agent who was now a Special Agent in Charge for the United States Forest Service. I'd met Kent Delbon in 1993, back when we were both law enforcement rangers at Yosemite. Working together had stoked our early romance, but Kent was now holed up at our Denver apartment while I was out alone in the backiest-backwoods of Southern California. Always the more sensible one, Kent reminded me there was no cell service at Mike's Place. "Returning to a remote locale to interrogate a potential suspect without backup could be dangerous," he warned.

"Like Clarice Starling down-in-the-basement dangerous?" I joked.

"Exactly."

But my husband knew better than to talk me out of going back. I had promised Chris's mother I'd get her some answers, and I couldn't stand not knowing what made McCoy clam up.

I sighed. "On this case, I need to think less like a cop and more like a hiker."

The next morning, I stopped at a local grocery store on the way to Mike's Place, where I purchased a case of beer, some Red Bull, Oreo cookies, a huge jar of peanuts, and a bottle of Jack Daniels.

It was ten thirty a.m. when I arrived at the remote outpost and knocked on the back door. Twice. No answer. I peered through a dirty window and detected no movement within the shadowy interior, so I poked around the compound instead. About fifty yards from the house sat an ancient wood shack and two dilapidated RVs only a cold, wet thru-hiker or the Unabomber wouldn't mind calling home. I explored the campers looking for clues, or some flash of insight, and found none. I walked around to the front of the main house. A wisp of smoke rose from a metal pipe on the roof. Someone was inside. As I stepped onto the porch, I spotted a dark figure moving on the other side of the screen door.

"Josh?" I called out. "It's Andrea, from yesterday. I brought some trail magic [free food] for the hikers."

"Hi, come on in." McCoy pushed the door open with one hand. In the other, he held a steaming beverage. "Have a seat."

For a man cave in the desert, McCoy's living space was cozy. Stuffing emerged from the arms of thrift store furniture positioned to face a window with a pleasing view of the chamise-studded ridgeline between Mike's Place and the PCT. I sat down while my host threw a stick on a tiny fire burning inside a wood stove.

"Can I make you a cup of tea?" he asked.

"Sure. Hey, I'm sorry for bugging you, but I have a few more questions."

McCoy looked me in the eye. "I want to help," he started, apologizing for yesterday. "I want the family to have closure, but I was worried our conversation would scare the lady hikers."

"No problem," I said, softening. "I'm sorry, too. I should have picked a better time for us to talk."

McCoy's little fire warmed the fall chill, and his manner toward me felt much more like that of a gracious host. In a sweet way. Not in an overly-charming-because-I've-got-to-win-you-over way. I felt completely safe and completely foolish for being suspicious of him. McCoy had a prickly side and, as I later learned, a deep-seated distrust of authority. But I now understood why many thru-hikers enjoyed this cluttered retreat managed by trail angels in the rough.

Once the mood had eased a bit, I laid out on McCoy's coffee table a trail map, some photographs, and my notebook. I then showed him a picture on my phone that I'd pulled off Chris Sylvia's Facebook page. In it, Chris wore a brown fleece hoodie with fake wool lining. Was this the coat McCoy found at the bottom of a dry waterfall?

"Nope, it was definitely a blue denim jacket."

Remembering our tense encounter the day before, I pressed McCoy to tell me why he was so certain Chris hadn't stopped at Mike's Place. He admitted that he couldn't have known for sure if Chris visited in February 2015 because he didn't start work at Mike's until months later.

Next, we talked theories. Maybe Chris walked off the trail despondent over his breakup with Elizabeth Henle. Or he skipped town and flew to Costa Rica. Perhaps, while looking for water or a cell signal, he got lost and fell or died of exposure—or, because his toiletries were rumored not to have been found in his pack, a mountain lion attacked him while he was relieving himself. Hey, maybe he joined a cult. *Yeah, right.* We both laughed at that idea.

Then McCoy offered another idea, one so real and scary it had made him clamp his lips shut yesterday to avoid frightening the lady hikers. Now that it was only the two of us, McCoy confided in me. The sunny skies and isolation along this section of the PCT had attracted a specific category of entrepreneur: guys who grew illicit crops and had business practices that often turned violent.

I assured McCoy I'd look into it.

McCoy welcomed me to stay at Mike's Place for as long as I liked, but I was eager to search some before it got dark. McCoy unloaded my bribe—trail magic—from my rental Jeep. "The hikers are going to love this." He smiled, eyeing the beer.

Back at the Sylvia gear site, I studied a ridge to the south—an enticement for further exploration. But once I stepped off trail to ascend the rocky slope, the thick brush fought back. I've endured enough cross-country travel through a variety of landscapes, vegetation, and weather conditions to have a sense of scale on the matter. Walking uphill through the scrub to peek under dozens of granite boulders ranked seven out of ten in terms of painful aggravation. What kind of person would spend more than fifteen minutes pushing through the brittle chamise and eye-poking shrubs to reach the top of this ridge? An escaped fugitive trying to avoid cops and hounds? Possibly. A suicidal person looking for a cliff? I doubted it. A bored young man wanting to pass time while waiting for a ride? No way. Pushing through the brush on these ridges was so horrendous I concluded that neither mountain lion nor maniac could drag a hiker's body ten yards through this crap without leaving behind a boatload of evidence.

I punished myself for over an hour before deciding to search elsewhere. I drove down and parked where a drainage hit the road. A mile walk up the dry creek brought me underneath the trail where Eric Trockman had spotted Chris's gear. Drainages have a way of collecting our debris, but this one was nearly pristine. I saw no sign of human existence, other than a few rusty parts from an ancient power line and a shiny Mylar balloon that had floated in from who knows where.

That evening, I returned to my one-room rental cabin in Warner Springs, poured myself a glass of California red purchased at the only store in town—a local quick mart/gas station—and opened my laptop.

Part of my process in attempting to track down Chris Sylvia was to study similar cases to try to find patterns and overlaps. The circumstances behind Louise Teagarden's disappearance in the late 1950s and the delayed recovery of her remains seemed relevant because she also went missing from the PCT corridor, approximately ten trail miles north from where Chris began his hike. Although it took thirty years for hikers to stumble upon her body, I imagined I'd do a quicker job of finding Chris. During my time with the NPS, I had taken part in a variety of search operations—searches for lost hikers, downed aircraft, flash flood victims, swimmers who went underwater, homicidal fugitives from justice, and suicidal subjects. Some of these people were located days, weeks, or months after they disappeared. A few were found by accident. But every case I worked was eventually resolved. As a professional searcher, I was taught to view a missing hiker case as a "Classic Mystery" in which we must look for clues as earnestly as we search for our subject, because people do not disappear into thin air. *Something* is left behind—we sometimes just have to work harder to find it.

Or so I believed.

In *Managing the Lost Person Incident*, a reference text for search professionals published by the National Association for Search and Rescue (NASAR), a lost person is defined as "a *known* individual in an *unknown* location, whose safety may be threatened." Typically, at the beginning of a search, a missing person's identity is known, but their personality and habits might not be. That's why, in a well-managed search effort, someone is assigned the role of "investigator" and the search investigator's first duty is to interview friends, relatives, and peers of the lost person. While gathering information for a "subject profile," the investigator develops a deeper understanding of the missing individual and, at least in theory, this helps us predict their behavior so that we can best determine where to search for them.

While researching other missing hiker cases for clues that might help me find Chris, two disappearances grabbed my attention: Kris Fowler and David O'Sullivan, the other men who had vanished from the PCT shortly after Chris. As I dove into the reports of their last known whereabouts, the mysterious circumstances surrounding their cases took hold of me.

It was nearly midnight by the time I closed my laptop and slid into the warm bed inside my Warner Springs cabin. Above me the blades of a ceiling fan whooshed, spinning round and round like my thoughts as I ruminated over all three of the PCT Missing.

What on earth had they been doing?

And what in the heck were they thinking before they went off everyone's radar?

# CHAPTER 4

# Border Fever:
# The Case of Kris Fowler

*In October 2016, thirty-four-year-old Kris Fowler disappeared near PCT mile 2301. Courtesy of the Aware Foundation of Virginia.*

**A**S HE NEARS THE NORTHERN TERMINUS AT THE US BORDER WITH CANADA, A PCT thru-hiker's zeal to finish is weakened only by weather. Especially in October, when the onset of winter in the Pacific Northwest creates a finer gratitude for warm, dry places of any kind, including spare bedrooms, cramped apartments, and office cubicles. However, the final sections of the PCT are also the most scenic—only the carnival of wildflowers, austere mountain passes, and snowy granite peaks in California's High Sierra can truly compete with the subalpine meadows, turquoise lakes, and glacier-carved amphitheaters in Washington's North Cascades—and Kris "Sherpa" Fowler didn't want to miss a mile of it.

Kris had a degree in marketing and once held a lucrative job handling logistics for a trucking firm, but a shake-up at his company gave him an opportunity to ditch his office career for more flexible work in construction. He was divorced, with no children, and had moved back, temporarily, into his dad's home in Beavercreek, Ohio. The divorce had been finalized for a little over a year, and although the split was amicable, the disappointment had catapulted the thirty-four-year-old into a transitionary period. Still, despite this unexpected turn of events, those who knew Kris Fowler said he was happy, popular, and adjusting well to this new chapter of life.

The reason he gave people for hiking a long trail was not complicated: he was seeking an adventure. Now that Kris was romantically and professionally untethered, it seemed like the perfect time to take on the PCT. As a bonus, his friend Colin Hurley wanted to join him. After Kris changed his Facebook workplace status to "started a new job conquering mountains on the Pacific Crest Trail," the friends began their trek in earnest on Sunday, May 8, 2016—Mother's Day.

Weeks into their hike, the men decided to split up and tackle the trail separately. Their parting was cordial, and the practice is common; friends who start off thru-hiking together often learn that it's better to hike your own hike at your own pace. Like a majority of thru-hikers, Kris was trekking northbound, or NOBO for short; only 10 percent of PCT hikers choose to hike the trail southbound (SOBO) because of the timing and the conditions since snowmelt comes late near the Canadian border. Another custom among thru-hikers is to take a trail name. While he was resupplying in Idyllwild, California (PCT mile 179), Kris Fowler was rechristened "Sherpa"—after he guided some fellow trekkers to the best hiker spots in town. When his new friends ran into him again a few days later, they called out, "There's our Sherpa!" and the name stuck. He'd grown fond of his trail name and the identity that came with it, but Sherpa knew that once he stepped over the Canadian border and finished the PCT, the magic of his thru-hike would be over. Then, like everybody else, he'd have to go by his real name, Kris Fowler, and get a job.

Five months and 2,122 miles after he left Idyllwild, Sherpa reached PCT mile 2301, near White Pass, Washington. He had approximately 352 miles to go before hitting his ultimate destination: a concrete monument at the PCT's Northern Terminus, on the Canadian border at PCT mile 2653. A seasoned thru-hiker could hike this distance in eighteen days, or less if conditions were good. But Kris wasn't in a great hurry to complete his journey. On October 5, while passing through Trout Lake, Washington, he wrote the following in a trail register: "Sherpa…last one to Canada wins!" He accented these words with a smiley face.

Sherpa, like most thru-hikers, did not view his walk from Mexico to Canada as a race or a competition. A PCT thru-hike was more of a pilgrimage—a journey to savor—a 2,650-mile walking meditation that changed you, often in profound ways. That's not to say it was an easy existential transformation; as with most forms of enlightenment, this one had to be earned. "Embrace the suck," a common PCT thru-hiker refrain, hinted at the physical trials hikers faced as they set forth on their quest. Blisters. Desert heat. Mountain snow. Days after days of grueling miles, rough terrain, steep slopes, and winding switchbacks. Hunger. Thirst. Bodies grimed with dirt, sweat, blood, rashes, and bug bites. And yet, despite these discomforts, the experience was so life altering, it wasn't uncommon for thru-hikers to be afflicted by what they called post-hike depression after they completed the journey and reintegrated into society.

Sherpa carried a lightweight backpack, black with orange panels on the sides. He hiked in sandals because he wanted to "feel every step" and slept in a hammock. In one of the last known photographs of Sherpa, taken while he walked across the Oregon border into Washington, a paperback is jammed inside an external pocket of his pack. The title, visible through the mesh, is *Wanderer*—a memoir written by the "New Hollywood"–era actor-turned-author Sterling Hayden in 1963. Among other things, the book details Hayden's violation of court orders when he escaped his debts and angered his ex-wife by sailing to Tahiti with his kids. Throughout the pages of *Wanderer*, the disillusioned actor ruminates on the soul-numbing confinements of capitalism, corporatism, and the modern American lifestyle in passages such as this:

> What does a man need—really need? A few pounds of food each day, heat, and shelter, six feet to lie down in—and some form of working activity that will yield a sense of accomplishment. That's all—in the material sense, and we know it. But we are brainwashed by our economic system until we end up in a tomb beneath a pyramid of time payments, mortgages, preposterous gadgetry, playthings that divert our attention for the sheer idiocy of the charade.

Even before he stepped on the trail, Kris had confided in a friend that "corporate America is not for me anymore." Now, as he neared the end of his hike, these ideas likely bubbled back to the top of his mind. Perhaps, on the trail, Sherpa had been able to free himself from Kris Fowler's more material daily concerns. But as the

Canadian border drew near, so did the troubles and responsibilities of civilized life. Everyday hassles like a busted phone charger, a
dwindling bank account, and other worries. How could he replen-
ish his savings without becoming a cubicle drone? Where could he
live that would give him the chance to experience natural beauty
every day, like all the magical scenery he'd photographed along the
PCT? Was there a woman who would join him—one who could be
happy living unattached to the comforts of suburbia? And beneath
all this lay a much deeper question: How does a thru-hiker reinte-
grate into society after spending five months on the trail?

Reading *Wanderer* may have brought these dilemmas to the
forefront of Sherpa's thoughts as he trekked toward the finish line
that fall, but we'll never know for sure where his meditations had
landed him. Because on the evening of October 12, 2016, the thru-
hiker entered the cold and dreary woods at White Pass and was
never seen again.

# CHAPTER 5

# Lucky Dave:
# The Case of David O'Sullivan

## MISSING PERSON

## DAVID O'SULLIVAN

IRISH CITIZEN  25 YEARS OLD
5'10" / 154 POUNDS / BLACK HAIR / BLUE EYES
LAST CONTACT WAS ON APRIL 7, 2017, FROM IDYLLWILD
CALIFORNIA

DAVID WAS HIKING ON THE PACIFIC CREST TRAIL, (PCT)
FROM CAMPO CALIFORNIA  TO CANADA.
DAVID WAS HIKING ALONE.

DAVID'S DISTINCTIVE BACKPACK IS PICTURED

ANY INFORMATION ON HIS LOCATION, POSSIBLE
SIGHTINGS OR ANYTHING THAT MAY HELP,

CONTACT CAPTAIN LEONARD PURVIS AT THE RIVERSIDE COUNTY
SHERIFF, HEMET STATION AT

FACEBOOK PAGE: David O'Sullivan / MISSING PCT HIKER
https://www.facebook.com/groups/140662906657636

*In April 2017, twenty-five-year-old David O'Sullivan
disappeared near PCT mile 179. Courtesy of Cathy Tarr.*

S IX MONTHS AFTER THE DISAPPEARANCE OF KRIS FOWLER AND MORE THAN TWO thousand miles south, David O'Sullivan was getting hungry. He had to walk a mile off trail to eat at the lauded diner, but the additional effort was worth it. West of PCT mile 151, along a lonely stretch of Southern California's Highway 74, the Paradise Valley Café had been feeding hungry travelers since 1939, and it did not disappoint. The manager was hiker-friendly, the beer selection impressive, and the portion sizes were big enough to fuel a weary hiker with 2,500 miles ahead of him. It was lunchtime when David walked up to the counter, so he ordered up his favorite dish: a hamburger.

Eleven days earlier, on March 22, 2017, the twenty-five-year-old from Cork, Ireland, had started his trek north from the Mexican border near Campo. Nerdy, studious, and refreshingly disciplined, David didn't exactly fit the Irish stereotype; he would have a pint now and then but didn't imbibe much. An avid reader with a black belt in karate, he had degrees in English and philosophy, after graduating with honors from the University College Cork. He excelled in geography, wore glasses, and liked to play medieval-themed computer games. He still lived with his parents and worked at a local garage, and this allowed him to save up $8,000 for this very trip—and he was excited to experience the trail on his own terms.

On April 3, while devouring his burger at the café, he met another thru-hiker going by "Beta" (real name: Daniel Winsor). To explain his cracked lips and peeling face, David confessed to Beta that he'd lost his hat a few days ago, hence the wicked sunburn.

Losing your hat in the desert is one of several rookie mistakes. Another is packing too heavily. David had been inspired to hike the PCT after reading *Wild* (he thought the book was better than the movie). Strayed's memoir warned about the perils of carrying a monster-sized backpack, but the Irishman had confused American pounds for English stones and purchased gear twice the weight recommended. Once on the trail, he learned quickly. An overloaded pack results in sore shoulders and a slower hiking pace. In Mount Laguna, the first town northbound thru-hikers visit, David went to a local outfitter and underwent a process known as "the shake-down," which lightens your load as it empties your wallet. To drop twelve pounds of pack weight, David spent a few hundred dollars on more suitable gear and mailed home several inappropriate items he'd purchased in Ireland. But he kept his Kindle and the unique backpack he had found online: a cerulean blue beauty with neon green accents.

During their lunch, Beta, an experienced hiker, and David, a novice, discussed hiking strategies. Rumors traveling among their fellow hikers hinted at the perils ahead. Two months earlier, back in February, five day hikers had slid off the trail near Islip Saddle (an elevation of 6,680 feet) in the San Gabriel Mountains, northeast of Los Angeles and about 230 trail miles north of the Paradise Valley Café; one of these hikers even died after plummeting a hundred feet down an icy chute. What's more, between the Paradise Valley Café and the San Gabriels lay the San Jacinto Mountains, where the trail reached elevations above 9,000 feet. Because of a record snow year, the San Jacinto section was known to have a few icy spots still, but Beta believed it was doable.

David's hiking style differed from Beta's. A "purist," Beta remained committed to hiking south to north without skipping any miles. David was more practical. He wanted to hike as much of the trail as possible but had no problem skipping hazardous sections. David already planned to hitch around the High Sierra and come back and do it later, when conditions were safer—a strategy thru-hikers called "flip-flopping."

When David and his new friend parted ways, Beta left first to catch a ride back to the trail. Hitching to and from trailheads can be a disheartening experience for tired, raggedy-ass thru-hikers. Before long, Beta gave up. He was feeling rejected on his "walk of shame" along the road back to the trail when he saw a silver car "zooming by" with David in the passenger seat. With a nod to the Irishman's good fortune, Beta christened David with what might have become his trail name: Lucky Dave.

Whether the nickname would've stuck is questionable. Three days later, "Lucky Dave" sent an email to his family. It was the last time they ever heard from him.

CHAPTER 6

# *Dots on a Map*

---

FELT A KINSHIP WITH ALL THREE OF THE PCT MISSING; AFTER ALL, WHEN I WAS around their age, I embarked on a similar adventure myself. In 1999, after I quit my ranger job, I spent five and a half months walking the entire Appalachian Trail (AT) from Georgia to Maine. My demanding, tragedy-filled stint with the NPS had left me burned out and disillusioned, so, like Chris Sylvia, I was in a funk and needed to get my head straight. Like Kris Fowler, I was an unemployed thirty-something seeking a new way of life when I started my solo thru-hike. And, like David O'Sullivan, I'm a studious, disciplined book nerd. But I also stepped on the trail armed with something none of these men had: an intense background in wilderness rescue and emergency medical care.

For me, thru-hiking the AT was a challenging but relatively safe endeavor that healed my existential wounds. And I'm pleased to report that the thru-hiking mystique I experienced on the AT in 1999 hasn't gone anywhere—even if there are more people walking alongside you. The scenery on a long-distance footpath is just as enchanting. You'll still run into trail angels, trail trolls, and trail magic. Hiker midnight will always fall somewhere between seven thirty and nine thirty p.m. Purists, slackers, ultra-lighters, fast-packers, flip-floppers, yellow-blazers, yogis, and hiker trash continue to squabble over proper technique while maintaining a tolerant credo of HYOH—Hike Your Own Hike.

But other aspects of thru-hiking and thru-hiker culture have changed dramatically over the last twenty years. For one, in 1999, we didn't carry cell phones and we looked down on anyone who did. During my own thru-hike, I heard there was a fellow AT hiker who had one, but he kept it hidden in the bottom of his pack, like contraband, so we didn't give him grief over the transgression. Today, it's rare, and perhaps foolish, for a thru-hiker not to carry a smartphone that they can use to hail rides, order pizza delivery to a trailhead, and share thoughts and photographs on YouTube, Instagram, or Facebook of nearly every moment of their adventure.

That's not to say tech doesn't come with its own risks and challenges. For example, the well-documented (and ever-growing) social media habit of many younger adventurers may be triggering a rise in backcountry fatalities, because more hikers are performing riskier behaviors in their attempts to obtain the most striking cliff-side selfies. However, our proclivity to document our outdoor excursions via smartphones and to share these experiences online can also help searchers track us down if we become lost. I witnessed this firsthand when Facebook—an investigative tool I couldn't have imagined using twenty-five years ago—led to some remarkable discoveries during my search for the PCT Missing.

While at home on my computer looking for potential links between the three cases, I discovered "Bring Kris Fowler/Sherpa Home," a Facebook group administered by Kris's stepmom, Sally Fowler. After I clicked "Join," I was launched into an online posse of eight thousand hikers, hunters, Good Samaritans, mountain climbers, and web sleuths who had rallied around the Ohio businesswoman with a no-man-left-behind intensity. As I watched them interact online, Sally's determination tugged at my heartstrings, and the exploits of her volunteer searchers fascinated me. Would this eclectic band of amateurs actually find him?

If you follow a missing hiker Facebook page long enough, you'll witness a social phenomenon that is both inspiring and pathetic. After the authorities suspend their search, a family member or a close friend will create a Facebook group, believing the online attention will pressure the police to work harder or bring in leads that will help solve the case. This publicity draws in well-meaning people who want to help, but the spectators contribute little more than glib advice and supportive platitudes. Meanwhile, the casual cruelty of social media trolls sucks the discourse into petty arguments, distracting the investigation and triggering those who have become overly attached to the cause. The fiercer the fervor, the more frequently the group stirs up false sightings, backseat drivers, and a few nutcases. Then, if you're lucky, you'll see someone special jump into the fray: a quiet hero with keen instincts and pure intentions— someone who sincerely wants to help the family track down the answers they so desperately seek.

In the Kris Fowler group, the member piquing my curiosity the most was a woman named Cathy Tarr. Close to me in age, the middle-aged mother of two did something that I rarely saw on social media. She didn't just talk with a get-it-done positivity; she acted on it. And even though she realized that the problem was systemic in nature, she was determined to do her part to help the families that needed her most. And so, in October 2017, Cathy posted that she was setting aside her volunteer search effort in Washington for Kris Fowler over the winter and would now travel to California to help David O'Sullivan's parents find their son.

Cathy's Facebook announcement stunned me for two reasons: the commitment and the coincidence. Hikers found Chris Sylvia's gear at PCT mile 127. David O'Sullivan's last known point was at mile 179. The two men had disappeared fifty-two trail miles apart and two women in their early fifties were starting searches for them during the same week. I introduced myself through Facebook Messenger, told Cathy about my work on Chris Sylvia's case, and convinced her to meet me for dinner so we could compare notes.

I drove an hour from my rental cabin in Warner Springs to meet up with Cathy at a Sizzler in Hemet. Our conversation had a tender chemistry. We both picked at our salads as Cathy got me up to speed on all that she'd done with the Kris Fowler search and what she planned to do for the O'Sullivans.

Cathy first saw a missing person flyer for David O'Sullivan while she was in Washington searching for Kris Fowler. Although the Irishman was last seen thousands of miles away, in Southern California, some were tossing around a theory that he may have stopped contact with his family in April and continued hiking north. It's not unusual for thru-hikers to escape family dysfunctions and drama by breaking off all contact during their hike, but there was no evidence that David had intended to do this. However, even his own family clung to the hope that the twenty-five-year-old may have continued his trek without communicating with them—because that meant there was a possibility that he could still be found somewhere, alive. In case this was true, members of the hiker community had posted missing person flyers for David in the North Cascades.

Through Facebook, Cathy learned that Con and Carmel O'Sullivan were heading to California to persuade authorities to work harder to find David. Cathy's grown daughter, who was pregnant with Cathy's first grandson, lived in Riverside County, a half-hour drive from Idyllwild. While at her daughter's house, Cathy decided to recon David's last known location.

"I was making no big commitment by driving to the San Jacinto Mountains," she acknowledged. She only wanted to inspect the trailheads, visit the bulletin boards at community centers and coffee shops, and satisfy her curiosity about what efforts were being made to find David. What Cathy discovered on that brief excursion to Idyllwild, however, upset her. In Washington, locals had rallied to assist Sally Fowler in her search for her son. Here in Southern California, it appeared that nothing was being done. No searching. No investigation. No missing person flyers. Nothing. How would David's family feel when they arrived all the way from Ireland and saw that the Americans had stopped making any effort to find their son? If she didn't step in to help, Cathy concluded, no one would.

Investigating missing hiker cases was a novel endeavor for the retired corporate-level Walgreens manager. Other than the three months she'd spent looking for Kris Fowler, Cathy had zero experience in search management or law enforcement. At some point after our last trip to the salad bar, I asked her why she didn't join a local search and rescue unit.

"They have too many rules. They are beholden to county politics. I can get more done working outside their boundaries."

Naive, perhaps, but not far from the truth. Once a missing hiker case has gone cold and the authorities have given up, one motivated individual could do more by working outside the confines of a government agency. Nevertheless, flying solo in the male-dominated world of wilderness search was a ballsy move.

As I listened to Cathy's stories, I saw capital-letter virtues. Courage. Selflessness. Idealism. I viewed myself as a woman who had too much of the first quality and an acceptable amount of the second, but the third? Forget it. On a good day, my reservoir of idealism hovers a foot or two above mud level. Yet, within an hour of meeting her, I couldn't help myself—I believed in Cathy. *This gutsy chick just might find him.* I persuaded her to let me observe and document the next day's lunch with the O'Sullivans and promised to stay out of her way.

We were both taking a leap of faith. Each woman presuming the other to be as honorable as she seemed. Before we parted, Cathy wanted my advice. When the O'Sullivans arrived, how should she handle a family dealing with this sort of tragedy?

Remembering my own experiences working with victims' families, I advised Cathy to be present with their sadness, to be honest about her intentions, and not to overthink it.

Then she revealed one more thing that was troubling her. By conducting a private search for David, was she giving his parents false hope?

I didn't know enough yet to answer that question, but the O'Sullivans, I told her, "will be grateful for whatever help they can get."

The following afternoon when a server came by to take our order for the second time, we hadn't even opened our menus, and Cathy Tarr's face scrunched with concern. The O'Sullivans were late, and our conversation was becoming awkward. We were strangers, basically, sitting at a large table chosen for the relative privacy it offered inside the Gastrognome, a quirky restaurant in the mountain hamlet of Idyllwild, California. Cathy and I had met the night before, and I knew our male companion, a retired homicide detective from Southern California, only from a Google search.

David O'Sullivan's parents, Con and Carmel, had arrived from Ireland the day before our meeting, on November 7, 2017. In Los Angeles, they'd consulted with the Irish consulate before meeting twelve officials with the Riverside County Sheriff's Office in Hemet this morning. After discussing their son's case with the authorities, the O'Sullivans had planned to meet us in Idyllwild at noon. Our watches and phones told us it was nearly one.

"If they changed their minds or were running late, I don't know why they wouldn't contact me," Cathy murmured.

"Maybe Riverside County told them not to talk to us?" I suggested.

Cathy frowned. It was a cynical notion in opposition to what she and I saw as indisputable. She wanted to help and could accomplish

LANKFORD                                                  43

more for the O'Sullivans than the authorities would ever do. Even so, David's parents might not have realized how true this was.

Every five minutes, Cathy left our table to check the parking lot for Con and Carmel. Each time she did this, I asked the male detective for more advice on the Chris Sylvia case. This was part of a strategy Cathy and I had devised last night. I would distract the former cop so that she could greet the O'Sullivans alone. Our scheme served several purposes. One: we didn't want to overwhelm David's parents with the three of us all at once. Two: the O'Sullivan family's initial communications had been with Cathy. Meeting her first would give them some space. Three: Cathy barely knew the detective, but she had gotten a sense that he might not be a team player.

Cathy was right to worry about the retired investigator, but he was easy to distract. All I had to do was ask him questions about himself. Regardless, I valued his presence and expertise. Sturdy for his age, this guy was a rare bird—a former homicide detective who had thru-hiked the PCT himself.

At 12:55 p.m., the O'Sullivans joined us inside the Gastrognome, much to our relief. After the introductions, Cathy outlined what leads she was following, which witnesses she wanted to talk to, and where she planned to search. She was organized and well prepared for the meeting; from a binder with color-coded sleeves, she retrieved documents, maps, and missing person flyers.

Unlike Cathy, the detective hadn't brought a notebook and didn't even try to write anything down. He was in his sixties, and though he spoke openly of his grown children, I noticed he didn't mention anything about a wife. Cathy, on the other hand, was in her mid-fifties, assertive and independent, yet easy to be around. She had ivory skin, hazel eyes, and shiny brown hair, attractive features that would later inspire another male volunteer to liken her to Susan Sarandon. Wary, I watched the detective watch Cathy. *Was he here for something other than the case?*

Despite the grim purpose of our meeting, Con and Carmel were gracious and forthcoming. *Salt of the earth people*, I jotted down in my notebook. With heavy Irish accents, they told us all about how the local authorities had mishandled various aspects of the case. But even so, their critiques were measured and fair.

To some degree, a failure to start a prompt investigation into David's disappearance was understandable because thru-hikers are expected to be out of contact with civilization for days, if not weeks. After David sent his last email on April 6, 2017, it took at least a week before the O'Sullivans became worried enough to get on the PCT Facebook groups to ask whether any hikers had seen him.

"People were very helpful," Carmel had initially told a reporter in Ireland. "However, there was a lot of misinformation."

More than once, a witness claimed David was staying at a particular hostel, but when the O'Sullivans called the establishment hoping to talk to their son, the man in question who picked up the phone wasn't David. On May 31, the couple requested help from Irish authorities, who discovered evidence of a recent bank transfer from David's account. The May withdrawal implied that David was alive after April 6, and this justified suspending the investigation. Weeks passed before it became apparent that the bank activity was a routine automatic transfer.

After another month passed with no word from David, the O'Sullivans contacted the Pacific Crest Trail Association looking for help. As the O'Sullivans recalled it, the spokesperson told them the PCTA was "not a babysitting service" and suggested they buy their son a GPS tracking device. This was an inarticulate and insensitive way of letting the O'Sullivans know that the PCTA's mission, as stated on its website, is "to protect, preserve and promote the Pacific Crest National Scenic Trail as a world-class experience for hikers and equestrians, and for all the values provided by wild and scenic lands." In other words, the PCTA funds trail maintenance projects. It educates hikers on safety and "Leave No Trace" practices.

The thirteen-thousand-member organization also develops strategies for managing the increasing numbers of people determined to thru-hike the trail. The PCTA does not, however, exist to provide useful guidance or assistance to the parents of missing thru-hikers.

When a loved one goes missing far from home, especially while visiting a foreign country, the family is at a distinct disadvantage. Frustrated and desperate, the O'Sullivans resorted to using channels of the familiar. They contacted the Irish Outreach, an Irish American advocacy group in San Diego. A member of this group knew an Irish American police officer working in Murrieta, a city fifty miles from the PCT, named Lieutenant Flavin, who reported the situation to a detective within his department. To his credit, the Murrieta detective didn't shirk responsibility because the jurisdiction for this case was unclear. He opened a case number and created a missing person flyer. He also drove up to Idyllwild and asked some questions. But David's disappearance did not occur within the jurisdiction of Murrieta PD.

So, whose case was it?

Two men reported that they had seen a hiker who looked like David at two separate locations near Cabazon, an interstate town west of the PCT along I-10. This put the northbound hiker in San Bernardino County. But no one could corroborate these sightings, and David's last email placed him squarely in Idyllwild, dropping the case into the lap of Riverside County. By the time this agency accepted the responsibility, it was the end of July, nearly four months after David sent his last email.

Since 1961, Riverside County has relied on the Riverside Mountain Rescue Unit (RMRU) to conduct many of its rescue missions in the San Jacinto Mountains. RMRU is a group of trained search and rescue (SAR) volunteers, who are unpaid and must buy all their own equipment. On July 29, several RMRU searchers scouted the PCT between Devil's Slide and the Deer Springs Trail looking for fall zones. On August 4 and 5, they searched several drainages and found a lone purple sleeping bag, which was later determined not to be David's. On August 12, they searched more areas north of Idyllwild, but "despite the team's best efforts," RMRU stated in its online report, "and the various agencies who have also worked to find him, [David O'Sullivan] remains missing."

Once Cathy had gone over all she wanted to say, I asked the O'Sullivans about David's hiking behavior as well as his general personality, an old habit from my ranger days filling out Lost Person Questionnaires. These comprehensive forms were up to nine pages long and tedious to complete. Besides noting all the identifying features of a missing hiker, a search investigator will ask loved ones for what might appear to be irrelevant details, like the lost person's education level, job history, swimming ability, and favorite places to visit.

Con said that David prepared for his PCT endeavor by hiking with weights up Knockoura—a 1,600-foot (490 meters) peak near his home. He carried an inexpensive GPS wristwatch, but his knowledge of outdoor survival was minimal. He had no experience route finding in snow. He wasn't a penny-pincher—he'd treat himself to a nice hotel room while on the trail—but he was smart with his money. Though David was friendly, he typically kept to himself. He had a black belt in karate and read up on Native American history before coming to the States. He liked hamburgers but didn't like pizza.

"Who were his favorite heroes?" I asked.

"I don't know," David's father said, "but he preferred underdogs."

Learning more about the Irish hiker hit me with a familiar pang. David O'Sullivan was intelligent, conscientious, and disciplined. A happy introvert with a dry sense of humor who favored the dark horses among us.

I would have enjoyed meeting him.

After lunch, the detective left to set up camp on the mountain. Cathy and the O'Sullivans met with the local press, and then I drove the four of us to a hiker-friendly pizza restaurant known for taking photographs of every thru-hiker who ate there. We reviewed over a hundred Polaroid portraits of 2017 thru-hikers—scruffy, bearded men and outdoorsy, athletic women with sun-blushed faces glowing from the achievement of having 170 miles behind them and the glory of having nearly 2,500 miles to go. Carmel was disappointed to find that her son's portrait was not among them.

From the restaurant, we walked next door to the public library where David had accessed the internet to send his parents that last email. The librarians directed us to a map of the world nailed to the wall in a back corner. Every thru-hiker who visited the library was instructed to place a sticker to show where they came from. Con and Carmel bent over to peer at Ireland and saw a red dot on Cork.

Carmel put a hand to her mouth and wept. Con placed his arm around her shoulder. I looked at Cathy. With a nod, she indicated that we should give David's parents a moment to be alone with the map. I walked over to the front desk and introduced myself to the librarians.

"Are you sure the stickers on that map are for this year only?" I asked.

"Yes," they replied. "Every dot was placed by someone who came here in 2017."

There was no indication that another hiker from Cork had trekked the PCT that year, much less visited the Idyllwild library. While there's certainly a slim possibility it could've been someone else, it's most likely that David was the one who placed that dot on the map.

Witnessing the O'Sullivans grieve in front of that map solidified our resolve to help them find out what had happened to their beloved son. Cathy and I knew we had accepted a mission we couldn't easily walk away from.

"I debated whether I should get involved in this," Cathy admitted to me a few days later. "But someone has to do something. Can you imagine telling Carmel, 'We're not going to search anymore? He can't be found. Sorry, but we did everything we could'?"

Not only could I imagine, I'd performed the sad duty myself— and suffered for it. Cathy didn't yet know this about me, and she had never led a multiday search effort like I had—the O'Sullivan case would be her first—but right from the start, the novice was anticipating the guilt that would befall her if she gave up.

A week after Cathy and I met the O'Sullivans in Idyllwild, a San Diego County deputy searched my shoulder bag as I went through the metal detector. Once cleared to enter, I signed a numbered list before sitting on a hard chair. My mood was sour. Any trip to the county records office was a guaranteed tussle with bureau- cracy and I was feeling impatient. Weeks earlier, I had coached Joshua Sylvia into filing a written request for a copy of his brother's missing person report, but we had yet to receive it. This in-person visit was intended to push things along. While I waited for some- one to call my name, I conjured forth a state of cheerful profession- alism using a jaded mantra: *People skills, people skills, use your people skills.*

When my turn came, I described the situation through a hole in a plexiglass window to the young clerk on the other side. She handed me a form through a slot because I needed to file another, separate request. I filled in the blanks one more time and pushed the new form back to her. She retreated to another room. A few minutes later, another clerk, an older woman, came to the window.

"Only the victim can request a copy of the report," she said flatly.

"The victim has been missing for two years. I don't think he's capable of filling out the paperwork."

She pursed her lips. "We have rules to follow."

I understood that. "Okay, then what are the rules?"

She gave me no answer, but her expression said, *Heck if I know, but rules are rules.*

Again, I explained the situation. The family lived in Maryland and they wanted answers. I was there on their behalf.

"Do you have a court document declaring you as their legal advocate?" the clerk asked.

Of course not. "I'm only trying to help the victim's brother get a copy of the report. Can I show you his email asking me to help? Can we call him and let him tell you himself?"

Apparently, none of that would do.

"Okay," I conceded, "I'll have the victim's brother request the report again by mail."

"He'll have to show proof that he's a family member."

"How does he do that?"

She didn't know.

Would a notarized affidavit swearing he was indeed the victim's brother work?

Yes, maybe, and he'd also need to send a photocopy of his driver's license. And he'd have to pay twenty-five dollars.

Could I pay the fee now?

No. I couldn't pay until it was approved. And it couldn't be approved until it was paid. Oh, and payment must be in the form of a California check.

Internally, I rolled my eyes. Chris's Maryland-based family obviously didn't *have* California bank accounts. I wondered what other obstacles prevented this family from obtaining information.

"Before I leave, is there anything else I need to know or do to ensure that the victim's brother gets a copy of the report?" For emphasis, I pushed my mouth inside the hole in the plexiglass. "Because I'm going to be persistent."

The clerk provided no response. I was dismissed.

I walked out to the parking lot, defeated. People shouldn't have to go through this much bullshit to learn some details about their loved one's case. The "rules" were vague, tedious, and intimidating. They were also nearly impossible to follow. Many people in search of these kinds of documents would give up, and although that may be the intended effect, it doesn't make it right. Everybody gets that law enforcement should keep certain aspects of their investigations from the public. Sure. But not the entire friggin' report on a case that was nearly three years cold and for which there was no strong indication of foul play.

A few weeks later, Joshua Sylvia received a three-page document. The report appeared to have been cut and pasted from what I hoped was a larger narrative. Instead of redactions made in black marker, this one had REDACTED typed in all caps. Twice in the same short paragraph.

The first page of Chris Sylvia's missing person report was stamped CONFIDENTIAL in red ink. Below that, stamped in black, was a note that "distribution of information contained in the report is restricted by the California Penal Code, a violation of which would be a misdemeanor."

A petty reprimand on a document revealing little you couldn't read online.

I'd wished for more. Among the details not released was an itemized list of the gear initially recovered from Chris's pack. The presence, or absence, of certain items would tell a story—one a thru-hiker would understand better than a suburban detective with no backpacking experience. San Diego County's refusal to release this information handicapped my investigation, but in the months ahead, I would hold in my hands a vital clue that the authorities had missed.

Something that *should* have been in Chris Sylvia's backpack— but wasn't.

# PART TWO

## SEARCH AND INVESTIGATE

CHAPTER 7

# Welcome to the Club

I F SALLY FOWLER HAD TO CHOOSE THE DATE WHEN SHE JOINED WHAT SHE CALLED "The Club No One Wants to Be In," it would be October 31, 2016. Halloween. That was the day things got so real she broke down and dropped an *F*-bomb on a cop. But it was Sally's ex-husband, Kris's biological father, who felt it first.

"I haven't heard from Kris," Mike Fowler said when he called her on October 14. "Have you?"

"It hasn't been two weeks." Sally had last talked to Kris over the phone on September 30, but he had texted a friend two days ago. "Don't worry."

"I'm worried," Mike insisted. "It's not good."

Sally and Mike had been divorced for years, but there was little drama between them. They were friends; their social circles and families remained intertwined. Mike's first wife, Kris's biological mother, had passed away. Sally was in her fifties and had no children of her own. To explain how close she was to her stepson, she told people, "I gave birth to him when he was ten."

When Kris announced his intention to quit work and backpack from Mexico to Canada, Sally couldn't say she liked the idea—spending six months hiking a rugged trail seemed like a dangerous endeavor—but Kris was thirty-four, a grown man, and she hadn't raised him to be a momma's boy. Mike, a Navy veteran who rarely took a sick day over the course of thirty years, struggled with it as well. Undeterred by his parents' concerns, Kris started his trek on May 8, 2016. A Sunday.

"Happy Mother's Day from the PCT," he texted Sally, along with a picture from the trail. "Here I go."

Five and a half months later, Kris's number was going straight to voice mail and his dad knew instinctively something was wrong.

To ease Mike's concern, Sally tracked down Amber Johnson, a "lady friend" Kris had met on the PCT. Amber said Kris had texted her on October 12 to let her know he was hiking north from White Pass, Washington. Cell service in the mountains was always spotty, so it was normal when a PCT thru-hiker didn't communicate with friends or family for days, even weeks, at a time. Amber wasn't worried.

Days later, though, when Kris still hadn't answered her texts, Amber started having second thoughts. She messaged Sally: "I'm worried now."

The following week was as hopeful as it was frustrating. Hopeful because Sally kept thinking Kris was going to show up. That any minute he was going to walk out of those mountains and—*boy oh boy*—would he be pissed when he found out how she and everyone else had made such a fuss.

Like most partners responding to a crisis, the Fowlers divided their labor. Mike phoned the cops and Sally investigated. As an account manager/buyer for a wholesale grocery, Sally's forte was business, not law enforcement. But her dad had been a cop, and the sleuthing gene passed down to her. While sitting at the kitchen bar in her Ohio home, Sally directed hikers in Washington to check for Kris's signature in all the trail registers. She persuaded a hometown banker in Ohio to give her information about her son's last ATM withdrawals and credit card charges. She contacted all the hiker hangouts, the outfitters, the coffee shops, the bars, the hostels, and the cheap hotels. On October 28, Sally posted a restrained plea for "hikers to keep an eye out" for Kris on the PCT Class of 2016 Facebook group. Two days later, Sally's Facebook posts displayed more urgency and increasing frustration. Her niece and nephew created the Bring Kris Fowler/Sherpa Home Facebook group on October 30. As it brought in more and more leads, Sally followed every one of them to the end.

While Sally collected all the details of Kris's last known movements, Mike was butting heads with the authorities. Sally believed she knew why the cops were giving her ex such a hard time. When a child, a pretty young white woman, or an elderly person goes missing, people react quickly. When it's an adult male, law enforcement typically concludes that the guy doesn't want to be found. She figured the police departments were all hoping the case fell into another jurisdiction. No agency wants to be the one to file the missing person report. No department wants to be the one incurring the expense of a major search effort.

The initial confusion and hesitation that occur when a loved one goes missing were compounded in this case because Kris was a thru-hiker. Thru-hikers aren't backpacking a loop in one national park or forest. PCT thru-hikers are hiking from Mexico to Canada on a 2,650-mile trail, traveling in and out of dozens of jurisdictions while crossing the borders of dozens of counties and three nations. Packwood, where Sally learned Kris had made his last credit card charges, was in Lewis County. But the store where a clerk told Sally she saw Kris make a phone call was in Yakima County. Once Kris hiked north on the PCT, his route traveled in and out of three counties: Pierce, Lewis, and Yakima. However, if he'd successfully reached his next prearranged mail drop at Snoqualmie Pass, he could be anywhere along the boundary line of two additional counties, King and Kittitas. And if he had made it all the way to Canada, the case became international.

Mike called representatives from all five counties and Canada, and each of them advised him to contact the others. *Pierce, Lewis,*

*Yakima, King, Kittitas. Pierce, Lewis, Yakima, King, Kittitas.* Round and round Mike went. Every day that passed without hearing from Kris, the bureaucratic carousel became more and more infuriating. In his booming voice, Mike started letting people know how he felt. The lack of progress, and the failure for anyone to take his son's case seriously, would have tried the patience of any parent. "The RP [reporting party] was very argumentative" is how a police report described Mike's calls, and "cussing at the call taker several times."

Sally and Mike were both losing sleep, increasingly anxious about what might have happened to their son. Locals in Washington said there had been some rough weather starting on October 13 and more was on the way. The situation felt dire. On the night of October 30, Sally and Mike changed their strategy. "Let *me* call them," she said, and Mike concurred.

On Halloween, Sally woke up early. She walked to the barstool at her kitchen island, sat down, and started making phone calls and sending texts. She doesn't remember eating or going to the bathroom that day, and she never changed out of her pajamas, an oversized T-shirt. Parents of other missing hikers—members of that sad club no one wants to be in—contacted her through Facebook, offering their counsel. "You need to get out there," one father wrote, "because it made a world of difference with the officials when we showed up." That evening, a friend came to Sally's home to help because a hundred trick-or-treaters were lining up at the door wanting candy; meanwhile, Sally was still sitting at that kitchen bar, pants-less, making phone calls and sending texts.

The Yakima County report verifies that Sally Fowler called their office on October 31 and left an "extremely upset message" on a deputy's voice mail complaining that the Sheriff's Office was "doing nothing" to find Kris.

Indeed, Sally was extremely upset, sleep-deprived, and desperate. She was also a successful businesswoman, a problem solver by trade, who knew how a strategically placed *F*-word can be a real attention-getter. By her recollection, the message she left with the Yakima County Sheriff's Office concluded with: "My father was a cop and I know he'd be rolling over in his grave at the fact that nobody is responding to this. And who the *fuck* do I have to talk to in order to make something happen?"

Thirty minutes later, someone called her back.

"Ms. Fowler, this is Sergeant Randy Briscoe, and I want to let you know I don't appreciate the message you left me." Others within his office *had* done some preliminary work on the case, he assured her, but Briscoe said he was "just now hearing about all this, so you go ahead and tell me what's going on."

Sally gave Sergeant Briscoe the lowdown. The bottom line was this: Kris Fowler was last seen by a clerk in a store known as the Kracker Barrel at White Pass in Yakima County on October 12. It was now October 31. Obviously, her son was missing, so why wasn't anybody looking for him?

"Ms. Fowler," Briscoe acknowledged, "I owe you an apology. We need to get this missing person report filed right now."

Sally's older brother came to the house after he got off work. No one would call Sally a shrinking violet, at least not to her face. "She embraces all kinds of people, but she's not going to tiptoe around you" is how a friend described her—but when Rick Guyton speaks, his little sister listens, and always has.

"You gotta go out there, Sally," her brother said, "and I'll go with you."

As Rick Guyton said these words, her son's disappearance became real, too real, and Sally Guyton Fowler fell apart.

In Washington, the elk are colossal and, like the suicidal squirrels constantly dashing back and forth across the roads back in Ohio, they are everywhere. Sally's driver, a sympathetic local hiker named David Wolfe, came within inches of hitting one of the beasts on their dark ride from the Portland airport to Packwood. By the time Wolfe dropped Sally, Rick, and Sally's boyfriend, John Stayton, at a dumpy motel on the main drag, it was nearly dawn. Exhausted from their travels, they slept only a few hours.

Upon waking in the morning, Sally stepped outside and her blue eyes took in the immensity of the mountains surrounding her. Most impressive was Mount Rainier. The "fourteener" provided a magnificent backdrop to Packwood, a tiny community nestled a little over a thousand feet above sea level and thirteen thousand feet below the mountain's snowy dome. Sally's search party of three ate breakfast at a diner next door to the motel. The first order of business was for the men to find maps of the area while Sally canvassed the town on foot. Her first stop was the hardware store. From credit card records, she knew Kris had purchased something there and the manager confirmed through his old receipts that Kris had bought starter firewood, matches, and fingerless gloves. After checking the hardware store off her list, Sally made her way through town, handing out missing person flyers at each and every business along the way and asking everyone she met if they had seen her son. At the post office, she and the postmistress determined that Kris had mailed a package from there. Records even revealed the approximate size by what Kris had paid to mail it. Later, Sally pushed the postmaster general to investigate the situation, but what Kris mailed from Packwood or to whom the package was addressed remains a mystery.

From the post office, she walked down the blocks to a historic inn at the far end of town. Unlike the seedier motel where she was staying, the Hotel Packwood was cute and inviting. Large wooden bears greeted you as you stepped onto the front porch. The establishment had a 4.5-star rating on Trip Advisor, where reviewers described the elderly couple who owned it as "sweet and helpful."

Sally first learned about Kris's stay at Hotel Packwood from two hikers going by the trail names Pickles and Forget-me-not, whom she had tracked down via trail registers and Facebook. Pickles and

Forget-me-not hiked with Sherpa along the notorious Goat Rocks traverse. In Packwood, Kris joined them for dinner at the Blue Spruce Saloon on October 10. Over their meals, the trio discussed their plans for the miles ahead. Pickles and Forget-me-not were going to hitch north—skipping hundreds of miles of trail—to reach the Canadian border before foul weather hit. Sherpa remained committed to hiking all of it consecutively, but his gear was better suited for balmier conditions. Before they parted, Pickles left Sherpa with his tent and some advice: the proprietors of Hotel Packwood would let him stay there for free if he was willing to sleep in an old trailer in the backyard.

Cold and wet from his snowy hike out of the Goat Rocks Wilderness, Kris walked out of the Blue Spruce and headed down the street to the Hotel Packwood. He hiked in sandals but wore neoprene socks to protect his feet from the chill. Behind the hotel, Kris found the old camping trailer Pickles had recommended. He tried the door, but it was locked. It may have been dark by then, and cold. Perhaps Kris knocked on the door of the hotel first and no one answered before he jimmied into the trailer so he could sleep inside. In the morning, he went out to do his errands. He left behind his backpack and gear because he intended on settling with the proprietors when he came back.

When the inn's manager, Marilyn Linder, entered the trailer to clean it, she discovered Sherpa's backpack inside. Frightened, she quickly informed her husband, David, who called the police. An officer responded, and Kris returned shortly after. Like many male thru-hikers, Sherpa, unwashed and shaggy, resembled a homeless person. The officer searched through the backpack and checked his identification. Kris had no criminal history, but his current predicament could change that.

"Am I in trouble?" the hiker asked, uneasy.

"Not at all, son," David Linder interrupted. "You just walked into a blessing because Jesus wants me to help you." The elderly couple dismissed the police officer and invited the dirty thru-hiker inside for a home-cooked meal. Sherpa had been leaning vegetarian, but Marilyn's meatloaf sandwiches were so delicious, he ate two. In exchange for another night's stay, he did a few chores for David while Marilyn washed his smelly clothes.

This couple, the epitome of trail angels, begged Kris to stay with them a third night, for free. A record-breaking "monster storm" was on its way, and heavy snow was predicted for the Cascades. But Sherpa was infected with border fever. No "stormpocalypse" was going to keep him from continuing his trek. In the morning, on October 12, Kris signed the hotel's register and headed back to the PCT.

Flash-forward a few weeks to November 2. Kris was gone and Sally was sitting inside the inn listening to David and Marilyn Linder retell their story, one they'd already told her over the phone.

"I could tell he felt awful for breaking into the trailer," David said. "I didn't want him to feel bad. It was freezing."

Marilyn pointed out Kris's signature on her hotel register, and Sally shed more tears. David was a joyfully religious man. Before Sally left, he clasped her hand and prayed for Kris. It was a small but kind comfort knowing that this loving couple had taken her son under their wings prior to his disappearance.

From the inn, Sally walked to the gas station on the east side of town, where an elk loitered at the pump as if it had as much right as anybody to be there. The clerk went through his receipts until he found one showing a purchase Kris had made for less than four dollars, most likely a candy bar or a soda.

Local news stations soon picked up on the story of Sherpa's disappearance. After Sally returned to the motel, a crew arrived with their camera and microphone. "We just want him to come home," Sally told the reporter with KIRO 7 News. "I hope he walks out and says, 'What the heck are you doing, Mom? What's all the fuss?'" She hadn't slept to any real degree for over a week and it showed, but so did her determination. Under her blue flannel shirt, she wore a black T-shirt imprinted with a steadfast slogan: I DIDN'T COME HERE TO LOSE.

The motel manager spoke on camera as well. "They pinged his phone," she said, the sign of her business displayed prominently behind her, "and as far as the ping is concerned it hasn't left White Pass, so we're going to concentrate on this area while Yakima [County] is concentrating somewhere else."

After connecting with Sally via Facebook, the motel manager had been unbelievably helpful. Later that afternoon, she gave Sally's group a ride to the Kracker Barrel, a mini-mart/gas station twenty miles up the road at White Pass. Here Sally re-interviewed a clerk who saw Kris on October 12. Sherpa had come in and asked to use the phone because his charger wasn't working right. He made a twenty-minute call to an 800 number, but the authorities could not trace it. He looked so hungry that the clerk offered him a foil-wrapped burrito, on the house.

From the Kracker Barrel, the motel manager drove Sally's group to the trailhead. At 4,500 feet, White Pass was much colder than Packwood, and the forest grew thicker as the PCT headed north, switchbacking deep into the conifers. A ridiculous urge to run up the trail and start yelling for Kris overcame Sally, her mind indulging in a fantasy of finding him right there in the woods. She considered White Pass—Kris's point last seen—to be ground zero. She expected to see searchers here, scraping the trail for clues, like something you'd watch on TV. But there was no line of people walking side by side with their eyes to the ground and beating the brush with sticks. Sally's little group were the only ones there.

After an hour or so at the trailhead, the motel manager drove them to another section of the PCT. Sally got out of the car and walked around to get a feel for it. Fungi, fleshy mounds of various colors and shapes, sprouted up all over the forest floor. Sally's brother picked one up to examine it. "Oh no!" the motel manager screamed, startling everyone. "That one is poison. Don't touch your eyes."

Rick Guyton foraged wild foods on occasion, and he thought the fungus in his hand looked like it could be edible. Suddenly, a Forest Service officer drove up. Sally waved the officer down and gave her some flyers. The motel manager advised the officer that the Yakima Sheriff's Office had given her friends permission to park their vehicles at this remote trailhead at night so they could search for Kris when they got off work. Normally, muddy pickup trucks with local license plates that are parked overnight at strange places might arouse a forest ranger's suspicion or concern, but the Forest Service officer said she'd advise her colleagues that the manager's friends were searching the woods for Kris in the evenings, and they should pay no mind to the men and their cars.

When the group returned to Packwood, Kris's lady friend from the trail, Amber Johnson, arrived with her sister, increasing the size of the impromptu search party from three to five. They laid out all their maps on the floor of Sally's large motel room, turning it into a de facto command post.

Meanwhile, the Bring Kris Fowler/Sherpa Home Facebook page had amassed over a thousand followers by then and was "going crazy" with clues and tips. A bear hunter claimed to have seen Kris on the PCT well north of Packwood on Blowout Mountain on October 22. Because he seemed credible and had provided a detailed description of the missing hiker's clothing and gear, the bear hunter's sighting shifted the official search effort to the north. But tips continued to surge in. A store clerk sold a candy bar to a hiker who looked like Kris in Mazama, the last town for resupply before the terminus, and officers were reviewing the store's security tapes. A bus driver believed he picked Kris up in Olympia, a city near Seattle. Everyone in the motel room had their phones going. The young women were the most adept at social media. Rick worked the maps. Sally put pressure on the cops, interviewed the witnesses who said they saw Kris, and patiently listened to every psychic with something to say. While Sally was busy with these tasks, a local police officer pulled her brother aside.

"Things are not as they seem," the cop said, nodding at the motel. It was an ominous warning, but Rick kept it to himself. His little sister had enough to deal with already.

It was all so exhausting. Things were getting foggy, challenging this capable woman's ability to cope. On the second day in Packwood, Sally melted down during breakfast. It was obvious what she needed; she was no use to anybody if she didn't get some rest. The men and the young women went back to White Pass to search for clues while Sally returned to her room, pulled the covers over her head, and cried herself to sleep.

When she woke up, her phone dinged with "a million" messages to follow up on. Alone in her room, Sally grabbed her notebook and started working. The dingy motel had seen better days. The carpet was stained, the walls were thin, and the latches on some of the windows had been pried back in a way that made it impossible to lock them. Sally glanced outside and saw people conducting mysterious meetings in the parking lot. She wasn't one to judge, but these guys appeared to be up to no good. They reminded her of the motel manager's boyfriend, who was supposedly searching for Kris after work, but couldn't look Sally in the eye when she thanked him. At that moment, a light bulb came on in her head. *Something is not right with this motel.*

Sally wasn't naive generally, but she had never been to Washington, and she knew how vulnerable she was. Her son was missing. She needed all the help she could get. When the motel manager had offered her help via Facebook, it had seemed like a godsend. This generous person was providing them a place to stay, driving them to White Pass, and instructing the forest ranger to let her friends park at the trailhead all night without suspicion so they could "search for the missing hiker" when they got off work. At first Sally thought to herself, *How nice of them.*

But were they really looking for Kris?

When the others returned, Sally voiced her concerns. Her brother now revealed what the cop had told him. Yes, the manager's friends may be spending time in the woods after dark, but he didn't think they were searching too hard for Kris. They were probably hunting for chanterelles. The sweet-smelling mushrooms, a delicacy, sold for as much as $250 per pound. Harvesting them in the National Forest without a permit is a criminal offense federal officers rigorously enforce. The motel manager's friends may have been using the search effort as an excuse to be in the forest after sunset, because it was the perfect cover to poach mushrooms.

"Let's go," Rick said. "Now."

The manager wasn't responding to Sally's texts, so she left cash in the room to settle the bill. "Like battered wives," they loaded their suitcases into Amber's car and left.

The next day, Sally rented an SUV and headed north, following the trail's direction toward the town of Mazama. On the way, someone posted on Facebook that Kris had been found. Alive! They pulled over so Sally could call Sergeant Randy Briscoe.

Ever since Sally had first pushed Briscoe to "make something happen" in their initial call on October 31, the Yakima County Search and Rescue coordinator had been extremely busy. The delay in initiating a search for her son would always bother Sally, but once Sergeant Briscoe took the reins, the official operation to find Kris exploded in scale. Thanks in large part to his efforts, at least seven counties, the Air National Guard, the Civil Air Patrol, and over a hundred searchers all over the state had sprung into action. Spearheaded by Corporal Ellis Nale, twenty ground searchers scoured the length of the PCT in Kittitas County. At least three counties, Chelan, Snohomish, and Yakima, flew over the trail, searching for signs of the missing thru-hiker. And Briscoe put boots on the ground, sending his troops over every foot of the PCT along the seventy-six-mile section in his jurisdiction. Before it was over, the multiagency search for Kris Fowler would be the largest collaborative search operation Briscoe had ever seen, and the combined cost must have approached six figures.

But from her position, out there alone with her little amateur search party, Sally couldn't fully appreciate how earnestly the professionals were working to find her son. Further complicating matters, the relationship between Kris's stepmom and Sergeant Briscoe had gotten off to a rocky start, but it would recover. Sally knew she needed Briscoe's help, and the deputy needed her cooperation. They were in this together whether they liked it or not. And it is a credit to both their characters that, only a few days after she dropped an f-bomb on Briscoe's voice mail, an enduring, mutual respect was already growing between them. Within minutes of Sally calling him to ask about the reports that Kris had walked out, Briscoe called her back to update her on the potentially promising news.

Unfortunately, Kris had *not* walked out of the wilderness. The Facebook post was false information shared online. The misunderstanding was rectified within ten minutes. Long enough for Sally's hope to skyrocket, crash, and then burn.

On November 8, another tip came in via Facebook. "My husband and I gave Kris a ride on October 12," a woman wrote. "He seemed very eager to get back on the trail and wanted to get some miles in before the storm." The woman sent Sally a picture she took before they parted. In the photo, a backpacker stood in the parking lot of the Kracker Barrel. He wore a knit beanie, a black raincoat, and rain pants. He carried the weight of his pack with ease. In one hand, he held a bag of merchandise most likely purchased at the hardware store. The other hand was raised enigmatically, perhaps in a half-hearted wave to the photographer. The hiker was good-looking and tall. His shaggy blond beard caught the fading afternoon light. Most striking was the soulful look in his blue eyes. It was Sherpa, proving beyond a doubt that Kris Fowler was at White Pass on October 12, 2016, at 3:30 p.m.

For ten days, Sally's unofficial search party tracked down several more leads, visiting many towns along the route. Winthrop. Mazama. Darrington. By the ninth day, they had logged 2,500 miles on the rental car's odometer and hadn't stayed in one place for more than two nights. Yet they were no closer to knowing what happened to Kris than they were when they started. Bone-tired and starving, they booked hotel rooms in Bothel. Someone ordered pizza. Sally was about to take another bite when her brother took a deep breath and announced, "We're going home."

She'd been ravenous, but her appetite instantly vanished. She was on the verge of losing it. Completely. "What do you mean, 'we're going home'?"

"Listen, everything you are doing here, you can do at home."

Rick Guyton had spoken, and his little sister had to admit it was true. They'd driven all over a humongous state with little to show for it. The biggest strides they'd made in tracking down her son had been accomplished over the phone or through social media—things they could do back in Ohio. Yet, when Sally set her mind to do something, she didn't take no for an answer. This was how she made things happen at work. Like the slogan on the T-shirt she wore in front of the news cameras, Sally Fowler did not come to Washington to lose. She came there to bring that kid home. Sally wept, convincing her brother she needed more time.

They flew back on the eleventh day. On the plane, Sally wrapped a blue scarf around her head to hide the tragedy written all over her face. She gazed out her window at the Cascade Range below. Her son was still down there, somewhere in those snowy mountains, and she was leaving him behind. It hurt. It really, really hurt.

When Sally first told me about her trip to Washington, I sensed how tough that flight home must have been for her. Later, she confessed that she couldn't bring herself to travel back to the North Cascades.

She felt others were judging her for this. Why would a woman who was serious about finding her son not return to the state he was missing from?

But I understood entirely. Flying home without a lost child is a pain no mother should have to endure twice. And Rick was right. Sally's best investigative work was done from home, through social media. And that's a heck of a lot easier and cheaper than putting another two thousand miles on a rental car.

Back in Ohio, Sally returned to her demanding job and continued to work her son's case late into the evenings. She had been home a month when, late one night in December, her nephew sent her an image making the rounds on Facebook—a picture of an unidentified man in his thirties who appeared to be unconscious. He had a full beard, blond hair, and a pleasant face, but his eyes were closed, and someone had pulled a white sheet tightly across his bare chest. Sally's heart raced. The man in the photograph looked like her son, and he was strapped to a hospital bed in Brazil.

CHAPTER 8

# The Man in Brazil

WHEN KRIS'S EX-WIFE SAW THE FACEBOOK PHOTO OF THE "MAN IN BRAZIL," SHE told Sally, "I can't say it's *not* him."

Sally agreed. The unidentified man was the correct height. He spoke English. His eyes were blue, and he appeared to have suffered a mental breakdown. Maybe Kris had lost it somehow, hit his head or experienced a psychological collapse, and ended up in Brazil. But before she booked a flight to a country notorious for kidnapping foreigners, Sally needed to know one more thing. Did the Man in Brazil have a tattoo on his back? For reasons she couldn't fathom, the Brazilian authorities were unable to answer this simple question.

Other families hoped the Man in Brazil was their own son. A mother in Scotland. A family in Germany. After those cases were ruled out, a "private investigator" with a heavy accent called Sally. "You fly to the country," he said. "I pick you up and take you there." For five hundred dollars. Instead of hiring the Brazilian "investigator," Sally requested help from someone she'd never met in person but completely trusted: an aspiring thru-hiker in Missouri named Morgan Clements.

Nine months earlier, back in April 2016, Morgan had attempted a thru-hike of the PCT but had to quit three hundred miles in because of an illness. Like many PCT hopefuls, Morgan stayed connected to the trail family or "tramily" via the PCT Class of 2016 Facebook group. In late October, he saw Sally's posts about her missing stepson. Morgan was in his late forties, more than a decade older than Kris, but he felt an affinity for the missing hiker. On October 30, he joined the Bring Kris Fowler/Sherpa Home group, the day it was created. A few knowledgeable locals, trail angels, and thru-hikers chimed in right away, offering a little advice and lots of thoughts and prayers in the comments, but Morgan kept his contributions behind the scenes.

The Missourian had a unique background and wanted to apply what he'd learned over the years to help solve the case. The horror of the terrorist attacks on 9/11 had inspired Morgan to start mapping worldwide occurrences of terrorist activity and sharing it on his website GlobalIncidentMap.com because he felt the government and the media weren't doing an adequate job of keeping the public informed. Before long, he was mapping other scary things, like mass shootings, arson-caused wildfires, outbreaks of contagious diseases, and natural disasters. Over time, Morgan's data became more valuable. By 2017, government agencies, the military, and corporate entities were among the clients contracting his services, and his company, GlobalIncidentMap, employed people all over the globe.

Looking at Morgan's maps instantly evokes urgency and alarm. Hundreds of colorful icons blink wherever fires, explosions, violence, radioactivity, and food poisonings threaten the globe. In 2008, this aesthetic inspired the Museum of Modern Art (MOMA) in New York City to display one of Morgan's terrorism maps in an exhibit. By then, his hobby-turned-business had grown to the point, he told a reporter, that he spent his days in front of eight computers in his Missouri basement making maps for "people who don't want to have their heads stuck in the sand."

The mapmaker's cynical humor veiled an idealism within. Perhaps if his company charted every incident of violence and horror in the world, others could use that information to prevent future incidents. Another example of Morgan's covert soft spot for humanity emerged when he contacted Sally Fowler and offered to help her find Kris pro bono. Neither of them could have imagined how much or how often Sally would depend on him. "Once I started talking to the mother," Morgan later said, "it became personal."

The length of Morgan's workdays crossed global time zones, but his hours were flexible. "I was in a unique position," he noted, "where I could dedicate several hours a day to help Sally." One of the first things he did was ask her whether she had access to Kris's laptop, and he recommended she contact an information technology professional for help. Prying into a loved one's online presence is a delicate matter, legally and ethically, and Morgan knew to tread lightly. "Understand," he later explained to other would-be sleuths, "accessing this sort of data without a person's permission is an egregious breach of privacy. One which could produce embarrassing or hurtful results."

Under the principles of "Leave No Trace," a hiker should "take nothing but pictures and leave nothing but footprints" while in the wilderness. Ironically, tracking experts believe that a single hiker will leave nearly two thousand physical signs per every mile they walk. "It's virtually impossible to pass through an environment without leaving some trace or evidence," write the authors of *Managing the Inland Search Function*, a text for search planners. "Tracks, scents, disturbances, discarded articles all mark the presence of humans in an area." Like a ground tracker looking for a snapped twig in the woods, Morgan looked for "footprints" left in "the clouds" of the Web. Just as you do when you walk through the brush, when you use the internet, social media, or a cell phone, you are dropping a trail of evidence others can follow. Hidden within our social media accounts, online purchases, and Google searches is a gold mine of potential clues, and Morgan Clements was talented at finding them.

He and Sally sifted through Kris's online activity and several intriguing discoveries rose to the surface. Kris had purchased *Wanderer*, the book about the disillusioned actor wanting to escape society, from Amazon. He was "couch surfing" Airbnb rentals. He had joined a mushroom-hunting group and made inquiries on Facebook about working as a cannabis trimmer. But the most surprising thing they learned was that Kris had been scoping out "woofing" opportunities in Argentina and Brazil before he disappeared.

*Woofing* is shorthand for World Wide Opportunities on Organic Farms (WWOOF)—a loose network of organizations that offer homestay farming opportunities, often for those on a budget. "Live and learn on organic farms" is the motto one group uses to attract idealistic young people wanting to travel the world while laboring on organic farms for free room and board.

Within minutes of seeing the Man in Brazil, Sally sent the photo to Morgan, who stared at his computer late into the night to compare facial features of the man in the photo to images of Kris. Unable to rule out the possibility the two men were the same, Morgan investigated further by using Google Translate to read Portuguese news articles about the unidentified man. According to these stories, the Man in Brazil had wandered into traffic and was begging for money before he was arrested and then hospitalized. Morgan was considering booking a flight to Brazil when a Brazilian thru-hiker in the 2016 group responded to his Facebook message that asked for help. The female thru-hiker, who wants to remain anonymous, made several calls before deciding to drive eight hours from her home in Brazil to visit the unidentified man in the hospital to see him with her own eyes.

Meanwhile, Sally shared all that she knew with Ellis Nale of the Kittitas County Sheriff's Department. From the start, Corporal Nale had worked Kris's case in cooperation with Sergeant Briscoe from Yakima County. Nale notified a government official in DC and that person contacted the American embassy in Brazil.

Once the Brazilian thru-hiker arrived at the hospital, she confirmed that the man in the photograph spoke English with an American or Canadian accent, but he did not have a tattoo on his back. The Man in Brazil was not Kris Fowler.

Moments after Sally received this information, an official from the American embassy in Brazil called. This might not be my son, she said, but he belongs to somebody and they are looking for him. She sent the American embassy official the Facebook photo and told him the man might have either an American or a Canadian accent. As soon as he was off the phone with Sally, the American contacted the Canadian embassy, where someone searched through a Canadian missing persons database and at least one mystery was solved.

The Man in Brazil was Anton Pilipa, a thirty-nine-year-old Canadian who suffered from schizophrenia and had been missing since 2012. Pilipa had worked for humanitarian relief organizations before his mental illness got the better of him and Canadian authorities arrested him for assault. Instead of showing up for his court date, Pilipa had fled the country. With no passport and little money, the fugitive claimed he had traveled from Vancouver, British Columbia, to Brazil—a ten-thousand-mile journey—by walking and hitchhiking.

For years, Pilipa's family had been searching for him. "I told myself he was dead," Stefan Pilipa, Anton's brother, confessed to a reporter, "because that was the only thing I could come up with [to explain] his absence."

To celebrate the reunion of Pilipa and his family, Sally shared the following post on her Facebook group:

**Sally Guyton Fowler**
January 7, 2017 · ·

So...the Brazil man....It all started because someone took a photo of a patient that seemed to not know his own name and didn't have any ID on him and sent it to a mom from Scotland whose son has been missing for over 2 years. This Mom knew right away it was not her son as the man in the photo did not have a tatoo on his chest that her son has. So, she posted the photo. A family from Germany then thought it was their son, who also had been missing for over two years. They hired a PI that found out his blood type, eye color, and height and this confirmed it was NOT their son. In the meantime one of my family members saw these posts, sent me the picture and so it began. During all of this, I Messaged with both of the families who's sons are also
Missing. Today, the Mom from Scotland messaged me to make sure I had heard the family of this Brazil man had been found. Like me, she was thrilled. Hats off to her for Sharing that photo on FB and starting this whole series of events. It gives us and many others hope.

If used properly, isn't FB an amazing vehicle ?! Without it, this man would still be missing from his family. Without it, we would not have most of the info about Kris that we have today. Without It, we would not have so much support from all of you. So happy that something good has come from all of this. I didn't sleep a wink for two solid days while this Brazil sighting first started. It was all worth it. Happy Endings are possible! #givesmehope. #ourdaywillcome

Hey Kris call me

👍👍                                          43 Comments  3 Shares

👍 Like            💬 Comment            ↪ Share

*Facebook post by Sally Fowler.*

Yes. If used properly, Facebook *was* amazing. However, using social media to find a missing loved one wasn't without its dark side. By then, the Bring Kris Fowler/Sherpa Home group continued to bring in leads and had accumulated over six thousand followers. Although most of Sally's followers were kind, helpful, and supportive, a few were critical and judging. Some were manipulative or narcissistic. Others were flat-out crazy. Like the guy who declared he had quit his job to look for Kris. At first, his posts came across as heroic. He was out there scouring the wilderness, carrying an extra pack on his back so he could give it to Kris when he found him. But, as members of the Facebook group cheered him on, the man's posts became more and more dramatic, as he vowed to "keep going" despite "feeling weak."

It didn't take long for Sally to suspect this whack job had never hiked a mile in his life and was staying at a Holiday Inn the whole time. His profile pic was obviously fake, but she ignored the bizarre game he was playing until the guy messaged her friend requesting money for a horse. "Unless he shows up looking like John Wayne," Sally told her friend, "don't give him anything." After that, Sally blocked this individual from the group. His delusions were distracting others from finding her son.

Sally didn't want her Facebook group to become a drama hub, but she also didn't want to push anyone away. For each catfishing wannabe, there was a selfless, skilled, serious person like Morgan who genuinely wanted to help without asking for anything in return. "Who knows," she shrugged, "the littlest thing could be the lead" that brought her son home. For similar, albeit more jaded, reasons, law enforcement monitored Sally's Facebook group under a fictitious account of their own.

Chasing leads while keeping the Facebook group active spilled over into Sally's day job at a large-scale grocery supplier, where, according to Sally, one mistake could lead to a million-dollar loss for her company. Normally, Sally was a detailed, organized person. The type who kept a neat house and religiously sent out thank-you notes. All that went to shit after Kris disappeared. She wasn't sleeping like she used to. She cried too much and too often. She had to stop wearing mascara.

The strain took its toll on Kris's father as well.

Five months after Kris disappeared, in February 2017, Mike Fowler came down with a severe case of laryngitis that hampered his ability to speak. A specialist diagnosed him with "vocal cord paralysis" due to stress. Months later, in April, the doctors figured out what really ailed him: an enlarged lymph node pressed against a nerve to his vocal cord. The node was swollen because a huge tumor resided in Mike's left lung. Sally waited in the hospital while a surgeon biopsied Mike's tumor. He was recovering from the anesthesia when the doctors met her in one of those little rooms, looking grim. She'd been in those depressing rooms before and had been on the receiving end of the dire news that is delivered there. But this felt different. The doctors had a peculiar look on their faces, like whatever they'd seen in Mike's lungs had frightened them.

Mike should get his affairs in order, the doctors said. He had lung cancer.

When Sally entered Mike's hospital room, he sat up and smiled. He was craving pizza and wanted to go home.

"What did the doctors tell you?" she asked, hesitant.

It became clear that Mike hadn't yet heard the news.

Sally gave him a choice. "Do you want to wait for them to give you the biopsy results? Or do you want to know what they told me?"

"Tell me," he said.

So she did.

Mike spent his last days at home cooking up a storm and mulching the yard. One day he overdid it. He pushed a button on an emergency response device Sally had given him. Cancer had reduced Mike's voice to a whisper. To communicate with 911, he had to clap numerical responses to their questions. They readmitted him to the hospital and he was in no mood for visitors, but he wanted Sally's stepmom, Sandy, to bring him some of her famous chicken wings.

Sandy Guyton became Sally's real mom "in every way" after her biological mother died of cancer when Sally was twenty-one. Their relationship mirrored the one she had with Kris. Both Sandy and Sally never had biological children. Sally became Sandy's only daughter, like Kris became Sally's only son.

Mike loved his former in-laws. Before Sally's dad died, he had lost his voice after a stroke. Mike wanted to tell Sandy that he now understood what that must have been like for his father-in-law. Sandy brought Mike some of her homemade chicken wings, just like he requested, and they had a wonderful visit.

It rained that day. On the way home, Sally's stepmom entered a bad intersection. Two cars collided. Hours later, Sandy died in surgery.

The tragedies kept piling on. Her stepson. Her stepmother. Her ex-husband. It was a nightmare. The kind that might send you to a dark corner of the house, rocking back and forth indefinitely. Days after her stepmom's funeral, Sally joined her brother Rick at Mike's bedside to say goodbye.

Mike Fowler first joined Facebook in June 2016, for the sole purpose of seeing the photographs and following the updates his son posted from his PCT thru-hike. Now, months later, he hoped to be reunited with Kris soon, but he would die without the peace of knowing what had happened. On the day he passed, Mike squeezed his ex-wife's hand. He wanted to tell her something.

Sally leaned in.

Mike whispered simply: "Find him."

Five months later, Sally was with friends, having dinner at a local restaurant, when her phone flashed with a "funny number" she didn't recognize. "I have to take this." Sally excused herself from the group, moving over to an empty table so she could hear better.

The caller was a cop from Washington. "We found a backbone in the woods," he said. They were running some tests. They would contact her once the results were in.

Sally thanked the officer for keeping her in the loop and walked back to her table. She confessed the grisly topic of the phone call to her companions, and, after a moment of sympathy, everyone returned to their dinner. Sally had received calls like this before. Her son had been missing a year by then and hearing terrible, hopeful news was becoming routine. She stared at the half-eaten meal on her plate and tried to unsee a mental image of a human spine lying in the forest.

As he'd promised, the cop from Washington called her back a few days later.

The spine did not belong to Kris.

"Part of my new daily life is to get a phone call while I'm eating supper at a nice restaurant with friends and somebody is saying, 'Hey, I want to let you know we found a human bone. It looks like a spinal column, and we're running tests on it.' It's unreal."

When Sally told me this story, she had already spent an hour detailing the facts surrounding her stepson's disappearance with a clear-eyed fortitude I admired, but after the words "it's unreal" came out of her mouth, she wept.

"I'm sorry," Sally apologized for breaking down. "It's been a hard week. I'm much better than I used to be. But...you know... the holidays."

"I hope I'm not pushing too many bruises," I said.

"I'm fragile," she replied, "but I'm not a fragile flower. I think it's helping me, but I'm sure I'll cry myself asleep tonight."

In response to this contradiction, Sally stopped crying, and we both laughed at the absurdity of it. *All* of it. The last fourteen months had broken Sally's heart six ways to Sunday, but her sense of humor remained intact. That had been the point Sally was trying to make with her spine-in-the-forest story. *Who gets calls like this?* and *How did this become my life?* Still, as much as Sally wanted to find her son and bring his body home, the spinal column didn't belong to Kris, and that meant he could still be alive.

Sally acknowledged the unlikelihood of his survival, but she wasn't ready to throw in the towel just yet. "My head thinks he's on the mountain, but my heart hopes he's braiding hair in a commune somewhere."

Members of Sally's Facebook group, Bring Kris Fowler/Sherpa Home, became somewhat aware of how dreadful 2017 was turning out to be for Sally when on June 22, she announced Mike's death on her page.

**Sally Guyton Fowler**
June 22, 2017 · 🌐                                                              ...

It is with a broken heart that I share with you our sad news about Mike, Kris's Dad. He lost his battle with cancer yesterday. I was privileged to be with him along with his dear friends and his amazing family as he peacefully went to be with God. Kris was sorely missed.

Kris truly got his love of the outdoors from his Dad. Mike loved Kris with every ounce of his being. They laughed, they yelled, they fished, they hiked, they camped, they went to Reds games and they even shared a few cold beers. I am proud to have raised Kris with Mike.  We both still love each other's families and maintained a friendship and were confidants on just about everything. Kris was so proud that we were still friends and liked each other's significant others. It just makes life easier. It wasn't always rosie, but we always worked it out.

The past eight months has been harder on Mike than anyone else on the planet. It was difficult seeing his pain concerning Kris. I so hoped we could have closure while Mike was still here, but God has another plan apparently.

I know this.  If Kris is on earth, and I still have hope that he is, Mike already knows where he is and will lead him to us or us to him. If Kris is no longer on earth, he is having one heck of a reunion with his Dad. Fishing and eating are involved.  Hugging, smiling and belly laughing too. Mike is already greatly missed. I don't know how I'm going to do this without you. Fly high Mike. I love ya.

Hey Mike....bring him home to me💕

Hey Kris...call me💕 — with **Michael Fowler** and **Kris Fowler**.

*Facebook post by Sally Fowler.*

Nine hundred people reacted to this post, many of them by clicking on hearts and crying faces. One crying face emoji represented the support of a silent follower, a woman in her fifties who, in two months' time, would end up becoming a major player in the search for Kris Fowler.

CHAPTER 9

# *The Volunteer*

---

**C**ATHY TARR WAS NOTHING IF NOT PREPARED.

"It's official!" she announced on Facebook. "My Pacific Crest Trail permit has been approved!" At fifty-four, she was older than most of her fellow thru-hikers; hiking was a new pursuit, but like most endeavors Cathy took on, she went at it with gusto. Over the course of two years, the retired mother of two had bagged forty-two peaks in New England, trekked a two-day pilgrimage in Ireland, and hiked two sections of the PCT near the Southern Terminus. In February 2017, when she got the word about her PCT permit, she was in New Hampshire during the frigid months of winter, because that's when the White Mountains were perfect for testing one's ability to hike in snow—in other words, strapping claw-like metal crampons to the bottoms of your boots and using an ice axe to arrest your slide down icy slopes.

In 2013, the Pacific Crest Trail Association (PCTA) instituted a voluntary permit system to disperse the environmental impact caused by an exponential growth in backpackers. During the prime thru-hiking season, it issued only fifty northbound permits for each day. It was something to celebrate when Cathy learned she had made the cut, although her given start date, March 19, 2017, was earlier than she wanted. As a northbound thru-hiker, Cathy preferred a start date in April, when the weather was warmer and the timing would allow her to trek across the High Sierra after the snow had begun to melt. For this reason, some hikers believed the PCTA's quota system was unsafe because it forced thru-hikers to start sooner than they should.

A few days after the PCTA notified Cathy of her start date, a friend invited her on a day trip to Maine to look at some real estate. The long drive gave them plenty of time for conversation, but Cathy doesn't remember what they were talking about when another car pulled out in front of them before her friend could avoid a collision.

It could have been worse. The first thing Cathy's friend said was, "Oh well. I need a new car anyhow."

"Call 911." Cathy couldn't catch her breath.

"Are you okay?"

"I don't know." She wasn't bleeding, but her chest hurt like hell and that scared her.

At the ER, they admitted Cathy into the Trauma Room because nothing else was available, she was told. A hospital employee remained in the room with her, distracting her with small talk. It seemed weird. Was her condition that serious? She told him she had a permit to hike the PCT. Her starting date was less than a month away. After she rolled through the MRI machine, two doctors came by. A male and a female. One stood on each side of her bed. "I hear you are hiking the Pacific Crest Trail in March," the male doctor observed.

Yeah, Cathy told him, that's right.

"I'm sorry to tell you this, but that's not going to happen." The physician shook his head sympathetically, pointing to her breastbone. "Your sternum is fractured."

This shocking news brought forth the tears. After two years of planning and preparing for her 2017 PCT thru-hike, Cathy's dream of hiking from Mexico to Canada had been crushed—right along with her sternum. It took a couple of weeks, but she did get over it.

*No, you are not going,* the universe had commanded. "It took an accident to stop me," she later concluded.

Over the next few years, I would become very familiar with Cathy's approach to setbacks. To me, it was straight-up Mary Poppins. Optimistically realistic in the face of any and every challenge life threw her way.

Cathy Short Tarr had been adulting for a long time. When she was ten in rural Pennsylvania, her mother died of cancer. She'd never seen her father cry, but when he broke down right in front of her, it hurt her deeply.

Her father's values were old-fashioned. His eldest daughter was already married, so once his wife Esther was buried, it fell on George Short's middle child, Cathy, to get her younger sister off to school and to have the house ready when he came home from work. When Cathy's grandmother started showing signs of dementia, she cared for her too. Then, when Cathy was twenty, her dad succumbed to a heart attack. Nine months later, her grandmother died. Before she could legally drink a beer, Cathy "knew the funeral director by name and how to pick out a casket."

Well prepped to establish a home of her own, she married young and raised two children before getting divorced. Newly single in her forties, she accepted a shipping and receiving position at Walgreens. The pharmacy chain recognized managerial potential in Cathy and quickly promoted her into its corporate ranks, moving her to different stores around the country. Cathy liked her job all right and she was respected. Mayors and the chief of police attended the corporate-funded community events she planned. But a vague longing pulled at her. Sooner than most, Cathy had learned an important lesson: life was too short to set aside your dreams only to sit all day inside an office with no windows.

In 2015, at the age of fifty-two, Cathy gave notice to Walgreens. She sold her home and most of the items in it. Living out of her car, she traveled across the United States and visited a half dozen other countries. She fell in love with the Pacific Crest Trail and the idea of hiking every mile of it—which is why it was such a bummer when, all of a sudden, her body wasn't up to the task. But there's not much you can do for a fractured breastbone other than take it easy for a year and avoid hiking superlong trails over nine mountain ranges while wearing a heavy pack. As she healed, nearly every day she read enviously about the other hikers' travels via their Facebook posts in PCT Class of 2017.

Among the trail dramas Cathy followed on the PCT Facebook pages was the search for Kris Fowler, which was brought to her attention one day when she spotted a post at the top of the group's page. As a mother of two and a hiker herself, Cathy identified both with Sally, the mother, and with Kris, the missing.

Then, in July 2017, a month after Mike Fowler died, Cathy was staying with her son in Arizona when a new post popped up in Sally's group. A local hunter from Washington named Andrea Kirkman had put out a call for volunteers to come to the North Cascades. Kris had been missing for nine months, dozens of professional and volunteer search efforts for him had failed, but Kirkman and her husband, Josh, remained committed to organizing a three-night/four-day search in August. "I've been talking to Sally," Andrea Kirkman wrote on Facebook. "My husband and I know the area well. We are looking for five groups of at least four per group. We all will provide our own food, water, and gear!"

And there it was. Like a sign from the universe that had told her to slow down months before. *This* was a way for her to stay connected with the trail and its community while making use of her preparation and the knowledge she'd accumulated, all in the pursuit of a truly meaningful goal: to help a family find their lost son.

And so, she drove up from her son's home in Arizona and joined the August search. Cathy and the other volunteers scoured the landscapes south of Snoqualmie Pass during the day. At night, they sat around camp and discussed every angle of Kris's disappearance, hoping that some small detail would reveal itself to be the lightning bolt of insight that solved the case. The camaraderie united them, and Cathy was impressed by many of the people she met. The outdoorsy locals knowledgeable about Kris Fowler's case and the mountains he disappeared in. The former search and rescue workers, mountaineers, backcountry horsewomen, and hunters. Not to mention the generous and caring people, like Andrea and Josh Kirkman, who had followed the case closely from the start. Others charted the moment-by-moment weather reports and detailed timelines of Kris's movements, sharing what they learned with Sally's Facebook group. A few even met with several witnesses who said they'd seen Kris and interviewed them.

For Cathy, one lead stood out. On November 1, the day Sally Fowler left Ohio for Washington, a bear hunter had called in a tip after seeing a story about Kris Fowler on the evening news. The hunter told Sergeant Briscoe of the Yakima County Sheriff's Office that he and a friend were walking south on the PCT scouting for bear near Blowout Mountain at nine a.m. on October 22 when they saw a hiker heading toward them from the opposite direction. The hunter said his friend walked ahead while he stayed behind to say hello.

"What are you hunting?" the hiker had asked.

"Bear."

"Cool."

After this brief encounter, they had parted, each going in the opposite direction.

The bear hunter's description of the hiker he'd seen matched the one Briscoe was looking for—about to a T. He was tall and slender, with a beard. He carried a large black backpack and wore a beanie. His pants had unique pockets, and there were two orange panels on his pack.

"Sarge," the bear hunter told Briscoe, "I'm pretty sure it's your guy." Then he added that the friend who was with him on October 22 was also confident that the hiker they saw was Kris Fowler.

In response to the bear hunter's sighting, the search operation shifted to areas north of Blowout Mountain, and at least two searches south of there were canceled. The bear hunter continued to involve himself in the case by communicating with Sally, both over the phone and through written messages. "I'm a Christian man," he assured her more than once. He also offered advice to the volunteers in Sally's Facebook group, including a comment he posted on November 1, where he referred to "the possible sighting...by some hunters."

That day, no one seemed to notice the peculiar phrasing he'd used.

In his own post, the bear hunter had referred to himself in the third person.

Ten months later, Kirkman and the other volunteers were searching an area north of Blowout Mountain, based on the bear hunter's tip. However, as Cathy became more and more familiar with Kris's case, she became less and less confident in the bear hunter's story. For one, the dates didn't work. Blowout Mountain was a three- to four-day hike north from where Kris was last seen on October 12 at White Pass. Even in poor weather, he should have hiked past Blowout Mountain a week *before* the hunter claimed to have seen him. But this wasn't the thing bothering Cathy the most. What really disturbed her was the amount of detail the hunter claimed to have remembered. In conversations with Sally, not only had the bear hunter described exactly what Kris was wearing, he identified the type of pockets on his pants and the colors of two panels on his backpack.

One day, Cathy tested her theory on two volunteer searchers hiking ahead. She watched them greet two PCT hikers coming in the opposite direction. As soon as the thru-hikers had left, Cathy caught up to the volunteers and asked, "Hey, what color were their backpacks?"

They didn't know.

"Were they wearing shorts or pants?"

They couldn't say.

Cathy suspected as much. Although the searchers had spoken to the hikers mere moments earlier, they recalled few, if any, details about their clothing or gear—after all, why remember so many precise details about a stranger when you've only crossed paths for a minute or two? Something was definitely off about the bear hunter, but whenever Cathy brought it up, people dismissed her with the same logic: It must be true, because why else would he report to the police that he saw a missing hiker? Why get involved at all?

To the dismay of both Kris's family and the volunteers, Andrea Kirkman's August search uncovered no sign of Kris. On the bright side, however, they had ruled out several areas north of Blowout Mountain and Cathy made new friends who, like her, had become engrossed in the case. The scenery grabbed her as well. Motivated to keep searching, she started looking around for a place to extend her stay.

The last resupply stop before the final push to the Canadian border is in Mazama, Washington, where a hostel owned and managed by Carolyn "Ravensong" Burkhart catered to hikers. To PCT fans, Ravensong was a rock star. In 1976, at twenty-one, she became the first woman to successfully solo hike the entire PCT. Now in her early sixties, the outdoor adventurer stayed connected to the trail through Facebook and hosted new generations of thru-hikers in what she called the "Hiker Hut." Nestled in the pines, the tiny cabin had a kitchen, a loft, and a shower displaying a large tile mosaic of the PCT emblem. Ravensong lived in the Raven's Roost, a larger cabin next door.

On the trail, news travels fast, online and off. United by their love of nature and common quest, hikers and trail angels share information about where you can get a hot shower, a dry bed, and a good meal, who you can trust, and when to watch your back. After a few weeks in Washington, Cathy established herself as a trusted member of the PCT "tramily." In the late summer of 2017, when Ravensong needed a caretaker for the Hiker Hut while she left town for a week, it didn't take long for someone to tell her that Cathy was the perfect choice.

During Cathy's stint in Mazama, she often sat near the campfire pit outside the Hiker Hut listening to thru-hikers' stories and, in doing so, learned more about the circumstances surrounding Kris Fowler's disappearance and the stretch of the PCT that spanned Washington. When Ravensong returned, Cathy moved into the Travelodge in Cle Elum, on the east side of Snoqualmie Pass, and based her own search efforts from there. She hiked as many sections of the PCT as her injury would allow. She gave thru-hikers rides to and from the trail. She carried a stapler in her car and posted flyers everywhere she went. Her commitment to finding Kris Fowler had started out casual, but, little by little, Cathy became so invested in the case that she couldn't auger her way out even if she'd wanted to.

One day she heard there was an amateur searcher stranded in a Seattle hotel room without transportation. Cathy had never met this hiker, but she knew he was from the Midwest and had spent several days searching the backcountry for Kris when wildfire closures forced him off the trail. Taking pity on this fellow searcher from out of state, Cathy called and offered to take him on a trip. Would he like to meet Ravensong and hear what she had to say about the case?

The next morning, Morgan Clements ducked into Cathy's silver Toyota RAV4.

*Wow, this guy is tall!* The mapmaker from Missouri who had helped Sally Fowler rule out the Man in Brazil was also lean, with close-cropped sandy-gray hair and a trim goatee. He looked like a cross between a businessman and an outdoorsman, someone who could pull off camouflage attire as well as he could a suit and tie. At forty-eight, Morgan was near Cathy in age, and like her, he had attempted to thru-hike the PCT but couldn't finish because of illness. Also, like Cathy, he had traveled a long way to help search for Kris.

Morgan was there to search an area of interest inside Mount Rainier National Park, between the PCT road crossing at White Pass and Chinook Pass, where the Laughingwater Creek Trail headed west before hitting pavement at Highway 410. This side trail descended three thousand feet over seven miles. While facing blizzard conditions in the high country, Kris may have been tempted to use the route as a bailout, but no one had checked it yet. So Morgan flew to Washington at his own expense to look for himself.

For a hiker unfamiliar with the Cascades, searching along Laughingwater Creek was an education. Lots of rain and lots of plants. A roller coaster of elevation changes tangled with fallen logs as thick as a couch. "You get out there and you're standing in it," Morgan later said, "and you're thinking 'Oh my gosh, if someone's thirty feet off the trail, they'll never be found.'" This impenetrable landscape of brooding mountains, unearthly lakes, and forests dark, deep, and dripping would make an epic set for *The Lord of the Rings*. Morgan was sleeping in his tent one night when he was awakened at three a.m. by a ghastly wail slicing through the forest gloom like a medieval war cry. Never in his life had the mapmaker from Missouri heard anything like it. It took a beat for Morgan to realize the source of this sound was nothing to fear, just a bull elk bugling for company.

As soon as he got up the next morning, Morgan continued his search across the congested terrain. He found some scraps of a blue tarp that could have been anyone's and a few beer cans, but little else. In case the odd bits he found might have been Kris's, he took pictures of the things he found so he could send them to Sally, who would later say none of these items appeared to have belonged to Kris. By the time he finished his search of Laughingwater Creek, Morgan was tired, wet, and frustrated.

On the long drive to Ravensong's, Cathy listened to Morgan bemoan how the strenuous trail had challenged his middle-aged body. *Oh boy*, she thought. Their differences became increasingly apparent the more they got to know one another—Morgan's views on politics, for one, diverged greatly from hers—but the mapmaker's heart was obviously in the right place, and they had one huge thing in common: neither of them could stop thinking about Kris Fowler's disappearance.

Inside Raven's Roost, Morgan, Cathy, and Ravensong huddled over a map spread out across Ravensong's kitchen table. While they discussed avalanche zones, witness sightings, and alternative routes, the women made quite the impression on Morgan. Ravensong was "sharp as a tack." And if Morgan had to give Cathy a trail name, it would be "Tenacious." The trio talked for hours. When it was time for bed, Ravensong headed to her sleeping loft. Cathy lay on the couch in the living room and Morgan got the floor. The next day, Cathy drove him to a hotel near the Seattle airport where the mapmaker caught a flight back to Missouri.

From then on, Cathy and Morgan messaged each other about the case almost daily. After a few weeks of this, once she built up the nerve, Cathy confessed something to her new friend via Facebook Messenger: she was sure the bear hunter was wrong about seeing Kris Fowler on the trail.

At first, Morgan dismissed her like the others had, but Cathy kept pushing him. "I know nobody believes me," she admitted. "I know it sounds insane, but the bear hunter's story doesn't work for me."

"Okay," Morgan relented. "Let me look into it a little."

A few hours later, he'd changed his tune. "Oh my God, you were right."

Within hours of looking into it a little, Morgan made a jaw-dropping discovery. The bear hunter's claim that he had seen a hiker matching Kris's description on the PCT on October 22 was indeed, as Cathy put it, "a bunch of bull."

"They were in Seattle on October 22," Morgan explained. "At a Huskies football game!"

Facebook remembers what we've done, even if we never posted about it ourselves. Morgan learned that the bear hunter couldn't have been where he claimed he was when he saw Kris Fowler by studying Facebook pages belonging to the bear hunter's friends. On October 22, 2016, a hunting buddy of the bear hunter shared a photo of the witness sitting in the stands at the University of Washington during a Huskies football game scheduled that same Saturday. To reach Blowout Mountain from the university required a three-hour drive (without traffic) and a long walk. One-way. It was practically impossible for the hunter to attend a Huskies game on the same day he saw a PCT hiker near Blowout Mountain. And these were just the first of many holes in the bear hunter's story.

The damning evidence triggered a vigorous round of messaging among Sally, Cathy, and Morgan. Once the three of them pieced together all the facts, Morgan put together a ten-page document calling into question the bear hunter's timeline and sent it to Yakima County's Sergeant Briscoe. And they all waited to see what would come of it.

A week or so after Morgan's email to Briscoe, Cathy decided to pursue another lead. During the 2017 hiking season, Kris Fowler's missing person flyers were so ubiquitous, you couldn't walk far on the PCT without noticing them. On or about August 17, a trail runner jogging a popular section north from I-90 at Snoqualmie Pass spotted backpacking gear scattered in the rocks below. When he stepped off trail to get a better look, the trail runner saw metallic and blue objects but didn't get close enough to inspect the gear because the items resembled things he'd seen on a missing hiker poster, which creeped him out. The trail runner reported what he'd seen to an official once he got back to the trailhead, but he'd been unable to take a picture or obtain the GPS coordinates of their location because his phone battery had died.

The official apparently never followed up. After a three-week delay, a hiker heard through the grapevine—or rather, the "trail vine"—about the trail runner's story and brought it to the attention of Sally Fowler, who contacted the witness for more information.

In an email to Sally, the trail runner described where he saw the gear: fifteen feet from the trail between mile 2408 and mile 2410 (these miles were gleaned from the 2017 edition of "Halfmile"—a popular app many hikers had downloaded onto their phones). "Where you come down from the switchbacks after the first descent," he explained, "after the [Kendall] Catwalk and before [south of] Spectacle Lake. . . . I think you'll find what you are looking for."

In the coming weeks, an official search team and a cadaver dog went in. Along with several volunteers, including Cathy, the group combed the area between miles 2407 and 2411. None of them found anything matching the trail runner's description of what he'd seen on a talus slope near the trail.

Morgan called this lead "the best thing we've got right now." In Missouri, he analyzed what the witness told Sally and the police. He compared every detail of the trail runner's statement with topographic maps and satellite imagery of the terrain between PCT mile markers 2407 and 2411 and decided something was off. Adding to the confusion surrounding this lead, PCT mileages varied each year as a result of trail reroutes, and there were inconsistencies between the official PCTA data book mileages and those listed on navigational software applications, but, eventually, it became clear. The mile markers given by the witness did not match his description of the terrain where he'd seen the items. Going by his trail description, the intriguing items were south (not north) of mile 2408. Once Morgan laid it all out in writing, his logic was undeniable. They had all been searching the wrong area. To find the gear seen by the witness, someone had to go back and search the trail between miles

2404 and 2407. But by the time Morgan figured this out, a September storm had dumped so much snow at the high elevations it was no longer safe to search there.

Cathy waited impatiently, keeping her eyes glued to the forecast. In mid-October, the weather lifted, and the snow melted. But another storm was on the way, giving her one good day to resolve the "trail runner lead" before a blizzard closed down the backcountry until spring. Cathy enlisted a new search partner to join her, a flight attendant named Laura Howson who she'd met during the August search. After studying their maps, the women decided the quickest way to the gear site was an obscure path up Mineral Creek.

The Mineral Creek Trail had a reputation for being a "son-of-a-bitch" route to the PCT. The drainage was prone to avalanches, clogged with tree blowdowns, and overgrown with nasty alder thickets. One blogger, who failed to reach the PCT during his ascent up Mineral Creek, called the route "evil." Another vowed, for as long as he lived, he'd never do it again.

On their way to the PCT, Cathy and Laura spent hours fighting the alder while crawling over downed logs. They waded several creeks and lost the path five times. When they reached a snow-covered clearing, Cathy saw no footprints. No path. No trail blazes. If there was a trail leading to the PCT from where they stood, the snow had obscured it. Two hundred trail miles south of the Canadian border, in mid-October, it gets dark by six. Cathy checked the time. This trek to the PCT was taking too long and their feet were wet from fording the creek. Cathy scanned the meadow for signs of which direction she should head and found no clues whatsoever.

Discouraged and confused, they needed a break. The women sat on a log and ate a snack while Cathy contemplated their next move. The day had started off with such hope. Now things looked bleak. Tonight, it would snow—a bigger storm than the one that hit three days before.

In Ohio, Sally kept her cell phone within arm's reach, waiting for news from Cathy. Did she find the gear? Does it belong to Kris?

The trail runner who saw something metallic and something blue among the rocks believed so. But even if Cathy found a way out of the clearing, there wasn't enough daylight left to search their target area. To get off this mountain before dark, she had to give up now, return to civilization, and make the phone call she was dreading—the call that would make Sally Fowler cry while Cathy listened silently, feeling helpless and vaguely responsible. The call that symbolically declared the end of the 2017 search for Kris Fowler.

Anticipating that phone call disheartened Cathy. When a big, messy ball of emotion, exhaustion, and frustration overcame her, she turned her face away from her search partner so the other woman couldn't see her tearing up. But true to form, she got over it. A day or two later, on October 16, Cathy posted a photo from the Mineral Creek route on Kris's Facebook group. In the picture, purple snowcapped mountains rose jaggedly above and behind a foreground of alders with orange leaves laden with snow. "Goodbye, beautiful Washington!" Cathy wrote. "You beat me on this hike, but let me tell you, I will be back!"

*CHAPTER 10*

# Hiker Box

---

L ONG BEFORE VOICE MAIL AND FACEBOOK, THRU-HIKERS DEVELOPED A WAY TO communicate with one another across time and distance: log-books. You'll find this unique communication system at trailheads, the front desk of hostel lobbies, hidden under cash registers in convenience stores, or sitting on a side table in a hiker-friendly café. In these smudged notebooks scattered all along the PCT, thru-hikers document the date they passed through, warn each other about hazards, and gripe about the weather. They also draw cartoons, share fascinating trail gossip, and wax poetic about the scenery or their mood. Similar to summit logs on mountaintops, but much more entertaining, these thru-hiker logbooks keep a record of information that is so valuable, the PCTA installs them at strategic locations to collect data on recreational use patterns.

In December 2017, once I returned home from my thwarted attempt to obtain official reports regarding the disappearance of Chris Sylvia, I studied the photographs I had taken of pages in the 2015 trail register at Mike's Place. The first entry was written by a lone hiker walking south from Idyllwild on January 6. There were no more entries until five weeks later, on February 17—the day Chris Sylvia failed to rendezvous with Min Kim at the Buddhist temple. On that day, a thru-hiker going by Big DogCruxen scribbled: "Pretty weather so far...bobcats growling, small bear tracks, but no attacks, so far, just hot, hot, hot coming through the Anza-Borrego [Desert]. Mike's is always a good place to take a zero day and rest those legs." A "zero day" is hiker parlance for a rest day with zero trail miles walked. Big DogCruxen stayed two nights, drank "four beers," and didn't see "a soul" the entire time he was there. Before leaving, he left twenty dollars in the donation jar and thanked the caretakers for the use of the "cozy camper" he had slept in.

On February 21, "Man Bear Pig" signed the register with no commentary.

The next entry was dated "February 20–24?" and written by a thru-hiker going by Hatchet, who must have been unsure of the exact dates (hence the question mark). "A storm rolled through," Hatchet scribbled. "Bunkered in trailer for 3–4 days....Look out for cats when shittin...they are definitely here!!!" This warning about "cats" refers to mountain lions and Hatchet's fear that one might attack a hiker who strayed off trail to go to the bathroom. On February 25, Hatchet implied that he and his hiking partner, Nostro, were continuing north to Idyllwild. "Thank you! Your trailer saved us from that storm. It's been crazy, but we felt safe here!"

Later, on February 25, "T-Rex" signed the register as well. "We've got 30–40 people out here to search for Christopher Sylvia," she noted. "San Diego Mountain Rescue, SD Sheriff's SAR, and Border Patrol."

Because she used her trail name on Facebook as well as the log, T-Rex was easy to track down. The SAR volunteer working with the county told me that her team had searched all the relevant high spots from which Sylvia may have tried to get cell reception. But there was little else about the case she felt at liberty to discuss without threatening her position on the official SAR team. By this time, Cathy had introduced me to Morgan Clements, so I could learn more about his involvement in the Kris Fowler case. The more I communicated with Cathy's Missouri partner, the more I appreciated the mapmaker's mind. He'd been working David O'Sullivan leads for Cathy and offered to take a peek at the Chris Sylvia case for me. Through emails or Facebook Messenger, I often bounced my thoughts off Morgan about all three of the PCT Missing. Every time, he came back with arguments that either supported or challenged my theories in useful ways. Many times, I took advantage of his skill at digging up useful information online about people.

With Morgan's help, I determined the identities of and contact information for the hikers who wrote in the trail register before and after Chris disappeared. I spoke to Big DogCruxen, who confirmed that he was alone at Mike's; a video Big DogCruxen had filmed during his stay at Mike's and posted online corroborated this claim. When I called Man Bear Pig, he said he'd left the trail and skipped ahead because he wasn't enjoying the company of Hatchet. He left the PCT at Mike's by hiking west on Chihuahua Valley Road until a local woman gave him a ride; after I tracked down the local, she verified this story as well.

Every hiker I contacted who had hiked in the area or visited Mike's Place in February 2015 confirmed one or more of the following conclusions:

1. There were no caretakers at Mike's that February including the time period between the afternoon of February 17 and when search officials arrived on February 24.
2. Mountain lions (or some other caterwauling beasts) were active nearby.
3. The weather was good prior to February 21, but a storm came through after that.
4. Water and shelter (and perhaps food and cash) were available at Mike's.
5. Chris Sylvia's gear was on the trail, but he was not seen by anyone known to be in the area between the evening of February 17 and the start of the search on February 24.

When meshed together, these five points suggested that Sylvia had most likely gotten into trouble or left the trail between the morning of February 16 (when he called Min) and the afternoon of February 17 (when Big DogCruxen arrived). I was getting the sense that nothing violent had happened at the hostel. But a major clue dropped onto my investigation like a bomb when I called Hatchet, the hiker Man Bear Pig wanted to avoid.

"I'm the one who found his pack," Hatchet said immediately, "and it was super weird."

Jeffrey "Hatchet" Lewis had hiked north from Campo on February 13 and arrived at Mike's Place on February 20 or 21. That night, he heard a horrible racket that—to him—sounded like "a mountain lion fighting a bobcat." The next day, he stumbled across a hiker's abandoned gear on the trail. In Hatchet's mind, it seemed like the owner of the abandoned items must have decided to "quit hiking and walked away, like he was pissed off."

A rainstorm forced Hatchet to hunker down at Mike's Place for three nights. On or about February 24, he and his hiking partner, Nostro, walked back to check on the forgotten gear. It was now damp from the rain, and that freaked them out. Since worse weather was on the way, they gathered up all the loose objects and stuffed them in the pack to protect everything from the elements. While doing this, Hatchet noticed an identification card for Chris Sylvia and one or two dollars, but no wallet. By Hatchet's recollection, he saw no cell phone, no toilet paper, no mess kit, and no canteen. In one pocket, there were several seed packets, the kind you'd buy at a hardware store to plant in your garden. Hatchet remembered them being seeds for carrots and wildflowers. He had seen similar seed packets inside the camper he slept in while at Mike's, which led Hatchet to the following conclusion: not only had Sylvia visited the hostel before dumping his pack on the trail, he must have slept at least one night in the same camper Hatchet had stayed in.

To keep the rain from damaging the abandoned gear, the thru-hikers carried Chris's pack to Mike's Place and huddled around it, worrying over what they should do. For sure, they needed to call the police, but there was no cell service. They climbed to the top of a nearby knob, hoping to find a signal. While up there, Hatchet spotted a police officer wandering around in a drainage below. The cop looked lost and appeared to be trying to raise a radio signal. Hatchet called out to him.

"Hey, Officer! We found a backpack."

The deputy told Hatchet about the hiker who had been reported missing, and once he reached a spot allowing him to communicate with his dispatcher, he called in this new information about the abandoned gear. By dark, a SAR team was assembling at Mike's Place, turning it into a command post—with Mike Herrera's permission. Over the next few days, nearly fifty searchers from San Diego, other nearby rescue units, and the US Border Patrol spent time at or near the compound while searching for Sylvia.

Someone from the Sheriff's Office interviewed Hatchet. It felt like an interrogation, but Hatchet understood that they needed to rule him out as a suspect. Most deputies are naive about PCT culture and PCT thru-hikers, and, after ten days on the trail and a few joints at Mike's, Hatchet must have looked and smelled rough around the edges. He informed the officer that, in addition to finding the abandoned gear, he had seen some things in the hiker box at Mike's Place.

Hiker boxes are a backcountry swap meet. "Leave a little, take a little" is the general ethos, but, if so inclined, you can live off all the food, clothing, camping equipment, and other unwanted items thru-hikers toss in hiker boxes. Most thru-hiker hangouts have a cardboard container, a large bucket, or a shelf designated for this purpose, but at Mike's Place, the hiker box was a screened-in storage closet attached to the main house. A day before the cops showed up,

Hatchet was perusing the goods when he noticed a pair of camouflage pants and a paperback novel, *Siddhartha*, sitting there for the taking. Hatchet had served a stint in the military. He recognized the camouflage pattern on the pants he'd seen. It was Marine Digital, the same design the missing hiker reportedly wore. He also knew *Siddhartha* was a Buddhist novel that appealed to thru-hikers, especially one who was asking to be picked up at a Buddhist temple. Hatchet assumed the police would want to know about the clues he saw in the hiker box.

"Did the Sheriff's Office collect these items?" I asked.

Hatchet wasn't sure, but he got the impression they hadn't because the officer appeared to not understand the significance of "hiker things."

As soon as I got off the phone with Hatchet, I emailed Joshua, Chris's brother, to ask whether Chris wore Marine Digital camo pants.

Yes, he did. Joshua was sure of this because he was a former Marine and had given his brother several pairs of Marine Digital pants. He added that the pants should have "Sylvia" written inside the waistband in black ink.

What about this book, *Siddhartha*? Would Chris be into a novel about Buddhism?

Yes, Joshua replied, his brother was into Eastern religions. He had the Chinese symbols for "accept, learn, and let go" tattooed on his torso. *Siddhartha* was exactly the kind of book Chris Sylvia would carry with him.

This was certainly a compelling circumstantial coincidence, but it didn't prove the novel belonged to Chris.

Around this same time, Chris's best friend, Min Kim, wasn't returning my emails. I suspected Min was wary because he didn't trust my intentions. On Reddit, some commenters had speculated that "the roommate" might not be an innocent party, and a family member told me that Min's behavior after Chris's disappearance had seemed cold and suspicious. Plus, Chris's mom was upset that he hadn't reported her son missing until a week after Chris failed to show up for their rendezvous. But I didn't see the best friend as a suspect, and according to news reports, neither did the authorities. Chris's original intent had been to hike for two weeks, all the way to Mexico. The Fowler and O'Sullivan families had both taken over a week to report their sons missing as well. Desperate to get a few simple questions answered, I asked Joshua to contact Min and ask him about *Siddhartha*. Did Min think Chris would be carrying that book during his hike?

Yes, Min answered through Joshua. He had given Chris a copy of *Siddhartha* to read on the trail.

The hair stood up on the back of my neck. Immediately, I relayed this discovery to Morgan, who had other problems on his mind.

"I am sick, sick, sick," Morgan messaged from his home in Missouri. "Influenza B of some kind. I think it's bioterrorism..."

I hoped he was joking about the bioterrorism because I knew Morgan tracked terrorist activity for the government, and during the winter of 2017–2018, a nasty variant was going around. Morgan was so ill that his wife, Julie, drove him to the hospital for treatment. "I can't concentrate on work right now," he apologized, worried he wouldn't be of any help to me.

"Take care of yourself." I assured him, "This can wait."

Despite his weakened state, the next day, Morgan emailed me twenty-seven images of *Siddhartha* book covers he'd found online. "If we are looking for the specific book Min Kim gave to Chris Sylvia," he wrote, "we need to rule out others we may come across, since this is a popular title among hikers, and various versions may exist in the trail libraries and hiker boxes." He also sent me a photo pulled from Facebook of Chris wearing camouflage pants in the Marine Digital pattern.

I sent the email with all of Morgan's book cover images to Joshua, who forwarded it to Min, who then picked out an edition with a purple cover as the paperback he had given to Chris. "It was in good condition," Min added, but "slightly worn. I think the inside might say $1....I picked it up at a used bookstore at the Vista Library."

I posted the image of the purple cover on two PCT Class of 2015 Facebook groups, asking if any of them recognized the book. Within minutes, I got a response from Jordan Babb, a 2015 thru-hiker, who said a friend had plucked that book—or, at the very least, one that looked just like it—from a hiker box at the Acton KOA and had given it to him. Babb was so fond of the novel that he'd carried it with him in his pack for the remainder of the trip, all the way to Canada. Through photos they had posted on Facebook, Babb and his friend verified the date and place they obtained the book—May 15, 2015, at the Acton KOA, at PCT mile 444.3, approximately 317 trail miles north of Mike's Place. It made sense the book would move north, and a thru-hiker could do the miles between Mike's and the Acton KOA in twenty-one days or fewer. There were eighty days between February 24 and May 15, plenty of time for *Siddhartha* to be picked up by another hiker on the way to Acton.

I asked Babb if he remembered any details about the book. Any price written inside? Any highlighted or underlined passages?

He said there were some underlined passages but wasn't sure about the price. He'd check when he got home from work.

"You still have the book?"

"Yeah," he affirmed, but it wasn't in the best shape after traveling two thousand miles in his backpack. Babb offered to mail it to me and I accepted.

I also posted a picture of Marine camouflage pants on the same PCT Facebook pages to see whether anyone recalled retrieving a pair from a hiker box, but no one responded.

By tracking down the book Chris had stuffed in his backpack before he stepped on the PCT, I had uncovered another uncanny coincidence. All three of the PCT Missing were reading stories about characters who "disappeared" in some fashion before they, themselves, disappeared. Kris Fowler had pocketed a copy of *Wanderer,* a memoir in which the author, Sterling Hayden, became a fugitive of the United States justice system when he violated a court injunction by setting sail from San Francisco to Tahiti. David O'Sullivan had been reading a paperback edition of *After Dark* by Haruki Murakami before he vanished. Set in Tokyo, *After Dark* occurs in a world with "inaccessible fissures" that "swallow people," and no one can predict when or where these "abysses" will spit them out. Although the cryptic novel leaves some readers unsatisfied, the philosophy major must have appreciated Murakami's metaphysical themes. So much so, he took the time and expense to place the book in a box and mail it home. And then there was Chris Sylvia, who was perusing a thrift store paperback version of *Siddhartha.*

In 1922, four years before those plucky Americans started creating a continuous multistate footpath across the western United States, a German writer named Hermann Hesse published *Siddhartha*—a novel exploring Buddhist themes. The tale, one that is now popular with thru-hikers, begins when Hesse's protagonist, Siddhartha, disappoints his father by leaving all his possessions behind to walk the path of the wandering pilgrims. In the forest, Siddhartha suffers from self-denial and pain, hunger and thirst, loneliness and despair. But one night, while camping on the aesthetic trail, young Siddhartha experiences an awakening. It's as if he is seeing the world for the first time. The river. The woods. The mountains. It's all so beautiful. So strange. So mysterious.

Passing through a village, Siddhartha meets a woman whose charms seduce him off the trail. They settle down and bear a son.

When the domestic bliss wears off, the preoccupations of civilized life stifle Siddhartha, and he becomes restless. Again, Siddhartha rids himself of his possessions, abandons his friends and family, and walks back into the forest. But, once alone in the mountains, Siddhartha's depression returns. Tormented by dark thoughts, weakened by hunger, he comes to a river crossing and stops. In the cold, fast water, he sees death as a release. Siddhartha lies under a tree and thinks about suicide until he falls asleep. When he wakes up, Siddhartha starts walking. Weeks later—or is it years?—he runs into an old friend on the trail, but Siddhartha has changed so much his friend doesn't recognize him.

*Siddhartha*'s ending is mystifying. When Hesse writes that the wandering pilgrim was "reborn" into another form, what does that mean? Did the hiker on the "strange and twisted path" reincarnate into a spiritual entity after contemplating suicide, or did he wake up like a regular guy, temporarily enlightened and refreshed from his long nap under a tree at the edge of a cold river?

> other teachings. I will learn from myself, be my own pupil; I will learn from myself the secret of Siddhartha.
>
> He looked around him as if seeing the world for
>
> At that moment, when the world around him melted away, when he stood alone like a star in the heavens, he was overwhelmed by a feeling of icy despair, but he was more firmly himself than ever. That was the last shudder of his awakening, the last

*These passages in Chris Sylvia's copy of Siddhartha have been underlined by an unknown hand. Paperback recovered and photographed by the author.*

The day *Siddhartha* arrived in the mail, I held the battered book in my gloved hands and, like an archaeologist examining a sacred artifact, turned it this way and that for meticulous inspection. In the cover photo, a Buddha sits serenely in front of a violet background. According to the back cover, the novel is an "iridescent tale" about a young man who embarks on a "spiritual quest." The tattered binding flaked off in purple strips. Inside, the wrinkled pages blossomed with yellow stains, as if the book had spent time in the rain. Eleven passages were underlined in ink by a wavy hand. Eight of the highlighted paragraphs were in the chapter titled "Awakening."

The first page had "50¢" written in faint red ink in the top right-hand corner. Through Joshua, I sent photographs of the book to Min who replied that it looked exactly like the one he had given to Chris, except more worn. Although he first remembered the price of the book to be one dollar, Min believed the fifty cents symbol written inside indicated a match, since he'd purchased the book for cheap at a used book sale and couldn't recall the exact price he had paid for it.

This must have been Chris's book. I was 97 percent sure of it, but even if I was wrong about that, I believed Hatchet's story. The grungy thru-hiker had spotted *Siddhartha* in the hiker box, but when he reported this to the authorities, a police officer dismissed a tip coming from someone who looked like another fine example of hiker trash. Dozens of SAR personnel and law enforcement officers tasked with finding a guy wearing camouflage pants who planned to rendezvous with his friend at a Buddhist temple hadn't noticed the Marine Digital pants and Buddhist novel sitting *in plain view* on the back porch.

I sympathized. From the news footage I'd watched, San Diego County spent thousands of dollars and deployed an impressive variety of resources during the time they searched for Chris Sylvia.

For at least five days, they gave their all to find him. I know from experience, in the heat of a multiagency search operation, it's easy to miss a key tip because you are distracted while wrangling scent dogs, search teams, helicopters, and media attention. I'm sure plenty of leads fell through the cracks on the cases I worked. But the fact remained that an opportunity—and an important one, at that—had been lost. Perhaps Chris had left other items behind in the hiker box. Things that would indicate what he had done and where he had gone. Evidence like this goes undiscovered when searchers fail to follow a crucial rule of search theory: look for clues with as much diligence as you search for your subject.

I called Brian Patterson, the San Diego County detective assigned to Chris's case, to tell him that I had Chris Sylvia's book in my possession. He responded with one syllable: "Hmm." Detective Patterson shared no information about the case with me. Nor did he have any questions about what I'd learned. I wasn't surprised; Chris's mother had complained that the detective wasn't returning her phone calls. I diplomatically let Patterson know that the family was eager to hear from him. At my insistence, he jotted down Joshua Sylvia's contact information. But Joshua says Patterson never reached out to him.

Since the detective assigned to the case expressed no interest in *Siddhartha*, I went elsewhere for advice on what to do with it. I contacted Dr. Monte Miller, a forensic DNA expert in Southern California with a PhD in biochemistry and over a decade of experience with forensic applications of DNA technology, and asked him if an old book left behind by a missing person would have any evidentiary value.

Dr. Miller ("call me Monte") said the book could still harbor DNA evidence from the missing person, but to fully comprehend the possibilities and limitations, I needed to understand the difference between touch DNA and fluid DNA. Touch DNA comes from skin cells left behind after we handle objects. The substance handled, and the length of time it was held, affect both the quality and the quantity of any DNA left behind. I'm oversimplifying here, but as Miller explained it, a sweaty or licked finger will deposit more DNA than a dry one, because body fluids are liquid DNA—a richer, stickier source. That's why you send a swab of saliva to the lab when you run an ancestry DNA test on yourself, instead of your fingernail clippings or a piece of paper you touched.

According to Miller, if you licked your finger to turn a page in this book, you may have deposited a DNA sample hardy enough to be detectible for decades. However, someone who handled only the outside of your book may not have transferred any DNA at all. And even if he had, that DNA would degrade sooner than the licked-finger DNA you left behind under favorable conditions.

Since the novel *Siddhartha* could have evidentiary value, I also asked Dr. Miller how I should store it. He suggested I place the book in a paper sack and tuck it away in a dark, dry place.

Excited to have made some progress, I shared my discovery with Cathy. She had already read *Wanderer* and *After Dark*. Now she bought her own copy of *Siddhartha* and read it, too, just like I did, so we could talk about it. Did our missing hiker emulate the novel's protagonist by walking away from all his possessions? Is that why Chris laid out his sleeping bag and other gear on the trail?

"You know," Cathy pondered aloud, a glimmer of hope in her voice. "I think Chris Sylvia might be alive."

CHAPTER 11

# Search Planning

---

**D**ETERMINING A LOST HIKER'S POINT LAST SEEN (PLS) AND/OR LAST KNOWN POINT (LKP) is a search planner's first, and perhaps most crucial, task. But this is more complicated than it sounds. For one, the PLS and LKP differ in subtle but important ways. The PLS is the last credible sighting of a missing person by human eyes. The LKP is the last place where a missing person left behind physical evidence that they were actually there—like a car parked at a trailhead, a hotel charge made on a credit card, a signature written in a trail register, or an email sent from a library computer. Sometimes, the LKP and the PLS are the same location, as is the case with Kris Fowler, where a cell phone ping and a photograph (evidence) taken by a woman (witness sighting) both prove he was at White Pass on October 12, 2016.

Other times, however, the PLS and the LKP are distant in both time and space. David O'Sullivan's PLS is where another thru-hiker, Beta, hiked past him on the PCT a few miles north of the Paradise Valley Café on April 3, 2017. But David's LKP is three days later and approximately fifteen trail miles farther north, in Idyllwild, where, in addition to writing an email to his parents, he may have placed a sticker on a map and signed a logbook inside the Idyllwild Post Office on April 6.

Using the PLS and LKP to choose an initial planning point (IPP) for conducting a search for Chris Sylvia is even more challenging. Chris's PLS is where Min Kim dropped him off at the Anza Trailhead on February 12. But what's his LKP? Is it where he made his last phone call on February 16? Is it where hikers found his abandoned gear at PCT mile 127.4? Or is it Mike's Place, where a hiker saw *Siddhartha* and a pair of camouflage pants in the hiker box?

Once a search planner determines their IPP from the missing subject's PLS or LKP, they will attempt to define the geographical boundaries of their search. This is called "containment" and it's a tricky business that often relies on professional experience and investigative assumptions. For example, a park ranger may decide their missing hiker could not or would not have crossed a natural barrier, like a raging river or an impassable mountain range. Or the search planner may use a distance traveled versus time passed formula to determine the furthest distance a human could have traveled on foot from the LKP. But this last method loses its worth when looking for a hiker who has been missing for months. And thruhikers commonly hitch rides from one trailhead to another. The colder your case and the longer your search, the bigger your search area and the higher the probability your subject has left it. Professional searchers call the nebulous zone outside the boundaries of their search area the "R-O-W," or rest of the world. During the early days of a search, to decrease the likelihood that a missing subject enters the ROW undetected, a diligent search operations chief will set up road or trail blocks. Or they may instruct ground searchers to create sign traps—patches of dirt swept clean so trackers can monitor them for new footprints. Another potential sign trap in the modern search investigator's arsenal, video surveillance and game cameras, is often overlooked.

Containment can be an art more than a science, but it's paramount to conducting an efficient search operation. Otherwise, we waste too much money and too many hours looking for a needle in the wrong haystack. When this happens, it's called a "bastard" or "bogus" search.

On Cathy's map of the San Jacinto Mountains, David O'Sullivan's LKP, downtown Idyllwild, is marked with a blue star circled in red. The retired pharmacy store manager wasn't trained in how to manage a search using the esoteric strategies of "search theory" like I was, but Cathy had taught herself a few tenets by reading *Lost Person Behavior: A Search and Rescue Guide on Where to Look* by Dr. Robert J. Koester, a well-regarded search expert with a PhD in "Determining Probabilistic Spatial Patterns of Lost Persons and Their Detection."

For decades, Koester's statistical analysis of fifty thousand resolved missing hiker cases has guided search managers on how to best deploy limited resources. His book, *Lost Person Behavior*, is a 385-page deep dive into complicated search methods that use mathematical formulas, probability theory, and copious charts listing various percentages pertaining to the behaviors typical of forty-one different categories of lost people. Some of the statistical pearls one gleams from Koester's work are counterintuitive. Take this one: Did you know that solo males have a higher fatality rate than solo females? Therefore, a woman is more likely than a man to survive being lost or injured in the outdoors. And it's shocking to learn that 50 percent of adult hikers are found less than two miles from where they were last seen, whereas lost toddlers younger than three have been known to travel over five miles on foot!

If you had any faith in Dr. Robert Koester's statistics, there was a 95 percent chance David would be found within eleven miles of Idyllwild, his LKP. And there was a 50 percent chance he'd be found within two miles of the library. "Never abandon the statistical search," Koester advises in *Lost Person Behavior*. "Make sure statistically likely areas get searched at some point, in spite of what initial investigative information might indicate."

If only it were that easy.

On the northern flank of the San Jacintos, at PCT mile 205.6, a security camera monitors a water faucet on the trail. After trekking the
arduous miles from Idyllwild to Interstate 10, most (if not all) northbound thru-hikers will refill their canteens at this faucet. This camera was an excellent sign trap and Cathy figured, if David made it
that far, it would have taken his picture. What's more, if the surveillance camera took a picture of David using the faucet at mile
205.6, she needed to shift her search effort north of the San Jacintos. The Riverside County Sheriff's Office told David's family they
had reviewed the footage from that camera, but when the O'Sullivans asked them what it revealed, an official responded that it was
"nothing useful." This confused all of us. What did "nothing useful" mean, exactly? Did the Sheriff's Office view images of every
hiker seen walking by that fountain over the course of several days
and determine none of them were David? Or did "nothing useful"
mean the camera wasn't working at all?

I called the utility agency responsible for the camera and spoke
with a sympathetic employee who assured me the footage had been
thoroughly reviewed for signs of David. But, like the O'Sullivans, I
lacked confidence in this statement. It seemed to me that if the footage had been meticulously viewed for David look-a-likes, the O'Sullivans would have been sent at least one image of a similar-looking
hiker to rule out the possibility it was their son.

As many families of the missing will attest, search officials can
be maddeningly oblique in their communications. Law enforcement's need to protect the integrity of their investigation is the go-to
excuse for not releasing information. But I know there's more to it
than that. When I was a young and harried first responder, I often
felt overwhelmed and clumsy when advising stressed family members experiencing the worst tragedy of their lives. And we've all
seen how withholding details can be an effective excuse to obscure

human incompetence. Regardless of why searchers communicate poorly with families of the missing, the effect is generally the same. Lack of transparency only intensifies the anxiety that things aren't being handled properly.

One sign trap, the ATM in Idyllwild, was missed by Riverside County investigators. According to bank records, David withdrew $200 from that ATM before he disappeared. But, by the time Cathy contacted the bank, the digital security tapes had been erased. Preserving footage from surveillance cameras should be a priority action on a missing person case. In addition to obtaining evidence and other valuable information, there's an emotional upside as well. Photos from the ATM would have given the O'Sullivans one last picture of their son.

Alas, the water faucet camera provided "nothing useful," and none of the witness sightings of David north of Idyllwild were deemed credible, so Cathy believed whatever happened to David must have happened on the first or second day after he left Idyllwild, before he could make another purchase with his credit card, sign another trail register, or run into several thru-hikers who would remember seeing him. Nonetheless, narrowing down her search area to an eleven-mile radius of David's LKP still left Cathy a massive amount of treacherous ground to cover.

To access the PCT from Idyllwild, northbound PCT hikers have six trails to choose from: South Ridge, Devil's Slide, Deer Springs Trail, Seven Pines Trail, Marion Mountain Trail, and Black Mountain Road. David could have taken any one of those six routes, but the quickest was the Devil's Slide and the safest was Black Mountain Road. Or he may have hitched ahead and skipped the San Jacintos altogether. Cathy interviewed dozens of thru-hikers who had hiked north from Idyllwild during the first three weeks of April 2017, including two who left the same morning she believed David did. One of the hikers who left Idyllwild on April 7 was so intimidated by the reports of snow and ice, he bypassed the San Jacinto section entirely by hitching around to Interstate 10. The other said he avoided the notorious trail conditions on Fuller Ridge by trekking to the PCT via Black Mountain Road.

The eight-mile climb up Black Mountain Road is relatively easy—for a hiker. For a vehicle, USFS Road 4S01, or "the BMR" as locals call it, is one hellacious drive. In the following years, Cathy would come to resent every rut, every hairpin turn, and every washboarded stretch of the BMR. But not so much on the early November evening after she met the O'Sullivans, when the volunteer's first expedition up the rocky road seemed more adventure than ordeal. By the time she reached Fuller Ridge Campground (7,700 feet), it was almost dark and super cold. The retired homicide detective who had offered to help was already there, warming his hands over a desperate campfire he'd built for the two of them. But the chill sent Cathy to bed early, and the wind threw such a hissy fit, her tent flapped in protest all night.

In the morning, the O'Sullivans drove up from Idyllwild, then Cathy and the detective guided them to where the PCT crossed Black Mountain Road on Fuller Ridge. At this elevation, conifers shaded the ground and the landscape could feel remote and claustrophobic, but wherever the terrain offered an impressive view down the north side of the mountains, civilization seemed near. Six thousand feet below, on the desert floor, massive wind turbines stood in formation along Interstate 10. At night, headlights of cars driving between Palm Springs and Los Angeles glimmered like veins of moving lights.

After seeing the PCT at Fuller Ridge, the O'Sullivans had returned to Idyllwild, where they did a little detective work on their own. At the Idyllwild Inn, they asked a clerk to review his files, and it didn't take long for him to find proof David had paid to sleep there for two nights, checking out on April 7. This lead—another one missed by the authorities—was uncovered by the O'Sullivans within thirty-six hours of their arriving in the States.

Meanwhile, Cathy received a tip from Hemet. A woman reported she had recently seen a homeless man with a blue back-pack resembling the one pictured on the many missing person flyers Cathy had posted. The detective and Cathy drove to Hemet, interviewed the woman, and visited the homeless camp, but they couldn't find anyone with a blue backpack. On their way back up Black Mountain Road, Stephen Aherne—from the Irish Outreach in San Diego—called Cathy's cell. He could send thirty volunteers to search during the weekend of November 18 if she wanted them.

Aherne's offer energized Cathy. With thirty people, she could cover lots of ground. But the detective seemed upset by this new development. Missing person flyers won't help find David, he lectured, referring to the fruitless tip they had just received, and he opposed using amateurs to search. This was the responsibility of county officials. There were rules about such things. Who would be accountable for the safety of these inexperienced searchers?

Cathy viewed the situation differently. The authorities had given up. She didn't see how looking for a lost hiker violated any laws, and she would organize the operation to ensure they did it safely.

Cathy's opinions may have ruffled the detective, because he told her he wanted no part of this.

You don't have to be a part of it, Cathy informed him. This was her thing. Besides, the Irish Outreach folks from San Diego wouldn't be there for two weeks. He could leave before they arrived. For now, he should stay and help her search for David along Fuller Ridge.

On their drive back up Black Mountain Road, he was uncharacteristically quiet. When they returned to their campsite, he packed everything in his truck and drove away, leaving Cathy alone on the mountain without saying so much as goodbye.

Stunned, Cathy drove to the nearest spot with cell service and called me to vent. The detective's behavior seemed odd and out of proportion. She didn't understand it.

I was in Los Angeles when I took Cathy's call. "This turned out to be more than he signed up for," I comforted her. "You're more courageous than he is. That must be hard for him to deal with. I don't think he was up there with you just to conduct a search."

"But the whole purpose of this is to find David!"

"Cathy…" After an awkward pause, I spelled it out. "I'm pretty sure the detective wanted to hook up with you."

"What? I don't have time for that!"

Single for sixteen years, Cathy admitted she could be oblivious to the motivations of men. But the detective was even more clueless than she was. After all, when wooing a woman on a crusade, you must at least *pretend* to support her cause.

Cathy was undeterred by the retired detective's moody temperament. After he left, a television news producer called wanting to interview the O'Sullivans right away. Cathy drove down Black Mountain Road for the second time that day to convince the shy couple they should do the media appearance. For David's sake.

On camera, the O'Sullivans appeared as I saw them—salt of the earth people made vulnerable by horrible circumstances. A few days after the interview aired, the O'Sullivans' new Facebook group, David O'Sullivan Missing PCT Hiker, had grown to over seven hundred members.

Whenever one of the PCT Missing received media attention, more people joined the Facebook groups, but this wasn't always a good thing. New members had an annoying habit of giving redundant advice without catching up on what has been ruled out already. ("Thank you, Captain Obvious," is what Sally Fowler muttered to herself whenever this happened.) Others suggested wild theories or asked the same questions over and over again. At first, Cathy would patiently answer their inquiries. Where was David last? *Idyllwild on April 6.* What about the sightings north of Idyllwild? *They are bogus.* What was he wearing? *We don't know for sure, but he had a blue backpack.* What was his trail name? *He didn't have one yet.* Which trail did he take from Idyllwild to the PCT? *We don't know.*

Others could be rude beyond imagination, like a couple of Facebook hecklers who made Carmel O'Sullivan cry in her kitchen during the early days of her search for David. No matter what she did, someone thought it was wrong. If she pushed too hard to get information regarding David's potential whereabouts, she was an overbearing, anxious mom who was smothering her son. If she waited patiently to hear from David, she was a bad mother who couldn't be bothered to track him down.

To avoid such irritations, I hesitated to create a Facebook group for Chris Sylvia. His family hadn't made one and I didn't encourage them to. I had more faith in my own abilities than I had in the Facebook mob. Also, Chris's friends and family didn't exactly fit into a cookie-cutter mold. His siblings had different fathers. His mother was homeless and struggled with addiction. In no way did this make Chris and his family less worthy of compassion, but my cynical mind told me increasing Chris's social media profile would gain us nothing while putting people I now cared about on a bull's-eye for harmful negativity.

I discussed my concerns about social media with Cathy, and, although she understood my position, she disagreed with my choice. Over the course of our weekly interviews, I was learning more about what made the volunteer tick. Cathy's primary motivation came from a deep well of empathy she had for the mothers, especially Sally Fowler and Carmel O'Sullivan. On several occasions, she'd pushed Carmel to post more heartfelt pleas in the Facebook group created to find her son. I believed Cathy did this based on caring instincts as opposed to manipulative intentions. Because it's a sad fact that no one can leverage their grief and inspire people to help more than the parent of a missing hiker, and this miserable power is strongest in and between mothers.

Years before David O'Sullivan disappeared, Cathy received a late-night phone call that her son had not returned from a hiking trip. All the worst-case scenarios had gone through her head.

"I imagined an animal chewing on his face. It was absolutely gut wrenching."

Michael Tarr eventually walked out of the woods, alive and well, but for a few hours Cathy suffered a mother's worst nightmare. These maternal fears galvanized other women as well. In 2017, a Texan named Sarah Francis lost contact with her PCT-hiking daughter. Fortunately, her daughter ended up fine—Sarah credited the happy ending to the GPS locator device she'd bought her daughter after reading the advice Sally Fowler had posted on Facebook—but the experience rattled Sarah. When she learned about David O'Sullivan (Sarah's daughter started the PCT two weeks behind the Irishman), she felt a deep connection to his parents. That next Christmas, when her husband asked what she wanted, Sarah said, "I want a trip to California to help search for David." Other women like Sarah lent a hand whenever their schedules allowed, including Jeanette Ragland, a single mom undergoing chemotherapy for cancer, who was too frail to hike but did her part by providing Cathy and other searchers rides to and from trailheads.

Sadly, not all volunteers were quite so empathetic. Like the detective, a few men who volunteered to search with Cathy appeared to bring different priorities to the endeavor. One guy asked her peculiar questions like "Will we be searching for him in a pretty place?" and "What color boots will you be wearing?" Some claimed that they were intimidated by the terrain, like the guy who agreed to accompany Cathy to search off trail below Fuller Ridge, until he looked at Black Mountain Road on Google Earth. That road is too rough, he protested in an email. He was scared to drive up it by himself. One of the nicest, most helpful guys brought Cathy a bottle of wine each time he came to search and warmed her back with his hands when she got cold, which, from him, wasn't creepy at all. Even Cathy dismissed it as "maybe he was just being friendly."

Other people announced on social media their noble intentions to join the search, but once pressed for a commitment, they admitted they weren't available because of jobs, illness, or other excuses. With or without help, Cathy marched forward. She posted dozens of missing person flyers at businesses, trailheads, and hiker hangouts between Idyllwild and Big Bear. She met with local experts, outfitters, trail angels, and hikers. She also contacted a woman with RMRU, the local rescue team, who promised to send maps showing where they had searched before she inexplicably stopped responding to Cathy's emails.

Several searchers associated with Riverside County were supportive of Cathy's cause in private, but when she followed up with them to glean more information, they voiced concerns they'd be disbarred if they shared details with unofficial searchers. Cathy reached out to scent dog handlers, but none were willing to take the case for her, even if they were paid. Certified dog handlers risked being cut from official SAR teams if they worked any case without approval from the Sheriff's Office, she was told. "Okay," Cathy persisted, "then let's get approval," but a dog handler told her that would never happen.

The runaround exhausted Cathy.

"I'm getting annoyed." She sighed. "Twenty-four/seven I'm on this case. I need all the info I can get."

To me, as a former SAR official now looking at it from the perspective of families, the bureaucratic hesitancy to cooperate with a nongovernmental entity like Cathy seemed excessive to a cruel degree. Thankfully, a private organization from San Diego was more than eager to help.

On Saturday, November 18, two weeks after the detective left Cathy alone at their campsite, thirty people with the San Diego chapter of the Irish Outreach descended upon Idyllwild like the cavalry. "Extending hands of caring and guidance to the Irish" was their motto and along with their thick accents they brought a hearty desire to search for their kinsman, David O'Sullivan. Each morning, Cathy briefed them on what to look for and what to do if they found a clue.

"Search as if this is your son or your mother or your dad," she instructed. "Search so that when you go to bed at night you have nothing on your conscience except that you did your best."

In addition to emergency whistles, Cathy supplied each volunteer with an orange vest and hat to wear so they were visible as they moved through the woods. She had them sign in each morning and then sign out when they returned to base. On Saturday's search, someone loaned Cathy eight handheld radios. For thirty people searching in squads, that was more than enough. The next morning, seventeen volunteers arrived, but the person with the radios was not one of them. This forced Cathy to use her Plan B, a code system she set up for them to communicate via their emergency whistles.

The retired detective's reservations proved to be unwarranted. The operation was safe and the amateurs did excellent work. While scouring the ground at least fifty yards deep on each side of the PCT, they uncovered gloves, a tent stake bag, and a sun hat. None of the items could be tied to David, but finding irrelevant clues was a good sign because it showed Cathy her volunteers were effective searchers. On Sunday evening, before the volunteers returned to San Diego, Cathy sent them off with a sincere thank-you.

"You eliminated an area," she congratulated them. "Now we can move on to other locations."

Being nearly as stubborn as Cathy, the Irish Outreach volunteers agreed to return, in December, to search again.

# CHAPTER 12

# *Exposed*

---

SQUEEZED BETWEEN TWO OF THE MOST ACTIVE FAULTS IN THE WORLD, THE SAN Jacinto and the San Andreas, the San Jacinto Mountains rise above two dry valleys like an island plateau set above a desert sea. Nestled against the mountains' southern edge, underneath two rocky prominences that look down upon the village like gigantic gargoyles, is Idyllwild, a small town with a population of twenty-five hundred. From town, if you look up and north, Suicide Rock is the gargoyle on your left, and to the right is Tahquitz (pronounced Tah-qwitch) Rock, otherwise known as Lily Rock, because the granite is so white. From a satellite's view via Google Earth, these pale outcroppings resemble bottom teeth erupting from forested gums. A short distance beyond the gap between those gargoyled fangs is Humber Park, the parking area for the Devil's Slide, the shortest and most popular route to the PCT.

Suicide Rock gets its name from a trite tourist fable—a fatal "lover's leap" cliché à la Romeo and Juliet—but a horrifying legend associated with Lily/Tahquitz Rock more than makes up for the pedestrian tale. Tahquitz is an indigenous name, and the Cahuilla (pronounced Cah-wee-ah) Tribe has bestowed it upon numerous geological features in the San Jacinto wilderness, including Tahquitz

Peak, Tahquitz Canyon, Tahquitz Valley, Red Tahquitz Peak, Tahquitz Creek, and Tahquitz Rock. According to Cahuilla legend, Tahquitz was a corrupt shaman who behaved so terribly that the tribe exiled him from their community and forced him to live alone in the San Jacinto Mountains. Furious, Tahquitz morphed into a resentful demon who, to this day, enacts his revenge through lightning strikes, earthquakes, green flashes of light, and bone-crushing boulders that crash down the jagged slopes. But that's far from the worst of it. If Tahquitz finds a lone human venturing into the remote recess of his mountain home, he kidnaps them, consumes their mortal flesh, and then, once he's done eating, incarcerates their doomed soul within a glass cave hidden in the granite. From this rocky tomb, Tahquitz's prisoners can forever look out, but the living can never see in.

This Tahquitz legend is printed on a USFS sign at the Humber Park Trailhead, but most hikers pay no attention to it, and modern trail construction has tamed the "Devil's Slide" to the point that it no longer merits the moniker. Nowadays, the 2.5-mile climb to the PCT is mild and well-graded. At the top, you reach Saddle Junction, a relatively flat area with five paths spoking out from a jumble of signs pointing to a perplexing number of destinations. In 2017, none of these signs indicated which of the five paths were the PCT—and this has led to more than a few dangerous ends for nature enthusiasts. Several times a year, weekend hikers from places like Los Angeles become so confused by this bewildering intersection, they lose their way and need to be rescued. And that's the best-case scenario. In 2005, an experienced PCT thru-hiker lost the trail near Saddle Junction and died.

Walking 170 miles from the Mexico border to Idyllwild is not easy, especially for novice backpackers. But in terms of elevation gains, the so-called desert section of the PCT is like kindergarten compared to the advanced education hikers will get when they reach California's High Sierra and Washington's North Cascades. It is during their spring trek over the San Jacinto Mountains that many northbound thru-hikers are surprised when they receive their first taste of the alpine conditions they weren't expecting to encounter until five hundred miles later, in the Sierra Nevada.

No one understands the unique hazards hikers face in the San Jacintos more than Jon King, a local mountaineer who has been hiking the area since the 1990s. A world-traveling ornithologist with a science degree, Jon was born a British citizen, but he now has dual citizenship and resides in Idyllwild. To PCT hikers, he is known as "SanJacJon." Others call him "King of the Mountain" after he bagged San Jacinto Peak a herculean 207 times in one year. Since 2015, the mountaineer has been keeping thru-hikers informed of the current trail conditions via his San Jacinto Trail Report on www.sanjacjon.com. To keep his report current, he spends nearly seven days a week, every week, jogging or walking the San Jacinto trails, and he takes meticulous notes.

On March 29, 2017, a week before David disappeared, Jon hiked the Fuller Ridge section of the PCT with the aid of crampons and an ice axe because the trail was under two to three feet of snow. "One should not attempt Fuller Ridge Trail at this time without ice axe, crampons, and good knowledge of how to use them," Jon advised in his trail report. "This situation is unlikely to change before late April at the earliest. The alternate route is to hike up the Black Mountain Road for eight miles."

Five days after SanJacJon posted this in his March 29 trail report, Beta was eating lunch with David O'Sullivan at the Paradise Valley Café.

The following afternoon, on April 4, while David O'Sullivan got off the trail and hiked into Idyllwild, Beta was making his way up to the higher elevations of the San Jacintos via the South Ridge Trail when he saw a handmade warning posted by Jon King. In a blog post about his 2017 thru-hike on www.hikerbeta.com, Beta called it "the sign of doom."

*The sign of doom. Photograph by Jon King.*

If David saw this sign, he might have done exactly what Jon King recommended. Beta, the purist, ignored this "overamped warning" (his words) and continued his climb to the PCT near Tahquitz Peak. However, once Beta reached the snowfield between Tahquitz and the PCT, "the sign of doom" seemed less overamped. "One trekking pole slip, one careless step," Beta wrote in his blog, would send a hiker pinballing "through pine trees and rocks" as he slid thousands of feet down an icy slope. With a humbling lump in his throat, Beta strapped microspikes onto his hiking boots and continued north, his respect for the San Jacintos increasing with every step.

Every spring, northbound thru-hikers fret over the snowy conditions they'll face in the High Sierra when they should be worrying about the San Jacinto Mountains they'll encounter first, especially the six-mile traverse along Fuller Ridge. On March 30, 2017, a week before David disappeared, a PCT hiker requested emergency assistance from RMRU after he slipped off the Fuller Ridge traverse one too many times. Conditions were so treacherous that day, the responders' 4WD vehicle bogged down in the snow on Black Mountain Road and rescuers had to continue the rest of the way on foot. Traction devices (crampons or microspikes) on the rescuers' boots helped them avoid slipping off the icy slopes, but they had to post-hole—plunging their feet in and out of the softer snow, leaving a track of knee-deep holes behind them—on their way to the banged-up, exhausted thru-hiker needing rescue. A few days later, on April 4, RMRU responded again—this time to save a day hiker who had walked off the trail near Saddle Junction.

Beta arrived at Saddle Junction on his second day. After postholing through crotch-deep snow, he hit a section of solid ice where he slipped and slid twenty feet, ripping a hole in his hiking shorts on the way down. Beta had barely recovered from this mishap when he met another "panicky" thru-hiker walking south.

"I've been lost for two hours," the man groaned. "This trail is unfollowable. I'm turning around."

Another thru-hiker, trail name Convict, came along soon after. The conditions on Fuller Ridge had frightened her so badly, Convict did something every thru-hiker loathes to do. She turned around and started hiking in the opposite direction. Beta persuaded her to partner up with him and try again. On their way north, they slipped off the trail several times. When it got dark, they set up camp in the snow on Fuller Ridge. At 8,500 feet, "the wind was whipping," and Beta's feet were soaked from "tromping" through the slush. The next morning, they were traversing Fuller Ridge when Convict yelped. Her microspikes had lost their grip, and she was sliding. Incapable of helping, Beta watched Convict's terrifying skid until she arrested her fall by jamming her ice axe into the hard snow.

After a series of more slip-and-slides off Fuller Ridge, Beta and Convict reached safety when they crossed Black Mountain Road.

North of there, they caught up with several thru-hikers who had bypassed the gnarly traverse by getting a ride up the BMR. On the way down to I-10, trail conditions improved rapidly. It was a relief to have Saddle Junction and Fuller Ridge behind them.

Beta initially dismissed Jon King's warning, but for Cathy, San-JacJon was a gold mine of information about this stretch of the trail. She met with the mountaineer often, either inside his log home or at a local coffee shop in Idyllwild, where they discussed scenarios and pondered over maps. If David used the Devil's Slide to reach the PCT, he would have experienced the same scary situation on Fuller Ridge that Beta documented in his blog. Or David may have erred on the side of caution and accessed the PCT via the BMR. Hitching around San Jacinto altogether to I-10 was another possibility. Cathy and Jon discussed these and other theories ad nauseam and—because there were no confirmed sightings of David on the trail north of Idyllwild—concluded the missing hiker must have either run into trouble while on Fuller Ridge or lost the trail at Saddle Junction, where other confused hikers had left behind a maze of tracks in the snow.

John Donovan, a cantankerous yet compassionate social worker who had thru-hiked the Appalachian Trail, was one of many confused hikers who'd lost their way at Saddle Junction. Retired at fifty-nine, the Virginian with Irish Catholic roots embarked on a PCT thru-hike on April 19, 2005. On May 3, two hikers saw him at Saddle Junction, where he was struggling to find the snow-obscured trail. Twelve days later, a friend noticed Donovan had not picked up the resupply package he had mailed to Palm Springs. The friend reported Donovan as missing and RMRU searched the west side of the San Jacintos, including the PCT route along Fuller Ridge, where everyone expected Donovan, a lost PCT thru-hiker, to be.

But Donovan wasn't anywhere near Fuller Ridge.

The social worker was still missing a year later when a young couple rode the tourist tram from Palm Springs to the top of the San Jacintos. Although the area around the tramway is often crawling with tourists, the two inexperienced hikers accidentally strayed off trail. Wandering through the woods while yelling for people who couldn't hear them, they became more and more lost. During this desperate trek through the forest, the couple stumbled upon an abandoned backpack. Inside they found matches and a journal belonging to John Donovan. Cold, scared, and hungry, the couple struck the thru-hiker's matches to ignite a wildfire that led to their discovery and rescue. After plucking the lost hikers to safety, RMRU returned to look for Donovan's body. They found his body fifty yards downstream from the backpack, many miles from the PCT, in a narrow drainage on the opposite side of the mountain. That ravine was arguably the last place in the San Jacintos you would look for a missing PCT thru-hiker.

If it weren't for Donovan's journal, we wouldn't know for sure what happened to him. Winter conditions had forced the thru-hiker to turn around and head back to Idyllwild, but he lost his way near Saddle Junction and headed in the wrong direction, hiking north and then east until he could see, far below him, the lights of Palm Springs. Donovan's resupply boxes were down there, at the post office, waiting for him to pick them up. Heading for the lights, he entered a gash in the landscape that he hoped would lead to civilization. Bushwhacking deeper and deeper into the ravine, he reached a hundred-foot waterfall that blocked his descent. Too weak to climb up the way he'd come, the thru-hiker was trapped. On May 6, he ran out of food. "Goodbye," Donovan wrote in his last journal entry on May 14, "and love to you all."

When she found John Donovan's final resting place on a map, Cathy was shocked. *How did he get over there?* On SarTopo, an online map-sharing platform, she'd seen the search tracks of an experienced backpacker, going by the name Hiker Jim, who had searched for

David O'Sullivan northeast of Saddle Junction with the John Donovan scenario in mind, but when Hiker Jim reached the brushy sections, he feared the San Jacinto rattlesnakes too much to go farther.

Some of Cathy's hardiest and most experienced volunteers were also giving up on finding David, like the highly motivated rock climber from Rancho Cucamonga. The rock climber did an impressive amount of research about mile 186, a remote section of trail where a wildlife biologist had detected an odor of decomposition. There, he bushwhacked through the dense vegetation during the weekend of the Irish Outreach search but didn't find anything.

When Cathy debriefed him at the end of the day, the rock climber seemed very down, negative. "At least we can eliminate that area," Cathy said, trying to prop up his spirits, but, as far as she knew, he never participated in another search for David. The failure rate when searching for a long-lost hiker can be demoralizing.

"I think [the rock climber] thought he could do a little research, then go out and find David in one day," Cathy sympathized, but "it doesn't work that way."

If there was a place Cathy could call home during November and December 2017, it was the Quality Inn in Hemet, California. Her bottom-floor room, near the ice machine, was her command post. Boxes of paperwork cluttered the dresser next to a laminator she'd purchased at an office supply store; it hadn't taken long for her to learn that David's missing person flyers lasted longer if she covered them in vinyl. An early riser, she studied maps and answered emails in the morning. Next, she stopped for iced tea and a bagel at Panera before leaving Hemet. The drive from Hemet to Fuller Ridge via Black Mountain Road was over an hour. At the end of a hard day of searching, Cathy returned to her hotel room, took a shower, and went straight to bed. Then she got up the next morning and started all over again.

Martin Carew, an expat member of the Irish Outreach born in Dublin, returned to Idyllwild to help Cathy on several occasions. One day, they focused on an area underneath the Fuller Ridge section of the PCT—an isolated place humans rarely went. Then again, as Cathy pointed out, "if David was where people go, he would have been found already." It was late November, and the winds were brutal, but Martin, who lived at a thousand feet above sea level, in balmy Temecula, had forgotten to bring a jacket.

Cathy retrieved an extra down coat and some gloves she kept in her car and handed them to Martin along with a walkie-talkie. They split up, each taking a parallel course along the craggy slope. Contouring underneath Fuller Ridge required trekking down into and out of several gullies. With their eyes to the ground, searching for clues, they lost sight of one another. Three hours before sunset, Cathy radioed to tell Martin it was time to head back to the car.

An hour later, they had still not reunited.

"How are you doing?" Cathy radioed.

"I don't know," Martin replied. "I got turned around."

"Where are you?"

"I'm not sure, but don't panic."

"I'm not panicking." But she was concerned. In Cathy's mind, if something happened to Martin, it would be her fault. She sat down on a rock to think.

Suddenly, Martin had an idea. "I'm going to text you a picture [of where I'm at]."

Cathy's sharp eyes scanned the photo of trees and rocks—a common view that told her nothing. She asked Martin to send her a screenshot of his coordinates from his smartphone's mapping program. The image he sent was a blue dot on an enigmatic field of green.

"Okay, that's not helping. I'm going to blow my whistle." Cathy blew as hard as she could, but the wind drowned her out. Temps had dipped into the forties. Wind gusts stole the warmth right out of her. She had to keep moving. How long did it take to die of hypothermia? Cathy wasn't sure. Jon King had mentioned something about the Survival Rule of Threes. What was it exactly? In a harsh environment, you can survive three weeks without food. Three days without water. Three hours without shelter. *Three hours?* It would be dark soon. Above 7,000 feet, the overnight low would drop below freezing. Throw in some windchill and the jacket Cathy had loaned Martin wouldn't be enough.

Once she reached her Toyota RAV4, Cathy hopped inside, turned on the ignition, and cranked up the heat. Thirty minutes later, Martin sent a new photo of his location—a crumbling homesite at the end of a road. Cathy recognized it. "Go to the chimney. From there, climb the dirt road to my car."

"Bloody hell," Martin texted back, tramping tenaciously back up the steep and rocky path.

On their drive back to Idyllwild, Cathy wanted to know what Martin planned to do if forced to spend the night out there. How would he have kept warm?

"I would have crawled in between some boulders," he said, "to stay out of the wind."

Cathy wondered if that's what David did—crawled under a log or squeezed into a tight space between two rocks. She had made a commitment to Carmel O'Sullivan to work the case until the end of the year, but if David's body was tucked inside a place like that, she knew there was a distinct possibility she might never find him.

CHAPTER 13

# By Land and by Screen

**W**HEN IT COMES TO COLLECTING DATA ON PEOPLE WHO HAVE VANISHED FROM PUB-lic lands, the federal government often does a poor job if it even tries at all. Many concerned citizens have noticed this over the years, including Jon Billman, author of *The Cold Vanish: Seeking the Missing in North America's Wilderness*, who believes the often-quoted total of "1,600 missing" from public lands is "*wildly* conservative." Missing person activists and *Missing 411* author and filmmaker David Paulides have pushed the feds to do a better job tracking wilderness disappearances, but, as Billman concludes, the current situation leaves any attempt at a geographical pattern analysis of hikers who have vanished from national parks and forests "to civilians and conspiracy theorists."

To establish some historical context for my areas of interest, I had to sift through news reports and nongovernmental databases—like the National Missing and Unidentified Persons System (NamUS) or the Charley Project—and create my own list of hikers who had gone missing from certain locations. As I write this, at least five have vanished from the San Jacinto Mountains since the 1980s. Randy Spring, twenty-eight at the time of his disappearance, a Vietnam Army veteran, disappeared while backpacking near the PCT in October 1988. Searchers found Joshua Best's wallet on Leatherback

Ridge in September 2000, but Best, thirty-six years old, is still missing. The third is David O'Sullivan. Then, in March 2020, Ray Prifogle, fifty-two years old, disappeared from the Webster Trail. Two months later, Melissa Lane, forty-one, a friend of Prifogle's who was last seen on Black Mountain Road, became the fifth hiker to vanish from the San Jacinto Mountains.

When a story about a woman missing or killed in the wilderness gets shared on Facebook, there will be at least one "gals-shouldn't-hike-alone" comment underneath it, although, as the above list indicates, the majority of missing hikers are men. One explanation for this is that there are more men than women venturing into the woods, thus more men go missing there. But even when you take that into account, remember that statistics compiled by Dr. Robert Koester led the SAR expert to the following conclusion: a solo woman is *more* likely to survive a perilous incident in the outdoors than a solo man. Yet, the average female hiker fears for her safety more than the average guy does. Ironically, this phenomenon, dubbed the Fear-Gender Paradox, may be why women fare better, because their angst makes them behave more cautiously. Meanwhile, their overconfident male peers are taking more risks and suffering the consequences.

Gender differences aside, the San Jacinto wilderness is no joke, and the steep drop-offs, confusing trail junctions, and tumbling boulders Cathy faced while searching there caused her dedication to waver. *Holy crap, what have I got myself into?* And she scared herself a few times. *Holy mackerel, this is a dangerous spot.* Thankfully, she took precautions. Clipped to her shoulder strap was a GPS locator device with a stubby antenna. Although it resembled a circa 1997 cell phone, her Garmin inReach Explorer was the most advanced satellite messenger for sale at REI in 2017. It had mapping software, satellite text communication ability, and an emergency SOS button that worked 24/7. The device weighed 7.5 ounces, too heavy for ultralight ounce-pinching backpackers trying to lighten their loads, and it cost damn near a fortune. Four hundred fifty dollars for the unit (plus a hundred on top of that each year for the satellite tracking subscription) is more than most thru-hikers can afford. Which might explain why Kris Fowler didn't pay the fee to turn on the SPOT emergency device someone had given him.

For Cathy, the inReach Explorer was well worth the expense. In Washington, while on a solo backpacking trip to look for Kris in a remote location near Spectacle Lake, she sprained her knee. She camped one night to see if it might improve on its own, but in the morning, it still hurt too much to walk. Instead of pushing the emergency button, Cathy used her inReach to text a specific request for assistance. Within hours, locals sent up a packhorse to her coordinates, and she rode it out. She also took advantage of the inReach's map-sharing capabilities. While searching for David O'Sullivan in California, she asked Morgan to track her movements in real time from his home in Missouri. An arrow moving across a digital map on Morgan's computer screen represented Cathy's position. One day, Morgan noticed Cathy's arrow had missed a fork in the trail, so he called to warn her. She was heading the wrong way. Another time, Cathy was in a ravine when the bushwhacking became unbearable. Texting through the inReach, she asked Morgan to find an easier way out. With a bird's-eye view of her location on Google Earth, Morgan saw things Cathy could not. He gave her three options. Go back to the trail, either by climbing uphill to the west or uphill to the east. Or she could head downhill, away from the trail, toward a road. Cathy chose the third option and headed down to the road, where she hitched a ride back to her car.

GPS tracking devices allow hikers to communicate with friends and family from cell service dead zones, providing a superior safety net. However, they also encroach upon a hiker's privacy, the desire to be free from technology, and their sense of independence in the wild. Still, for some hikers, it's worth it. Morgan carried an inReach during his 2016 attempt to hike the PCT. He chose settings that allowed his wife to know when he was moving, where he camped, and how many miles he hiked each day. She could also text him as many times as she wanted to.

Morgan liked it that way and it came with clear advantages. But for some, including myself, this much connectedness feels smothering. Today, hikers carry these devices to comfort family back home only to create more anxiety because parents and spouses are observing every move their loved one makes on a map. In 2019, several mothers freaked out when GPS tracking indicated their adult child hadn't moved (on the digital map) for an hour. When one of these mothers posted her fears on Facebook, experienced hikers advised her to relax—*step away from the computer*—your thru-hiker is only taking a break.

A backpacker can avoid the eyes of overwatchful loved ones by leaving their inReach at home, but every time we use a phone or get online, we are under some form of surveillance and/or are leaving behind a record. When Morgan coached Niall O'Sullivan on how to access his brother's email accounts, they found three selfies David had sent to himself. Taken within the first hundred miles of trail, the selfies reveal David from the midtorso up. In all three, he wears a bright red T-shirt, a short beard, and prescription glasses. In two photos, he's wearing a cobalt blue windbreaker that is too flimsy for the conditions ahead of him.

Despite the beard and glasses, in his selfies David looks younger than his years. His blue, almond-shaped eyes gaze directly at the lens, but his half-smile expression is hard to read. Morgan thought he looked sad. From his own experience on the PCT, Morgan knew the first miles are rough and painful. Perhaps David believed he would make trail friends right away but still hadn't connected with any fellow hikers.

Cathy disagreed. The pictures were in no way sad. They were more like *Yay, I'm on the PCT!* "People don't take sad pictures of themselves," she pointed out. Sure, David looked a little tired, but these photos captured him in the evening light, after a long day of hiking. He probably took them to preserve his good memories on the trail. In support of Cathy's take on David's emotional state, his family denied seeing any indication of depression. According to them, the Irishman's twenty-five years on this earth had been happy and relatively stress-free.

In Arthur Conan Doyle's short story "A Scandal in Bohemia," Sherlock Holmes advises Dr. Watson that "it is a capital mistake to theorize before one has data. Insensibly one begins to twist facts to suit theories, instead of theories to suit facts." It was the same thing with David's selfies, which caused us to read things into his expressions based on our own experiences. Then again, they also provided the kind of "data" Sherlock Holmes favored. For example, now we knew what clothes David had been wearing before he disappeared.

Indeed, details in David's selfies became invaluable at least twice. When someone found a pair of prescription glasses on the trail well north of Fuller Ridge, they sent us a photo. On first inspection, these glasses looked exactly like the ones David wore. That is, until Cathy's team superimposed a photo of the frames found by the hikers on top of the glasses in David's selfies and discovered they were not a match. In a similar fashion, her team ruled out another lead by comparing the zipper pulls on David's jacket and backpack to a zipper pull found among some abandoned backpacking gear that had been burnt beyond recognition in a wildfire.

Another relatively new technology making headway on the search front was unmanned aircraft systems (UAS), aka drones. Wanting to take advantage of this resource, Cathy posted a request for drone operators on Facebook. Several UAS pilots called her immediately, offering to help, and they had lots of questions. What were the coordinates and the range of her search area? Which agency had jurisdiction? How far would they have to walk? Cathy struggled to provide these pilots precise answers to all their queries. At that time, she had no idea what drones could or couldn't do.

One caller, Gene Robinson with Texas EquuSearch, took the time to educate Cathy. A nonprofit devoted to finding missing persons and funded by private donations, Texas EquuSearch never charged families for their services and had recovered the remains of over two hundred people by various methods. Robinson's expertise with using his drones to help locate the missing had earned him a reputation as "the grandfather of drone search and rescue."

As Robinson explained, a drone pilot can search for a missing person in real time by watching a live video from his drone. He can also search later, at home, by reviewing (and re-reviewing) the high-resolution images taken of a search area. Two methods, artificial intelligence (software) or human eyes, were then used to search these images for bodies or clues. Robinson admitted the software was still a work in progress, so he used human volunteers, as well, to review his drone images. He called these people "squinters" because they spent hours squinting at photographs on a large computer or television screen, looking for signs of missing people.

Like image squinting, capturing thousands of images with a drone was a time-consuming operation requiring a team of methodical and experienced pilots with problem-solving skills. First off, drone batteries have a short life of less than an hour of flight time. To keep their aircraft flying, pilots often need to land the drone and switch batteries. Second, Cathy's area of interest was a complex landscape with narrow gorges and forested ridges. To search mountainous locations, pilots must program their drones to capture high-resolution photographs while flying a precise "lawnmower" grid over elevations that fluctuate. The San Jacinto climate—wind, rain, snow, and fog—added even more layers of trouble. When Cathy sent one UAS pilot a map of her search area, he told her that "it would take forever to do this with a drone."

Despite the odds, Robinson believed searching for missing hikers using drones had a promising future and told Cathy about a case he'd worked back in 2012. That March, two-year-old Devon Davis had wandered away from his home in southeast Texas while his mother napped. Searchers scoured the area for days before Robinson's drone took an aerial photograph that showed the child's body floating in an algae-covered swamp. Sadly, the boy had died—but at least his family knew what happened and could bury him.

"I'm willing to come out [and look for David]," Robinson added. "All I ask for is airfare, a hotel room, and something to eat." Cathy was ready to book a flight for Robinson when he called her with bad news. "I just realized we are searching in a national forest and a state park," he said. "I won't be able to bring my drones."

Robinson's relationship with the Federal Aviation Administration (FAA) was complicated. Since 2005, Texas EquuSearch had located the remains of eleven missing people using his radio-controlled aircraft to search areas that were difficult to reach. But their civilian use of drones for search and rescue had triggered the FAA's mission to prevent unmanned aircraft from colliding with manned aircraft. Frustrated, Robinson believed the FAA was being too strict when, in 2014, "the agency of no" ordered the nonprofit to cease its efforts using drones to find missing persons. Robinson and Texas EquuSearch filed a lawsuit requesting that the FAA overturn its decision. "It is incomprehensible," an attorney for EquuSearch, Brendan Schulman, said in an official statement, "as a matter of policy and common sense, that the FAA would deem 'illegal' the use of a technology that can reunite missing people with their families."

Much of Cathy's search area lay within the boundaries of a state park and a federal wilderness area—places where drone use was prohibited. And, while already in the FAA's crosshairs, Gene Robinson wasn't willing to risk flying anywhere *near* a restricted airspace.

All of a sudden, Robinson came up with another idea. A friend of his in Southern California owned a plane equipped with a high-resolution camera. Unlike drones, fixed-wing aircraft fly over public lands at higher, less-restricted altitudes. For $200 and the cost of fuel, Robinson told Cathy, his friend could fly over her search area, legally, while getting her the images. Did she want him?

Yes, Cathy wanted him.

The guy Robinson recommended was a California pilot who'd flown Lady Gaga in a wearable drone for a publicity event, but Gus Calderon did more than hover pop stars over a stage. He'd also coauthored a book titled *An Introduction to Small UAS Deployment for Emergency Responders*, and his business, Airspace Consulting, collaborated with Richard McCreight of Near Earth Observation Systems (NEOS Ltd.). McCreight founded his airborne imaging company after developing four light aircraft systems for several of NASA's research projects in 1995. His client list included the US Navy, Raytheon, and the National Park Service—to name a few. Thanks to Irish generosity and sympathetic people in the United States, the O'Sullivans' GoFundMe account could afford the fuel Calderon needed to fly over the San Jacinto Mountains while McCreight operated the specialized cameras mounted to Calderon's Beechcraft Bonanza A36.

This would be the first time the two men used their equipment to find a missing person. Working with Cathy, they planned an aerial survey of fifty-six thousand acres (an area larger than Washington, DC) while flying a fourteen-mile-long grid at altitudes ranging from 8,000 to 12,000 feet above sea level. They aimed to capture

1,235 color images at four-inch resolution, and these photographs would then be georeferenced, making it possible for ground searchers with a GPS device to get within sixty feet of any clues detected in them.

The David O'Sullivan Missing PCT Hiker Facebook group radiated with excitement.

I was proud of Cathy. The novice searcher had stuck her neck out to help the O'Sullivans. She'd taken charge and created something powerful. Her Pollyanna approach appeared to be paying off. Two months ago, nothing was happening; now, thanks to Cathy, nearly a hundred people, and several renowned experts, had joined her effort to find David. The O'Sullivans were so optimistic that they booked a flight to California to be there for the event. Intrigued, Sally Fowler wanted to know whether Cathy would consider organizing a similar operation to find Kris.

Cathy said she would. But first, she needed to prove the innovative technique would *work*.

Calderon posted a well-produced video of the operation on Vimeo. Set against a poignant piano soundtrack, the film introduces Calderon and McCreight, displays a map of the search area, and shows off an aerial view of the San Jacinto Mountains. After the flight, the video closes with a tear-jerking caption on a black background. "We're still looking for you, David."

Calderon flew over the northwest side of the San Jacintos on December 15, 2017. But Cathy and her team were surprised when it took days for all the images to be downloaded and then months for them to be reviewed. During that same weekend in December, the Irish Outreach volunteers conducted a second fruitless ground search while the O'Sullivans waited nearby in Idyllwild, anxious for any news.

It saddened Cathy to watch the O'Sullivans leave the States without getting the answers they so desperately craved. Leaving Washington without finding Kris had tortured Sally Fowler in 2016.

Now, Cathy saw firsthand just how miserable it was for Carmel O'Sullivan to fly home, a second time, without finding her child.

Meanwhile, in Texas, Gene Robinson reviewed the photos from Calderon's flight. What he observed disheartened him. The image quality wasn't as good as he'd hoped. The software struggled to distinguish blue, the color of David O'Sullivan's backpack, from shadows thrown off granite boulders. Nevertheless, he sent Cathy some coordinates for one blue item detected by the software. GAIA, a navigational app on Cathy's phone, led her to a tarp discarded in the wilderness, but this blue item found by the software had no connection to David.

Not wanting to put all her eggs in the software basket, Cathy asked some of her new online friends to review thousands of images with their own eyes. Morgan Clements, Gloria Boyd, Aaron Samuel Wheeler, and Sarah Francis spent hundreds of hours staring at digital photographs, scanning every one of them for the faintest clues. I participated in the review process as well. Whenever the squinters saw something interesting, they snapped a screenshot and asked me and the other squinters for a second opinion.

By this time, Sally Fowler was calling Morgan, Cathy, and me the "A-team" because she knew whenever she gave a tip to the three of us, no stone would be left unturned. One of the more interesting leads sent to me were photos of odd things ground searchers had discovered in the woods. I was the most convenient "expert" to review anything found that looked like a bone, thanks to the anatomy course with real cadavers that I'd aced in nursing school, along with the wildlife anatomy I knew from my Forestry degree.

I must have inspected a dozen photos of what turned out to be elk or deer bones recovered by ground searchers. However, the "bones" squinters found in the aerial photos were more challenging for me to rule out, so I reached out to a physician colleague and friend, Dr. David Kipper, who pitched in to help. This meant my phone could ping with a "could this be a bone?" image at virtually any time of the day, given our busy schedules. Dr. Kipper and I would study photographs of these strange things in the forest—curved branches that looked like "ribs," white "limbs" with intriguing knobs, and skull-shaped blobs—zooming in and peering at the images from several angles, looking for facets, angles, curves, and grooves that were anatomical slam dunks. Sometimes, we could tell right away the items weren't relevant. But there were also times when we couldn't say with any certainty that the bone-like object wasn't human.

When a squinter found something that looked like a bone or a tent or a backpack, the other squinters would analyze it until it became apparent that the item was nothing more than a stick, a rock, or a weird shadow. Occasionally, a squinter couldn't accept that his or her object had been ruled out and the debates got heated. At the end of this process, if an item in question remained compelling, Morgan plugged the coordinates into Google Earth. By comparing an older satellite image to the photo from Calderon's flight, he could determine whether an item was there prior to David's disappearance. If so, the lead was dropped. GPS coordinates for any object surviving our rule-out process were sent to Cathy, who would then send in ground searchers.

In the end, the squinters located abandoned cannabis farms, discarded furniture, old tarps, blue Mylar balloons, a bear, and even a wayward kite, but they did not find David. Our frustration grew day by day. Scrutinizing thousands of images and then inputting hundreds of leads on Excel spreadsheets fatigued our eyes and stressed our minds, while the repeated leads that turned out to be nothing exhausted our souls. The woman from Texas who wanted a trip to search for David for Christmas, Sarah Francis, later claimed that she lost 50 percent of her private business income that year because she devoted so much time to image squinting.

After months of watching them work, I admired the commitment of these squinters but eventually lost confidence in their

technique. Like searching four thousand gravel pits for one mar-
ble, scanning aerial photographs for a missing hiker seemed to be
a painfully tedious exercise in futility. Undeterred, Cathy and Morgan kept on doing it, ever hopeful that one of these shots would be
the break we needed to solve the case.

Eric Trockman sits where he found Chris Sylvia's abandoned gear. Chihuahua Valley Road is visible in the distance. *Photograph by Andrea Lankford.*

Kris Fowler crosses a bridge as he hikes north along the PCT. *Photograph by Amber Johnson.*

Cathy Tarr takes a selfie while on a trail near Lake Tahoe in 2016. *Photograph by Cathy Tarr.*

A selfie that David O'Sullivan emailed to himself during his early days on the PCT in Southern California. *Photograph courtesy of Carmel O'Sullivan.*

David O'Sullivan stands next to his parents, Carmel and Con, on the day he graduates from the University College Cork in Ireland. *Photograph courtesy of Carmel O'Sullivan.*

A missing person flyer for Kris Fowler seen by hikers as they walk the trail in Washington. *Photograph by Andrea Lankford.*

A PCT trail register in Washington with an entry by Sherpa dated October 5, 2016. *Photograph by Amber Johnson.*

Chris Sylvia's gear is found abandoned on the PCT at mile 127.4. *Photograph by Eric Trockman.*

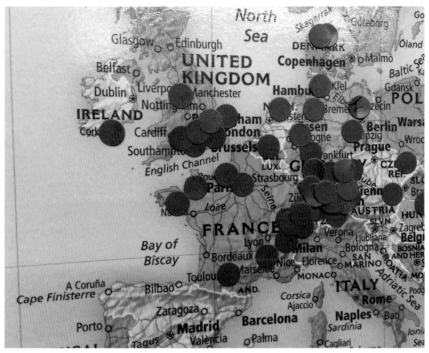

A red dot on Cork, possibly placed there by David O'Sullivan in April 2017, is on this map inside the Idyllwild Library. *Photograph by Andrea Lankford.*

The game camera image of a mountain lion shown to the author when she visited the Hawk Watch Winery on Chihuahua Valley Road. *Photograph by R. J. Stewart.*

The Irish Outreach
volunteers hold hands and
pray before they initiate a
search for David O'Sullivan
in 2017. *Photograph by Gloria
Boyd.*

Sally's Packwood
"command post" during
her 2016 search for her
stepson, Kris Fowler.
*Photograph by Sally Fowler.*

The Lieu Quan Meditation Center on Chihuahua Valley Road. This "Buddhist temple" was described as "awesome" by Chris Sylvia during his last phone call with Min Kim in 2015. *Photograph by Andrea Lankford.*

In 2018, Cathy found "David" carved into this log while searching for O'Sullivan in the San Jacinto Mountains. *Photograph by Cathy Tarr.*

Jon King aka "SanJacJon" and his loyal hiking buddy, Anabel, on the Devil's Slide Trail. *Photograph courtesy of Jon King.*

Pam Coronado and Aanjelae Rhoads use their emergency blankets to keep mosquitos at bay while unexpectedly overnighting in the San Jacinto wilderness. *Photograph by Aanjelae Rhoads.*

The photo of a pyrocumulonimbus cloud Pam texted to Cathy when she and Aanjelae were lost in the San Jacintos. *Photograph by Pam Coronado.*

Poster seen by the author when she and Cathy visited the Yellow Deli in Vista, California, in 2018. *Photograph by Andrea Lankford.*

From left to right: Mackenzie Pollard, Cathy Tarr, and Sally Fowler prepare to board a helicopter to search for Kris. *Photograph by Sally Fowler.*

A remote section of the PCT where Wayne Frudd's search team found a backpacker's ditty bag buried in the mud. *Photograph by Wayne Frudd.*

Sherpa and Ultra Violet take a break. Sherpa preferred hiking in sandals so he could "feel every step." *Photograph by Randy Godfrey.*

Prayer circle for Kris and Mike Fowler on the PCT at the White Pass Trailhead. *Photograph by Marcia Meyer O'Rourke.*

Sally and Marcia pose for a photograph with the helicopter pilot who flew Sally above the PCT during the 2019 search for Kris. *Photograph by Cathy Tarr.*

From left to right: Theresa Sturkie, Marcia Meyer O'Rourke, Sally Fowler, Cathy Tarr, and Andrea Lankford at the PCT trailhead at White Pass in 2019. *Photograph courtesy of Sally Fowler.*

This trail sign on the PCT, where northbound hikers begin their trek along Fuller Ridge, is nearly buried in the snow. *Photograph by Jon King.*

A snowy view of Suicide Rock as seen from the Devil's Slide Trail. *Photograph by Jon King.*

The last photo known of Kris Fowler was taken on October 12, 2016, at White Pass, Washington.

This orange cap, given to Sally by Andrea and Josh Kirkman in 2019, is signed by a team of volunteers searching for Kris in 2017. *Photograph by Andrea Lankford.*

The author on Mount Katahdin as she reaches the northern terminus of the Appalachian Trail in 1999. *Photograph by Kent Delbon.*

The author enjoys a Maine sunset on the Appalachian Trail in 1999. *Photograph by Andrea Lankford.*

A glorious sunrise on San Jacinto Peak. *Photograph by Jon King.*

Tahquitz Rock as seen from the Suicide Rock Trail. *Photograph by Andrea Lankford.*

# PART THREE

# FACT AND THEORY

CHAPTER 14

# *Predator*

---

E VERY NEW LEAD, INCLUDING THE OUTLANDISH ONES, NAGGED US FOR ATTENTION. Some weeks we received several tips in a day, which could get overwhelming at times, and, although we'd have dry spells on occasion, the unresolved leads piled up. One Facebook tipster kept pressing Cathy to investigate Inchworm, a thru-hiker who'd crept his way along the trail in 2017. The tipster described Inchworm as a "trail troll." Drawn to the PCT lifestyle, trail trolls don't thru-hike as much as they take advantage of the free accommodation, free food, and easy camaraderie offered to anyone claiming to be a thru-hiker. Some trail trolls exhibit signs of emotional instability. Others are prone to stalking female thru-hikers. A few even steal gear from unsuspecting trekkers when no one is looking.

In some people's minds, Inchworm's reputation as a trail troll automatically made him a person of interest in David's disappearance. Cathy wasn't ready to go that far, but she was curious enough to ask Morgan to provide her a summary of Inchworm's movements. The information Morgan plucked from social media convinced us that Inchworm couldn't have met David. The timing was off. But the relentless determined tipster wouldn't let it go. According to him, not long after David went missing, Inchworm caused a scene at Mike's Place. The tipster implored Cathy to go out to the remote hostel to ask the hostel's caretaker for more details.

It was a dreary, low cloud day when she drove her Toyota RAV4 past the Buddhist temple and up the bumpy five-mile stretch of dirt road leading to Mike's Place. Shortly after crossing the PCT, she pulled into the compound and parked her car. There was no internet or phone service at the site, so the caretaker, a guy she'd never met, hadn't been expecting her, but Cathy preferred it that way. In case she needed to loosen him up, she'd brought a twelve-pack of beer.

As soon as she stepped out of the car, she walked over to the garage because someone told her the caretaker lived in it. Upon closer inspection, the garage didn't look like a place *anyone* would live; instead, it was full of old junk and tools, including an ominous chain saw. Poking around the cluttered space, Cathy noticed something that startled her. A shotgun was propped up against the garage door, as if the owner intended to retrieve it at any moment. On the ground next to it were two bloody quail. Resisting the urge to flee, she returned to the Toyota and grabbed a miniature cylinder of pepper spray she kept in a secret spot. *Hmm . . . pepper spray versus a shotgun?* The odds did not seem to be in her favor.

Although it seemed pointless, she tucked the pepper spray in her pocket and walked back to the front porch. Through the screen door she saw someone inside watching television. She knocked, and a man spun to face her.

"I know you weren't expecting me," Cathy quickly introduced herself. "But I have some questions about PCT hikers."

"Oh," the surprised caretaker opened the door. "Hi. I'm Josh. Come on in."

First and foremost, after that long drive, Cathy really needed to pee, so Josh McCoy directed her to the bathroom. Like I had felt the day Josh McCoy first hosted me in his man cave a month earlier, Cathy's instincts told her she was safe, but not without some allowances. When she returned from the bathroom, McCoy was rolling what looked and smelled like a cannabis-laced cigarette. "Let's go outside and talk," he suggested.

On the back porch, McCoy pulled up a cheap plastic chair for Cathy to sit in. Less than ten yards away, the shotgun still leaned up against the garage. McCoy told Cathy a little about his hermit-like existence at Mike's Place. Whenever he needed to communicate with the outside world, he drove several miles up the road to a secret spot—a weather station—where he knew how to log on to the free Wi-Fi. Other than the sounds of nature, the entertainment options were limited. There was no cable, but an antenna on the roof picked up two television channels. McCoy explained that, at this exact moment, if she wanted to watch TV, they could choose between two shows—*The Bold and the Beautiful* or *The Talk*.

Cathy handed over the twelve-pack. McCoy opened a can and offered one to his visitor, but she declined, impatient to jump into the purpose of her visit. "Hey, have you heard of a hiker called Inchworm?"

"Yeah, I know Inchworm." McCoy sipped his beer. "He's not allowed back here."

"Why not?"

McCoy confirmed what the Facebook tipster had told Cathy. The night Inchworm stayed at Mike's, there had been major drama. A male hiker watched Inchworm take money out of the donation jar and had called the trail troll out for it. Others joined in on the scolding. Then a lady hiker accused Inchworm of stealing her pee rag—a cloth female hikers use while backpacking to clean their private parts—and the confrontation escalated. When McCoy first heard about David O'Sullivan's case, he'd assumed it was Inchworm who had gone missing, because so many hikers were mad enough to strangle him.

"When did Inchworm stay here again?" Cathy circled back.

"I can tell you exactly when if you hand me that book," McCoy replied.

Cathy handed McCoy the 2017 trail register. He flipped through it until he found the place where he'd torn several pages from the notebook to remove the profane entries vilifying Inchworm. From the pages left behind, he could pinpoint the date of the incident. The timing validated what Morgan had already determined: David and Inchworm could not have crossed paths. Cathy had officially reached the dead end of this lead.

McCoy had finished his second beer and was rolling another cigarette when Cathy decided it was time to go.

"Why don't you stay for dinner? I just shot two quail."

"No, thanks," she waved him off. "I'm a vegetarian."

McCoy accompanied her out to the car. They had met only two hours ago, but their parting was tender.

"If I ever get lost," McCoy said, "I want you to search for me."

I'd grown fond of Josh McCoy, but in line with what Cathy had experienced, whenever I visited Mike's Place, I caught McCoy in the middle of what appeared to be a menacing act, like running a chain saw or tending his beehives or shoving a mysterious item into a stone oven in the backyard. One afternoon, he baked me a pizza in that oven. I watched his homemade crust rise while enjoying one of the cheap beers I'd brought along, likely Natural Ice (McCoy's favorite). While I enjoyed my slice, the trail angel educated me about PCT Team Green, a cannabis delivery service for PCT hikers. When I hiked the Appalachian Trail in 1999, marijuana use was common but illegal. Eighteen years later, much had changed; a PCT hiker could order flower, vape pens, and edibles through Facebook and a PCT Team Green associate would deliver it right to them on the trail.

McCoy and I revisited details about the Chris Sylvia case, then I brought up the other hikers missing from the PCT: David O'Sullivan and Kris "Sherpa" Fowler. Did he know about them?

As a matter of fact, he did. McCoy believed he'd met the Irishman when David hiked through in March 2017. And he'd seen the flyers for Sherpa, who went missing in Washington the year before. "Maybe there's a serial killer prowling the trail," McCoy wondered aloud, glancing at me out of the corner of his eye to gauge my reaction.

This was fodder for conspiracy theorists. Homicide was a rare event on the PCT. The AT was another story. Psychopaths carrying either a gun, a knife, a hatchet, a machete, or a car jack have killed eleven on that trail, but, as far as I knew, a PCT thru-hiker had never been murdered.

After three slices of McCoy's delicious pizza, I got up to leave.

"Andrea, before you go, show me the bottom of your boots."

McCoy's request unnerved me, but I lifted my foot and, like a horse needing a pedicure, I presented him the back of it.

McCoy grabbed my foot to inspect the sole. "Hmm."

"What are you doing? Tracking me?"

"It's not you."

"What's not me?"

"I saw tracks down the road. Small footprints, like a lady hiker. I know you've been poking around. So I thought it was you, but your tread has lines where she has crosses. And your feet are bigger. I'm glad it wasn't your footprints I saw."

"Why?"

"Because I saw tracks made by a huge lion walking the same way."

On the way out, I drove down to where McCoy said he noticed the mountain lion tracks. If Chris Sylvia had walked down toward the Buddhist temple to meet Min Kim, this would've been the route he took. I slowed down where a drainage crossed the road. There, in the soft sand, were cougar prints large enough for me to see from the car. Intrigued, I hopped out to examine them. McCoy was right; the lion's tracks were as big as tea saucers, and they were following the trail of a hiker with small feet.

I continued my drive west on Chihuahua Valley Road. While bouncing over the rutted route through scrubby, oak-studded chaparral, a tree in a different creek bed caught my attention. I parked the car and walked up the claustrophobic wash to take a better look. At the base of a cottonwood, I found something weird: a knee-high mound of bark, four feet long and too well constructed to be a mountain lion cache (a stash where the cats store food for later—essentially a puma pantry). With sticks, then my bare hands, I pulled it apart, bit by bit, my mind reeling with what might be inside. I kept digging, all the way to the center of that mysterious mound, but all I found was more bark and more dust.

When I told McCoy about it later, he explained it was probably "pack rats."

I'd seen plenty of rat nests before, but nothing like that. "Damn, though, it was huge."

"Yeah, they do that here."

The same day I saw the lion tracks and the bark house, I stopped at Hawk Watch Winery—a little vineyard where Chihuahua Valley Road hits Highway 79—for some wine tasting. While sipping a creamy Viognier, I asked the winemaker what she thought about Chris Sylvia's case. She grabbed her phone, swiped the screen a few times, and handed it to me, showing off a photo of an adult cougar strolling along a sandy drainage that had been taken by a game camera near the PCT. The animal was big but thin, and it had a desperate, hungry look in its eyes. The winemaker said locals believe Chris wandered off the trail and a lion like the one in this photograph attacked him.

It wasn't impossible. Over the last one hundred years, as of 2020, mountain lions had attacked at least 126 people in the United States, killing 27 of them. And three of these deaths *did* occur within lion range of the PCT. A birdwatcher was dragged off a trail in a California park within five miles of the PCT in 2004, and two different lions killed two people within twenty miles of the PCT in 2018—a female hiker near Mount Hood in Oregon and a male mountain biker north of Snoqualmie Pass in Washington. I watched online videos and read blogs by thru-hikers who had been approached by mountain lions. Two women claimed a cougar stalked them while they huddled in their tents at night, and a male thru-hiker reported being charged by a lion at dusk. Terrified, the hiker let out a visceral scream so primal that the lion peeled away. These stories were harrowing, but still, a cougar had never killed a PCT thru-hiker. At least, not that we knew about.

Sylvia, Fowler, and O'Sullivan had all been hiking through cougar habitat. But *Puma concolor* does not drag its prey far. The leftover bones from a substantial meal like a human should typically be found within a quarter mile of the attack site. What's more, there were no drag marks near Chris Sylvia's gear. Nor blood. Nor signs of a struggle.

But mountain lions aren't the only animals that hikers need to worry about. Black bears (*Ursus americanus*) also live along the entire PCT. Their size is intimidating, and human–bear conflicts are common in the Sierra, to the extent that thru-hikers must carry a bear-proof container to store their food. However, West Coast bruins are relatively laid-back. They have mauled a few people—during my time as a ranger in Yosemite National Park, whenever a bear attacked a backpacker it was always over improperly stored food—but 1974 was the last time a wild black bear had killed a human in California or Washington, at least that we're aware of. Most people know grizzlies (*Ursus arctos horribilis*) are more dangerous than black bears, and a few of these bears do live along a short section of the PCT near the Canadian border. Luckily, thru-hikers rarely see them.

Next on my list of potential man-killers from the animal kingdom were snakes. A highly venomous rattlesnake lives (where else?) in the Tahquitz-cursed San Jacinto Mountains. "Idyllwild snakes," a form of the Southern Pacific rattlesnake (*Crotalus oreganus helleri*), have dusty black scales broken up by pale yellow bands. Biologists theorize that the rocky ridges in the San Jacintos allow rodents to easily escape their predators by scurrying under boulders. Needing to drop their prey quickly, Idyllwild rattlers evolved to have a neurotoxic venom containing paralyzing proteins that attack the nervous system of their prey, while the grassland snakes got by with the more common and less deadly hemotoxic or "blood destroying" venom. Nearly every year, a thru-hiker survives being bitten by one of the less venomous lowland snakes, but if you are bitten by an Idyllwild snake while in the San Jacintos, you may not survive. CroFab, the antivenom carried by most hospitals in the United States, is "notoriously" ineffective against the venom produced by Idyllwild rattlesnakes, according to toxicologist and snake venom expert Bryan Fry.

"People have to be kept in the hospital for up to a week," Fry explained to *National Geographic* in 2016, where they receive "continuous infusions just to keep them alive."

Not to mention, if you are bit while trekking a remote section of the PCT, the extended delay in reaching treatment will harm your chances of recovery. CroFab is a specialty antivenom designed for treating humans bitten by a snake with neurotoxic venom, and it's supposed to be given within six hours of the bite. What's more, you better have excellent insurance because this critical treatment is going to cost you. The sticker price for one vial of CroFab is over $3,000 and the math is not in your favor; to recover from a neurotoxic snake bite, many patients need *at least* two dozen vials.

With this in mind, it is distressing to remember that Idyllwild snakes are crawling all over the San Jacinto Mountains. During one week in 2016, an animal control expert removed twenty-five of them—seven were inside homes—from the properties of Idyllwild residents. While searching for David, Cathy spotted a dusky specimen coiled up under another hiker's car, and I watched a baby one dragging a cute little rattle on its caboose slither through the leaves beside the Marion Mountain Trail. In July 2020, Jon King was conducting research for his San Jacinto Trail Report with his canine friend, a Jindo–German Shepherd mix named Anabel, when a large black rattler struck Anabel's paw. A dog bitten by an Idyllwild snake has an extremely poor prognosis. If it weren't for Jon's quick action (he ran down the Devil's Slide Trail with Anabel's limp body across his back), three days in a veterinary ICU, several bags of intravenous fluids, five vials of VenomVet (an antivenom veterinarians use to treat dogs bitten by a hemotoxic snake), and a Hail Mary dose from a $5,000 vial of CroFab that was being reserved for humans at a nearby hospital, the mountaineer's beloved hiking buddy would have died.

Although lions, bears, and snakes take up more space in a hiker's nightmares, insects, canines, and cattle can be just as scary. On the north side of the San Jacintos, at PCT mile 202, along a heavily bouldered and shrubby section of trail, a nasty nest of carpenter bees lies in wait. Each year hikers blog or vlog about their painful ordeal of being chased and stung by this hive of bees with an apparent grudge against thru-hikers. A few miles north of the evil bees, across Interstate 10, the PCT enters a landscape inhabited by menaces of another kind. In March 2018, the *LA Times* published a story titled "Feral Cattle Terrorize Hikers and Devour Native Plants." That same year, Don Line, a trail worker for the PCTA, was conducting some trail improvements in this area when a massive bull, likely agitated by the intrusion, aimed its horns at the volunteer's belt buckle and charged. To save himself from being gored, Line hit the bull upside the head with a fence post. Not long after this attack, officials closed that section of the PCT—but not because of the bull. Hikers had reported several nerve-wracking conflicts with feral dogs and, like hyenas devouring gazelle on the Serengeti, a pack of them were taking down the bull's offspring. Worried the beasts would go after humans next, rangers blocked off that section of the PCT until the canine hoodlums could be removed from the premises.

To mention these dangers is to overstate them. If you encounter a wild animal on the trail, the experience is exponentially more likely to be a source of pleasure than peril. As far as we know, not one PCT thru-hiker has been killed on the trail by wildlife—neither mammal, reptile, nor insect. The odds of dying by water (ice, snow, raging rivers) or the lack thereof are *significantly* higher. But there is one more predator prowling the PCT that I must warn you about. And I doubt the species will surprise you.

At Paradise Valley Café, I was warned: Do NOT park in the parking lot at the Anza Trailhead. "Park on the south side," my waiter urged, "in view of traffic on the highway or your car might get broken into."

I took this advice seriously; I'd seen the memorial.

On the PCT, a few steps north of the Anza Trailhead, is a stone monument for Andrew "Andy" Elam. An excellent student who ran cross-country, Elam was nineteen on June 17, 1989, the day he went for a day hike along the PCT with his parents. The Elams left their dog in the car, and Andy, a runner, jogged the trail north from the Anza Trailhead with his parents for a short distance before heading back to the car to let the dog out. Later, when his parents returned to the trailhead, the dog was running around loose, their vehicle had been broken into, a window was smashed, and there was no sign of Andy. The Elams searched for an hour or so for their son before calling the police. Not long after the deputies arrived, they located Elam's body in the brush within three hundred yards of the trail. Detectives believed the young jogger surprised the person or people breaking into his family's car. According to news reports, the thieves had beaten Andy to death. Elam was a trail runner, not a thru-hiker. Because of that distinction, this tale escapes the finer parameters of thru-hiker lore, but the fact remains: Andy Elam was murdered while wandering the PCT. Plus, as of this writing, his case remains unsolved.

Dedicated urban dwellers may not feel it, but the siren song of a long trail casts a wide spell. Especially for anyone seeking respite from the judging eyes of civilization—like, say, criminals needing a hideout. In 2007, Michael Bresnahan fled Massachusetts after sexually assaulting a retired schoolteacher while holding a knife to her throat. Bresnahan evaded capture for nearly a year until someone observed him purchasing camping gear in an Oregon Walmart on August 4, 2008. Later, the US Marshals discovered the rapist had managed to evade authorities by living on the PCT near McKenzie Pass and occasionally hitching into nearby towns for food and gear. Bresnahan was sentenced to forty years.

Another violent fugitive used the PCT as a travel corridor for a crime spree during 2015, the year Chris Sylvia went missing. Benjamin Peter Ashley had a diagnosis of paranoid schizophrenia and a habit of camping where he shouldn't. Evidence of Ashley's criminal activity stretched from San Diego (robbery) to as far north as Yosemite National Park (warrant for resisting arrest). He was thirty-four, with curly black hair and intense blue eyes. Intending to blend in with his surroundings, he donned olive drab clothing, which is what he was wearing during the summer of 2015 when he raided cabins along the PCT for supplies. On July 28, the son of a local property owner and his two friends drove out to check on a cabin near Southern California's Jawbone Canyon. When they arrived, they found Ashley squatting on the property. He pointed a sawed-off shotgun at the young men and took them hostage. They complied with Ashley's demands, but once he was distracted, they made a run for it and alerted the police, who initiated a manhunt that would last three weeks.

Two days after kidnapping the three young men, the fugitive entered another cabin ten miles away. When the owner—a retired dentist—arrived, Ashley shot him dead on the spot. The next day, on August 1, two Kern County deputies cornered the fugitive and a firestorm ensued. Ashley wounded the two deputies in the gunfight and fled. The dragnet quickly intensified. A hundred or more officers descended upon the area, scrupulously checking cabins and combing the woods. To keep people safe, the sheriff closed a sixty-five-mile section of the PCT. Ashley's Wanted posters were plastered everywhere, from the trees of the trail to the national news.

On August 15, two weeks after Ashley's gunfight with the two officers, a hungry backpacker entered a mini-mart east of the Sierra Nevada with three duffle bags strapped across his back. The dusty backpacker claimed to be a PCT thru-hiker. "He didn't look like the big, bad boogeyman," the store clerk later told a Bakersfield reporter. But the clerk did recognize the hiker's face. Quick on his feet, he sent a surreptitious text to his sister to call 911. A deranged killer on the sheriff's Most Wanted list was browsing the aisles of his store, prowling for junk food.

Ashley made his purchases without incident and walked away from the convenience store. As he was heading back to the PCT, deputies confronted him. The fugitive pulled a 9mm from his waist, and the law brought out their AR-15s. Before the cops could kill him, Ashley panicked and fired the pistol into his own mouth.

Two years later, in July 2017, this same section of trail made headline news once again. A pair of SAR volunteers searching for a dehydrated thru-hiker stumbled upon two men carrying rifles and handguns. The armed bandits robbed the rescuers of their radios and ordered them to leave the area. To rescue the ill thru-hiker, the sheriff had to deploy a SWAT team. The bandits were never caught, so their motive remains unclear, but in news reports, a deputy speculated the two rescuers had accidentally wandered into an illegal cannabis farm.

This may explain the following warning posted on the PCTA website:

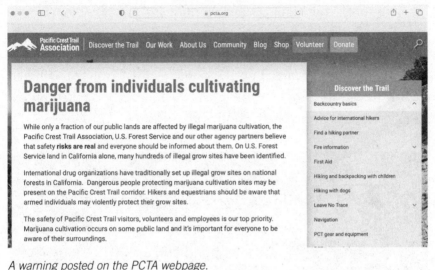

Danger from individuals cultivating marijuana

**Discover the Trail**

Backcountry basics

Advice for international hikers

Find a hiking partner

Fire information

First Aid

Hiking and backpacking with children

Hiking with dogs

Leave No Trace

Navigation

PCT gear and equipment

While only a fraction of our public lands are affected by illegal marijuana cultivation, the Pacific Crest Trail Association, U.S. Forest Service and our other agency partners believe that safety **risks are real** and everyone should be informed about them. On U.S. Forest Service land in California alone, many hundreds of illegal grow sites have been identified.

International drug organizations have traditionally set up illegal grow sites on national forests in California. Dangerous people protecting marijuana cultivation sites may be present on the Pacific Crest Trail corridor. Hikers and equestrians should be aware that armed individuals may violently protect their grow sites.

The safety of Pacific Crest Trail visitors, volunteers and employees is our top priority. Marijuana cultivation occurs on some public land and it's important for everyone to be aware of their surroundings.

*A warning posted on the PCTA webpage.*

David O'Sullivan was hiking toward an area known to have illegal marijuana farms, as well as a few opium poppy gardens, when he disappeared. Looking for a fast way to refill his wallet with spending money after finishing his thru-hike, Kris Fowler had made inquiries into working as a trimmer for a legal farm before he vanished. And, in hushed tones, several locals told me they feared illegal growers could have murdered Chris Sylvia, too. When I hiked Chris's route south from Andy Elam's memorial at the Anza Trailhead, I counted three cannabis farms visible from the trail within the first two hours of my walk, and nearly every year, the Sheriff's Office responds to homicides associated with farms in this area.

One hiker, who prefers to remain anonymous, shared with me a frightening encounter he had while hiking the PCT near Anza. After accidentally taking a path off the main trail, he came upon three men carrying firearms and holding back guard dogs. The growling dogs pulled so hard on their leads that their front feet leapt off the ground.

"I'm sorry," the hiker apologized. "I'm lost."

"Back the hell out of here," one man warned, unsympathetic.

The hiker did as he was told.

This incident occurred on the same section Chris Sylvia hiked before he disappeared, in an area where another hiker photographed a note pinned to the trail with rocks:

*Handwritten warning seen on the PCT. Photograph by Trace Richardson.*

When contemplating foul play theories, surly marijuana cultivators were not the only gardeners who popped up on my radar of suspicion. Stories had begun to trickle in about another sort of agriculturalist who patrolled the PCT in Southern California. But unlike the armed cannabis growers, when these farmers met a thru-hiker, they were *exceptionally* friendly.

# CHAPTER 15

# Cult Farmers

---

THE MORNING HE TOOK OFF TO HIKE THE PCT, CHRIS SYLVIA COOKED HIS FORMER roommate Elizabeth Henle breakfast, traded his compass for her flip phone, and told her to keep an eye on his good luck charm until he returned.

Years later, Elizabeth still holds on to that compass, waiting for her chance to give it back to him.

If memory served her correctly, the last call Chris made with that flip phone was the one he placed to Min on February 16. I asked Elizabeth to describe her roommate's state of mind before he disappeared. "I still have hope he's alive," she replied, "but he was so lost, I mean figuratively, when he left for that trip. He wanted meaning and approval so badly. I thought he could have easily fallen prey to some sort of cult-like thing. It was one of my first thoughts when he was gone without a trace."

*Fallen prey to some sort of cult-like thing?*

From the beginning, I had laughed off any suggestion about a member of the PCT Missing getting roped into a cult. Then I revisited Joshua Sylvia's Reddit thread and an unusual lead regarding his brother's case jumped out at me.

"Is there a chance he could have joined the Yellow Deli group?" a Redditor questioned the group. "They have compounds in Vista and Valley Center... [and] that would be the one way to disappear and start a new and entirely different life."

The theory wasn't totally out of the question. Chris had lived in Vista before he disappeared and Valley Center was less than an hour's drive from the PCT, but what in the heck was "the Yellow Deli group"? Until I did an internet search of my own, I hadn't the faintest idea.

Yellow Delis are cafés run by a religious community called the Twelve Tribes of Israel, or the "Twelve Tribes" for short. According to their website, the Twelve Tribes have three thousand members, fifteen cafés, and nearly fifty "self-governing" communities in countries all over the world, including Germany, Canada, New Zealand, Spain, and Brazil. The group's founder, Eugene Spriggs, opened the first Yellow Deli café in Chattanooga, Tennessee, in 1973. Forty years later, the Twelve Tribes manage cafés nationwide where they serve patrons simple home-cooked sandwiches, yerba mate tea, and wholesome desserts inside restaurants on trendy (expensive) streets in cities like Boulder, Colorado; Oneida, New York; Rutland, Vermont; and—you guessed it—Vista, California.

In promotional pamphlets published by the Twelve Tribes, they often describe themselves using bee metaphors. Individual members make up "a body" that lives within "the hive" and works in cooperation as "one mind and one heart." In the 1990s, the community expanded into San Diego County because, as one elder told a reporter, "there were a lot of lost people" in California. They opened two delis in the state, one in downtown Vista and one in Valley Center near a sixty-acre farm they called Morning Star Ranch, where they grew avocados and organic vegetables. Besides these properties, the Twelve Tribes also owned a cabin in Mount Laguna, a short walk from the PCT, where they fed thru-hikers and hosted them overnight.

On the webpage www.hikershostel.org, the Twelve Tribes advertised six hostels catering to long-distance hikers around the world: one near the Appalachian Trail, one along the Camino de Santiago in Spain, two along the Continental Divide Trail, and two on the PCT in Southern California. I read numerous blogs written by Appalachian Trail thru-hikers who have accepted the Tribes' generosity. "Hikers are like us," a community patriarch preached to one lady hiker during her stay. "We're both looking for something. We are searchers."

To draw hikers into their hostels, the group deploys young members to parse the trail. Traveling in pairs, these backpack-hauling evangelists are called "walkers." Male walkers can lure you into conversation by giving you an organic snack they call "green bars." If you accept their offer to sleep at one of their properties, the plainly dressed women will serve you a homespun meal and encourage you to attend prayer circles twice a day, every day, throughout your stay. There are dancing and music on the farms, but no movies or books. For hikers with an interest in WWOOFing (World Wide Opportunities on Organic Farms), like Kris Fowler, that opportunity is also readily available. If you decided to work on the farm, they would give you shelter, food, and acceptance. They also showered you with attention while asking gentle but probing questions: Are you married? No? We can fix that. Are you homeless? Jobless? Lonely? Disillusioned? Addicted? We can fix all that too. We love you. God loves you. "Come stay on our beautiful farm for a day...or forever!"

On Facebook, I found a 2016 photo of a canvas teepee erected on the PCT at the Anza Trailhead, where Chris Sylvia had begun his hike the year before. From the teepee, the Twelve Tribes handed out refreshments to thru-hikers and offered them shelter for the night. In another picture taken that same year, I noticed a PCT thru-hiker sitting next to two walkers in Warner Springs, a village on the trail south of where Chris disappeared. Through social media, I identified the thru-hiker in the photo and contacted him.

Paul Lockey described the walkers he met as "a little odd but nice." They were in their twenties and invited any and all hikers to come stay at their farm. Curious about their beliefs, Lockey asked them countless questions. The male walker told him they were not Christian, but added that if he joined them, he must take a Hebrew name. When Lockey directed another inquiry to the woman beside him, she looked at her male partner before speaking. "Go ahead," the male encouraged, "you can talk to him." Lockey characterized their recruitment method as casual. "Come to our farm," they offered. "You can stay as long as you want." Lockey observed one thru-hiker go with them, but he passed on their offer.

Another PCT thru-hiker I spoke to, trail name Jet Fighter, had also encountered members of the group she called "the cult farmers" between Idyllwild and the Anza Trailhead. People react strongly to the term *cult*, but the Twelve Tribes meet the definition to a T: a religious group with a charismatic leader and followers who are isolated from the mainstream. After finishing her hike in 2016, Jet Fighter grew anxious when a hiker she'd met from Japan, who spoke little English, left the trail with the cult farmers. She feared the language barrier made the international hiker vulnerable. When Jet Fighter heard the Japanese hiker (trail name Ping-pong) had returned to the PCT after his visit with the cult farmers, she was notably relieved.

I also spoke with a section hiker named Elana who met two walkers on the PCT a year later, in 2017. The walkers carried backpacks and offered her a free "green bar" and a religious pamphlet. The bars were green because the Twelve Tribes added mate, an olive-colored herbal tea with stimulant properties. The walkers spooked Elana because she knew someone who had joined the Twelve Tribes—and not necessarily for the better. A year or so before, she'd been shopping at a farmers market in San Diego when she ran into an old friend at a vegetable stand. He was selling organic produce grown at Morning Star Ranch in Valley Center. He told Elana he had a new name now. He didn't look the same.

Members of the Twelve Tribes appear to follow a strict and conservative dress code. For the men: it's jeans, plaid shirts, beards, and shoulder-length hair kept back in a short ponytail. For the women: it's long skirts, high-necked, long-sleeved blouses, long hair, and no makeup. Much of the group's legal trouble and bad press revolve around their child-rearing philosophy, which is small on conventional education and big on corporal punishment. "If you spank a child too lightly," advises a 348-page child-rearing manual published by the Tribes in 2000, "it has the negative result of strengthened rebellion, and they will never know that you love them." Others decry the group's racist, sexist, and homophobic rhetoric. In investigative reports released by the FBI, an ex-member reported that the community baked hallucinogenic and/or stimulant substances into "ritual" bread and fed it to members. It's worth noting that this could be an overly dramatic reference to yerba mate, the legal and benign herbal caffeine alternative they add to their green bars, but it's hard to know for sure.

Ex-members also complain about the Tribes' heavy-handed manipulations. According to thru-hiker videos on YouTube, when a thru-hiker stays at a Twelve Tribes hostel for more than one day, a walker is dispatched to "accidentally" run into the targeted hiker farther up the trail, again and again, in a way that makes the meetings seem serendipitous, like a divine intervention is at hand. If they decide to stay at the farm for a longer term, new recruits must submit all their possessions and financial assets to the community. By compelling you to work long days for free while forcing you to disconnect from friends and family who aren't members, they anchor you—physically and emotionally—to the cult.

As nefarious as all this sounded, I wasn't jumping to any conclusions. In June 2015, three months after Chris Sylvia disappeared, a Twelve Tribes member residing at Morning Star Ranch was kidnapped—not by the cult, but by his own family. That summer, his three relatives abducted their loved one, who they claimed had been "brainwashed" by the religious commune. But when questioned by the police, the kidnapping victim insisted that he had a wife and child, who were also members, and they had been living happily within the Twelve Tribes for five years. Police had no choice but to arrest the three well-meaning family members for kidnapping and the victim was allowed to return to the Tribes. A few weeks later, the kidnapping charges were dropped against the family members who thought they were "rescuing" a "brainwashed" loved one.

Six years earlier, in 2009, a missing four-year-old was discovered at the same California ranch. Again, it was the girl's own family who had kidnapped her, not the Twelve Tribes. Apparently, the girl's mother took the toddler from her grandmother (her legal guardian) in Ohio and ran off with her boyfriend, a known sex offender. On the lam from authorities, the couple drove thousands of miles across the country and joined the Twelve Tribes at Morning Star Ranch. The fugitives benefited from the Tribes' hospitality for a week before a member recognized the child's face on a billboard. The member informed an elder and, like any good citizen would, the elder immediately phoned the police. Soon after, the mother and her pedophile boyfriend were arrested by the US Marshals. When the girl was returned to her grandmother in Ohio, she'd been missing for twenty-seven days.

Although this story redeemed the Twelve Tribes from some suspicion, I relayed all this to Joshua Sylvia in an email and asked him for his thoughts on the matter.

"Chris is absolutely the type who would be sucked up by one of these recruiters," he wrote back. Of all the theories he'd heard, this one "made the most sense" of what might have happened to his brother. "Some people are susceptible to the idea of cults. Others, I feel it's something they might need. For Chris, I don't see a cult being the worse thing for him" because at that time, he was seeking a place "to belong, or fit in."

Joshua forwarded my email to Min Kim, who had a similar reaction. The Yellow Deli in Vista was within two miles of their apartment, but, if Chris ever ate there, Min doesn't remember it. However, Min "absolutely" believed Chris would be attracted to the new life the Twelve Tribes could provide him. Tory Strader, Chris's ex-girlfriend from Maryland, agreed. "He talked about living in a commune," she said regarding something he had said to her while they were dating when he'd suggested "if we wanted to travel by backpack, we could live in little communes as we go."

The specter of the Twelve Tribes came up in the Kris Fowler case as well. In April 2018, Sally Fowler noticed an unusual post on the Bring Kris Fowler/Sherpa Home Facebook page. The post, titled "Please Read," included a link leading to a Twelve Tribes website. The profile of the sender, "Karli Looney," looked fake, so Sally ignored the tip. Then, a few days later, when she went back to take another look, the post had been removed, and Karli Looney's profile had disappeared.

Short of going undercover by joining the cult myself, I didn't know how to rule out that one of the PCT Missing had joined them. I contacted Shelton Browne, a podcast producer in Tennessee with sources within the Twelve Tribes headquarters in Chattanooga. Right off the bat, Browne wondered whether Chris Sylvia was "spiritually curious."

Very much so, I answered. He'd been reading a religious book before he disappeared and was openly excited about seeing a Buddhist temple. But I had really called Browne hoping he would give me an excuse to drop this lead. "So, tell me," I asked, "after explaining the situation, should I continue to follow this? Or are you like, nah, no way is one of these missing hikers with the Twelve Tribes?"

"From what you've told me," Browne replied, "I wouldn't rule this out. I'd keep looking. It's not a dead end."

Next, I emailed an ex-member named David Pike, who left the Twelve Tribes in 2004 and now administered a private Facebook group for former members of the cult. I asked Pike for a favor. Would his group of over a hundred people help me rule out the possibility that Sylvia, Fowler, or O'Sullivan could be with the Twelve Tribes?

"Their families are worried," I urged him, "and they just want to know what happened."

"If they are with the TT [Twelve Tribes], they are not in danger and will be taken care of. Worked like hell, but treated okay," Pike assured me. He agreed to post pictures of Sylvia, Fowler, and O'Sullivan in his Facebook group to see if anyone recognized them because "we want to help these folks who are afraid/concerned for their kin."

Pike received one response, which he shared with me. A female ex-member who had lived and worked at Morning Star Ranch and Vista over the last ten years confirmed members would walk the PCT giving out religious pamphlets to thru-hikers, but she did not recognize Chris Sylvia's face.

If she was telling the truth, this was a compelling rule-out. I asked to speak to her directly, but Pike replied, "She does not care to talk to you."

When the former cult member claimed she didn't recognize Chris Sylvia, it felt like a bit of a letdown. I would have been *thrilled* to learn that he was alive and well with the Twelve Tribes. But her unwillingness to talk to me also left residual doubt in its wake. Pike, on the other hand, remained patient and forthcoming. He agreed to answer the following question from Sally Fowler. "How would the Twelve Tribes keep a new member from contacting their family?"

"Well," Pike considered, "I guess it depends on the person. They tell you that all Christians are going to the Lake of Fire unless they join. They tell you to be careful who you give [one of their publications] to because if a person receives a 'freepaper' from a 'disciple' and does not join, they are surely cursed. So, some people do not speak to their kin. [Members are told] their relatives are of Satan and not of God. . . . So yes, many people who join consider their friends and family [to be] dead."

Pike's answer was crystal clear: the Twelve Tribes *encouraged* their flock to cut ties with family. And, at the end of our correspondence, the former cult member had one final message for me to pass on to the loved ones of the PCT Missing: "Tell the families there is still a possibility of them being there. They might have visited Morning Star Ranch and then went to any of the other communities across the nation or the world for that matter.... Hard to say, but possible."

CHAPTER 16

# Weird Science

F AMILIES OF THE MISSING LIVE IN AN AWFUL, FLUCTUATING LIMBO BETWEEN HOPE
and hopelessness. They want *and* don't want to know what happened to their loved ones. They want *and* don't want news that a
body has been found. They occasionally get angry at the missing
person for causing them so much pain *and* these feelings—however
normal they may be—induce crippling guilt. After a while, loved
ones might tell them, "You need to move on," even though the very
idea of "moving on" seems impossible. As long as there is no body,
even if the head can conclude a child is probably dead, the heart
says that there *may* still be a chance. Perhaps, if they keep searching, they might find him alive. Trapped within this dreadful conun-
drum, Carmel O'Sullivan suffered—as the other mothers did—and
it wracked her nerves to the core.

On the day late in 2017 when Martin Carew—a volunteer
searcher with the Irish Outreach—lost his way while searching
under Fuller Ridge, he and Cathy had been out until dark, and
they returned to their hotel rooms late. Cold, grimed up, and dusty,
Cathy showered first thing. After drying off, she grabbed her laptop
and saw a fresh email in her inbox from Carmel, sent at two in the
morning Irish time. From the email, Cathy could tell Carmel had
been up all night, pacing around, her mind racing through all the

worst-case scenarios, until she convinced herself that the volunteers had found David's body, but the American authorities wouldn't let them call.

Cathy felt a horrible, heavy burden. As if the responsibility of finding (or failing to find) David O'Sullivan was hers alone to carry.

In a way, it was.

"The [American] police, they don't do anything," Carmel had once lamented to Cathy, voicing her frustration with the lack of effort and cooperation she received from Riverside County.

There was some truth to Carmel's complaint. The Forest Service had millions of acres to patrol and, unlike the National Park Service, the USFS didn't consider missing-hiker cases as falling under its purview. The FBI was the government agency responsible for investigating serious crimes on most federal lands, but the politically driven bureau rarely got involved except when the case was super-high-profile. The responsibility of finding missing hikers on Forest Service lands primarily falls onto the local Sheriff's Office. In David O'Sullivan's case, the agency left holding the bag was the Riverside County Hemet Substation, a small underfunded department in a high-crime area. And searching for a (presumed) dead hiker from another country would never be a top priority for a locally elected sheriff dealing with tons of problems.

This left it up to Cathy to insist that David's file make it into the National Missing and Unidentified Persons System (NamUS). The NamUS database, a nationwide system, kept a massive list of DNA and other data on file so that experts would have a better chance of matching unidentified human remains to a missing person. No one had listed Chris Sylvia in NamUS's public database, either, until Joshua Sylvia and I pushed for it. Inputting a missing person in NamUS is (or should be) a standard protocol, but if it weren't for Cathy and me, it might have never been done in these two cases.

It was clear to Cathy that once an official search effort has been suspended, there's a hole that needs filling. Government-funded search and rescue organizations are focused on finding people *alive*. When a hiker goes missing, a government agency might search for a couple of days (or maybe a week), but after that, when the odds for survival turn bleak—*good luck*—the victim's family is on their own. Even worse, once a search is suspended (called off), detectives distracted by other responsibilities often fail to respond to tips.

Another perpetual problem is communication—or the lack thereof. Many police officers and SAR personnel are so overwhelmed with their normal duties or are so lacking in people skills, they become awkward when explaining things to the victims' loved ones. A few, like the detective assigned to Chris Sylvia's case, clam up completely and don't return phone calls. And many agencies become reticent to an unwarranted degree, denying Freedom of Information requests for official reports and sharing so little information that the victim's family can't tell whether officers are actively following leads or not.

Within this atmosphere, what can families be expected to do? Just sit back, relax, and trust bureaucratic, noncommunicative, cash-strapped government entities to do the right thing? It should hardly surprise us when a family, given the lack of assistance families so often receive, resorts to desperate, even vigilante, attempts to find their loved one.

Unlike a government agency juggling many responsibilities, Cathy saw value in locating David O'Sullivan—not only to offer his family some resolution, but for the rest of us to learn what happened. *Every* life is valuable. Besides, cold-case searching also provided an opportunity to test innovative search techniques to see whether they worked and could be applied to future searches.

In January 2018, Cathy called me with exciting news. Following up on a Facebook tip, she had contacted a former police officer and cadaver dog handler in California who wanted to help her find David. His name was Paul Dostie and he claimed his dog, Buster, had found the remains of over two hundred people. Unfortunately, Buster had died a few years earlier, and Dostie, who was now in his sixties, couldn't hike far, but he knew someone else Cathy could hire. Dostie had a friend, a famous forensic anthropologist, who—for a fee—could find David O'Sullivan's remains with a yet-to-be-patented device. The anthropologist's name was Dr. Arpad Vass.

Dr. Vass had all the right credentials. The PhD in forensic anthropology. The experience providing expert testimony for the prosecution of a high-profile murder case. An inspiring TED Talk. Associations with the FBI, the National Forensic Teaching Academy, and the revered Dr. William Bass from the University of Tennessee's famous Body Farm. Impressed by Dr. Vass's curriculum vitae, Cathy expressed high hopes that with this new technology Dr. Vass could locate David O'Sullivan from the air using something called "DNA frequencies."

This sounded extraordinary. "I'm trying to wrap my head around how they can pick up DNA frequencies from the air," I confessed during our phone call.

"He says everything resonates a frequency," Cathy replied, repeating to me what Dostie told her. "It's a new science. No one understands it." But ultimately, Dostie said it worked and only cost a couple grand. All Dr. Vass had to do was put a DNA source (such as fingernail clippings) from a relative (such as David's mother) into the device and search for the correct frequency.

"What do they call this machine, again?" I asked.

"They call it 'the device.'"

This conversation left me perplexed by this apparently cutting-edge technology, but I was also infected by Cathy's enthusiasm for using it to find David O'Sullivan. I had never heard of Vass, but as a University of Tennessee (UT) alumna, I was familiar with Dr. William Bass and his prestigious Body Farm. I surmised that any forensic scientist associated with the UT Anthropology Department and the Oak Ridge National Laboratory was doing legitimate work.

So I went online and watched the TED Talk that Dr. Vass gave in 2012, simply titled "Forensics." In his speech, Vass (rhymes with *gas*) introduces himself as a man who has "dedicated the last quarter century of his life" to trying to give "a voice" to the dead. With gruesome yet fascinating slides, he highlighted his work with cadavers on the UT Body Farm. Using innovative technology to find clandestine graves, Vass explained, we could provide justice to the victimized and the missing. I had to admit, the forensic anthropologist had a quirky sense of humor and a nerdy appeal.

Near the end of his fifteen-minute presentation, he showed a slide of the LABRADOR, a machine he invented that, like a cadaver canine, could "sniff" out chemicals of decomposition. The LABRADOR looked like a handheld metal detector and, not unlike how a bloodhound announces he's on the scent with a mournful bay, the LABRADOR communicated its analysis with plaintive beeps and tones. At the end of his presentation, Vass played a recording of the LABRADOR detecting decomposition, calling it "the sound of death in the key of C." The eerie electronic music produced by what Vass claimed was the LABRADOR hitting on human decay induced a chill down my spine.

"The dead can talk," Vass said in closing, "and they can be heard."

Vass's TED Talk ended on a moving note, but I still couldn't fathom how he—or anyone else, for that matter—could detect specific human remains from a helicopter using familial DNA from fingernails. I was aware of forward-looking infrared (FLIR)—thermal imaging—being used to locate people from the air, but even this well-known technology had a limited success rate in finding missing hikers—especially those who are dead—because their body temperature doesn't contrast enough with that of the surrounding environment. If Vass could find human remains with his new device, why weren't SAR teams using it routinely? When I asked this of Cathy, she explained that Dostie told her Vass was being secretive about how his new device worked until the patent was approved.

I tracked down the patent application. Besides Vass, three more names were on it: two UT Knoxville agricultural engineers and a former Knox County sheriff. "Under the principles of quantum theory," the patent read, Vass's "matter detector" sensed "electromagnetic radiation" emitted by an object. When the machine recognized the "unique electromagnetic signature" of the target object, two L-shaped antennae "cooperated" to point it out.

Quantum theory? Electromagnetic signature? Two L-shaped antennae that cooperate? Right then, my own yet-to-be-patented bullshit detector sounded its alarm.

*I'll be damned. That geek is dowsing for graves!*

I envisioned a man in Depression-era clothes walking across a drought-battered field with two twigs in his hands, hoping to discover water, or oil. If the tragedy behind our current case wasn't so real, and the cost of hiring him wasn't so expensive, Dr. Vass's offer to dowse for David O'Sullivan using little more than a divining rod would be quaint.

I held hope that Dr. Vass could be on to something, but not for long. Remember, I have two science-based degrees—one in Forestry and another in Nursing. I'm also a skeptic who prefers cold facts over warm sentiments. However, I'm still human—and I do have weaknesses. The first is a superstition that the dark warnings in Native American legends may be rooted in something very real. The second is my fondness for people who believe in things I don't. Cathy is one of these people. Her go-to, faith-based beliefs involve the guiding power of numbers, signs from heaven, and divine timing. And I guess there's a part of me that's drawn to the optimism and imagination I see in people who believe in such things. With that said, Cathy isn't a full-tilt mystic. She still responds to facts and values the power of logic. I knew I had to warn her. I sent her an email explaining why I believed Vass's gadget was nothing more than a high-tech divining rod and that hiring him was akin to hiring a psychic.

"Boy oh boy," she responded. "What a crazy situation."

Understatement of the *year*.

We both worried about the O'Sullivans. If your son disappears and a famous forensic anthropologist arrives on the scene confidently stating he can locate your child's remains using DNA from your fingernail clippings, there appears to be nothing, other than a few thousand dollars, to lose. Cathy forwarded my email to Paul Dostie, adding in her own concerns. "I am open-minded," she wrote to Dostie, "but I don't want to waste other people's money and give the O'Sullivans false hope."

Dostie didn't flinch. "This is not dowsing. It is a very advanced sensor technology Arpad developed over a period of twenty years....It passed its first patent test in detecting explosives [and] has been used by several law enforcement agencies back east.... Neither Arpad or I would put our reputations on the line if it did not work."

My skepticism was unshaken. A document emailed to Cathy made it clear that Dr. Vass and his company, avaSensor, LLC, "cannot and does not guarantee a positive outcome or success for every search." It seemed to me that Paul Dostie and Dr. Vass were peddling false hope under the guise of science, and for that, I wouldn't pay ten cents. Con, David's father, was as suspicious as I was, but Carmel and Cathy believed it was worth trying because maybe, just maybe, the renowned anthropologist knew what he was talking about.

Here, I faced a real dilemma and was forced to ask myself a key question: What was *my* role in this situation? When Cathy first allowed me to observe her search for David, I had promised to stay out of her way. But, as a former ranger, I had to express my concern that Vass would give us "some sketchy info that isn't factually true," and this would distract the group "from searching where David might actually be." My experience as a nurse told me to allow Carmel O'Sullivan the space and freedom to act in a way that eased her pain, as long as no one got hurt in the process. Dr. Vass's flight to California was already booked and paid for. He was set to arrive in a few days. I didn't know what to do other than book a flight for myself. In the off chance the forensic anthropologist did find David O'Sullivan with his peculiar machine, I wanted to be there to observe it.

As soon as my flight from Denver landed, I received a text. "It looks like he made it after one trip to Home Depot," Cathy wrote about the mysterious device. She was spending the day driving Dr. Vass all over the San Jacinto Mountains. That evening, I met up with them as they arrived at the Hemet Quality Inn, the inexpensive motel Cathy had practically lived in since she began her quest to find David O'Sullivan. Vass stepped out of Cathy's car holding a strange contraption constructed from white PVC pipes, a plastic funnel-shaped thing, metal wires, strings, and knobs. Grabbing a paper sack from In-N-Out Burger, Dr. Vass fumbled with the device. Something fell off, hit the asphalt, and rolled away. I immediately dropped to the pavement to retrieve the coppery component from under Cathy's car.

"That's very important," Vass thanked me as I handed him the errant bolt.

The doctor was in his fifties and appeared to be genuinely concerned for David's parents. Tired and hungry after flying across the country early that morning and spending all day with Cathy on the mountain, Vass preferred to eat alone in his room. We left the dark-haired anthropologist at the hotel clutching his grease-soaked bag of fast food in one hand and the strange device in the other. Right then in struck me: Dr. Arpad Vass would be well cast as an absent-minded, slightly mad scientist with good intentions that go awry.

Leaving Vass behind, Cathy and I proceeded directly to the nearest restaurant promising alcoholic beverages. Over watermelon mojitos, she filled me in on the day's events. Whatever this Vass thing was all about, the O'Sullivans had funded it and, by God, Cathy would make sure they got their money's worth. She had driven Dr. Vass straight from the Ontario airport to her search area, and then handed Dr. Vass clippings from Carmel's fingernails, which had been FedExed to her straight from Ireland. Vass placed the clippings in a tiny glass tube that he screwed in the device.

Holding the device as one might aim a laser gun, he scanned the terrain with his instrument while laminated cards with obscure charts dangled from strings around his neck. In the parking lot for the Devil's Slide Trail, the device detected something behind a shrub. Vass said that the hit was weak and suggested David must have relieved himself there. Next, they drove up Black Mountain Road to scan the southwest side of Fuller Ridge—Cathy's area of highest probability—but the Vass machine detected nothing. Next, she drove him along a paved highway to overlooks that featured views of the trail as it descended the northern side of San Jacinto Peak. Aiming his device from one viewpoint, Vass hit on several spots in a distant area on the mountain's flank. He mentioned a disclaimer—something about his reading being the result of "bounce." Cathy had no idea what this "bounce" meant, but nevertheless, she marked the spots on her map.

Early the next morning, Cathy sped Vass and me over to a small local airport. Using funds from the O'Sullivans, she had chartered a small helicopter to fly Vass and his device over the PCT between Idyllwild and Big Bear. Paul Dostie and his new dog met us on the tarmac where we waited while Vass was in the air. Cathy had warned me ahead of time that the former Mammoth Lakes police officer was "a talker." True to form, Dostie's gab was a gift that kept on giving. As an added bonus, his new scent-dog-in-training, a gorgeous black lab named Boscoe, was as affable as his owner. The cadaver dog pulled at his lead to greet us with his wet nose.

The pilot flew the anthropologist and his device over the PCT. While in the air, Vass texted several GPS coordinates to Cathy that implied "hits" for David's body and "Caucasian bone." When plotted on a map, the hits were along the same ridge as the "bounce" locations Vass had detected the day before.

Once Vass landed, we headed over to Idyllwild, where a team of volunteer searchers was standing by. These people had generously given their time to search any location detected by Vass and his device. After lunch, in a parade of vehicles, the unofficial search party drove to the north side of San Jacinto Peak to recon the ridge in question. The group hiked a mile or so (south) up the PCT toward the summit. From the trail, Vass used his machine once more, before pointing to a remote area halfway up the mountain. Vass said the signal from his machine could be another "bounce," repeating his disclaimer once again, but he insisted that David's remains were somewhere on the mountainside above a narrow canyon—I also heard Dostie say his dog had alerted on "decomp" scent coming down that same gorge—barricaded to foot travel by a four-hundred-foot waterfall.

*Shit.* I grimaced. The area Vass pointed to was halfway up the mountain where there were no trails, no paths, and no discernible landing zones for a helicopter.

The waterfall appeared to be a major obstacle, and when I looked it up later, I learned I had good reason to be wary; back in 1939, a college student fell to his death while attempting to climb around it. I estimated it to be a three-day expedition for a strong and experienced searcher to reach the Vass coordinates, comb the area for clues, and come back. No way could Cathy's volunteers go up there that day, if at all.

As soon as Cathy paid Vass, in cash, he and Dostie left to work another case. Their abrupt departure rubbed Cathy the wrong way. In addition to travel expenses, the O'Sullivans paid Vass *three thousand dollars* to come to California to search for David. In the end, he worked for approximately twelve hours and stayed one night.

The volunteers headed home, and Cathy and I returned to Hemet to find dinner. Even though Panera was one of her favorite restaurants, she barely touched her food. She slouched in her seat, her eyes rimmed with red. I recognized the look. The held-back tears of a capable woman experiencing fatigue, frustration, anger, and confusion.

*What just happened?*

What Cathy needed now were comforting words from a friend, not an I-told-you-so from a skeptic. I compared our situation to a predicament I'd experienced several times as a private-duty nurse. This was like when a desperate patient requests a controversial new medical treatment, I told her. Sometimes you have to let them try a doctor's questionable and expensive therapy. Even when you think it won't work.

That night, I hoped my medical metaphor might help Cathy feel less alone, less responsible. Later, it became even more fitting. Controversial treatments on vulnerable patients can bring on nasty side effects that leave countless victims in agony, just as the fallout from Dr. Vass's activities would afflict more than a few well-intentioned people in the months ahead.

CHAPTER 17

# *Fracture*

O UR INABILITY TO IMMEDIATELY FOLLOW UP ON THE LEAD PROVIDED BY DR. VASS tormented David's mother. In emails, Carmel O'Sullivan pushed Cathy to do something—in case there was *any* chance he could be right. I was sympathetic to Carmel's hopeful thinking, but, to me, the "science" behind Dr. Vass's instrument was extremely flawed, and his coordinates made no sense. For David to be where Vass said he was, the novice hiker would have had to traverse several impressively rugged, perhaps impassable drainages on the wrong side of the mountain. Yet, I had to admit, it tracked with some of the gruesome incidents I'd already uncovered during my hours of extensive background research; after all, the doomed PCT hiker John Donovan who lost his way in the snow at Saddle Junction had done the same exact thing.

As misfortune would have it, the Vass coordinates were also outside the zone of aerial photographs from Gus Calderon's flight. Determined to help Carmel get past the Vass lead, Cathy hired Calderon and his aircraft a second time to obtain aerial images of the area Vass had hit on.

Meanwhile, I did some further research of my own and discovered a way to get to the elusive spot—an obscure route mountaineers used to summit San Jacinto Peak via its north face. This route traveled within a half mile of the Vass coordinates. This was not a trail, per se, but an intricate bushwhack used by mountaineers prepping for more famous summits, such as Denali or Mount Everest. From the desert floor (1,200 feet) to San Jacinto Peak's highest point (10,834 feet), the route gained 9,600 feet in seven miles, an ascent that is steeper and longer than climbing out of the Grand Canyon. Near the top, a steep couloir held enough snow that brave alpinists have skied down it. Theoretically, if David pulled a John Donovan by wandering too far east, he could have entered the watershed, slid down the snow-filled couloir, stumbled his way along a ravine filled with car-sized boulders, and collapsed near the Vass hits. There was little chance David did this—the terrain was too complex—I placed the odds at less than 1 percent—but the scenario was within the realm of human possibility.

"Don't send anyone up there unless they know what they are doing," I warned when I told Cathy about the route I'd found. With its steep ravines, rocky pinnacles, and rattlesnake breeding grounds, the north face of San Jacinto was one badass piece of topography—basically a death trap for a novice searcher. An expedition to the Vass coordinates called for the skills, fitness, and abilities of an expert hiker—and even then, it wouldn't be easy.

Hiring Gus Calderon and his plane to obtain more aerial images was a much safer alternative, and Cathy's team of squinters was eager to help. Scanning for clues on their computer screens, the image squinters spotted intriguing patterns among the rocks. A black cross shape in the granite. A cluster of shadows bearing a disturbing resemblance to a human body slumped over a boulder. For weeks, the squinters scoured these new images, methodically ruling out every compelling item they saw.

Although the squinters found nothing of significance in the end, Paul Dostie never wavered. He remained certain that David died on the mountain at a site near the Vass coordinates. If we didn't find him at that location, he theorized, it was because wild animals had scattered the remains until there was nothing left, a process the dog handler called "disarticulation."

"That's bunk," Cathy pushed back against Dostie's excuses. "David's gear, at least, would still be there."

Like Dostie, Carmel wanted to believe the forensic anthropologist— with a self-proclaimed 85 percent success rate for finding graves with his device—had detected her son's location. In Carmel's mind, a famous American anthropologist had found David's body nestled within the treacherous gorge below San Jacinto Peak, and no one was brave enough or willing to go up there and retrieve him.

I hated the whole situation. To help Cathy, as well as to ease the mind of David's mother, I volunteered to trek to the Vass coordinates and prove the missing hiker wasn't there. Cathy suggested I call her friend Jon King to learn more about the route. The Idyllwild mountaineer gave me excellent advice, including instructions on how to avoid trespassing on private property, where to make camp overnight, and where to find water. I booked another flight to Southern California near the end of March, when the weather would be pleasant for me but too chilly for the rattlesnakes.

On the day before my expedition, Cathy and I visited the Warner Springs Community Center, a hiker hangout south of where Chris Sylvia had disappeared. The spring NOBO thru-hiking season was in full swing and Patrice Mallory, a hardworking volunteer at the center, was busy catering to the needs of newbie hikers. She introduced us to Mary "Pillsbury" Scudder, a young woman selling lightweight hiking gear out of an Airstream camper converted into a mobile outfitter. I asked Pillsbury if she knew of the Twelve Tribes. Yes, she confirmed, she had seen them "many times" in Mount Laguna. With their rustic clothes and wholesome grooming (beards, no makeup), the cult farmers resembled PCT hikers to the unaware. However, according to Pillsbury, you could pick Twelve Tribes members out of a crowd by looking for "the shine" in their eyes.

From Warner Springs, we headed to Valley Center to eat lunch at the Twelve Tribes café near Morning Star Ranch. On my way to the bathroom, I overheard a Tribes member offer a vagrant a job picking avocados for $12/hour. Once inside, I grabbed some pamphlets from a shelf and stuffed them in my purse to read later. Our waiter, a nice-looking guy in his thirties, seemed distracted or stressed as he took our order and brought us our sandwiches. On the way out, I purchased one of those green bars I'd heard so much about to take on my hike.

The next morning, a Friday, Cathy and I were on the north side of the San Jacintos. We ran our eyes from my starting point here on the desert floor to the snow-covered summit. From this vantage, we could see five ecological life zones, from Desert to Arctic-Alpine. The north face of San Jacinto Peak is one of the steepest escarpments, or long slopes, in the Lower 48. I would only go halfway up, but with over thirty-five pounds strapped to my back, I still dreaded the ascent. Reluctance battled against sense of duty, while the Tahquitz mythology fed my unease. "If I'm not out by three p.m. Sunday..." were my parting words to Cathy, "something is wrong."

With that ominous farewell, I stepped out into the wilderness. After crossing the desert floor, I forded a swollen creek and started to climb, relying on my hands, butt, and knees to scramble over and around many car-sized boulders. Several of these rocks were stained from an old fire-retardant drop. The brick-red spatter poured off the granite in large red drips, as if a giant had been murdered there and no one had bothered to clean it up.

By the top of the first ridge, I was growing hungry, so I nibbled on the green bar. The grass-green snack was a sweet and hearty fare any weary hiker would enjoy. I took a route too low on the ridge before finding a more gentle grade as I made the long traverse deeper into the gorge.

After hiking for hours, I was low on water and feeling fatigued when an inconspicuous stone rolled out from under my boot, causing me to twist my ankle and fall. This should have been no big deal, but my left ankle landed on another insidious little rock in precisely the wrong way. I felt and heard a snap. Pain flashed through me. On the ground, I examined my leg. The swelling was both immediate and severe—and this alarmed me. I was in a cell service dead zone in complex terrain. *No one* hiked here. If I yelled, no one would hear me. My canteens were nearly dry, and the nearest water source was a mile away. According to the Survival Rule of Threes, if I couldn't reach that creek, I might be dead before Cathy started worrying about me at three p.m. on Sunday.

I stood up and put weight on my injured leg. The pain was a click shy of excruciating, but I had no choice. I had to limp, crawl, and scoot my way through the brush and rocks until I reached water. The going was slow and at one point during my stressful bushwhack, I had to scoot along the base of a rocky cliff, using my hands and my bottom to take some weight off my ankle. With my face closer to the ground, I spotted a dusty old bone. I picked it up for examination—a fractured rib from a decent-sized mammal, obviously not human. The poor critter had either fallen from above or had been dragged there by a predator. I tossed the bone aside and slid farther down a narrow ravine, the only safe access to Falls Creek.

Reaching the pristine brook was a tremendous relief. I had shelter. I had food. I had a water source that would never run out. For the pain, I rationed a flask of brandy and a handful of ibuprofens. *My ankle wasn't broken*, I assured myself, *only sprained.*

Lying in my sleeping bag that night, I stared at the stars through my tent's screen door and brooded over the chain of events that had brought me here. Dr. Vass was nuts, and I felt like a fool for pursuing a bullshit lead. What were we doing, Cathy and I? Were we really helping these families or were we only prolonging their agony? And, as my current predicament made painfully clear, following leads puts searchers at risk, too. How far should anyone go to find a hiker who has been missing for months? How much should we sacrifice for another's sense of closure? My thoughts churned as I grumbled at my misfortune. A conspiracy between two little rocks had taken me down, and here I was, injured and isolated, on the north face of a mountain range cursed by a demon. If Tahquitz wanted to drag me to his gloomy cave and imprison me there forever, now would be the perfect time.

In the backcountry, trouble comes hard and quick. You can do everything right—be in excellent shape, come well prepared for all conditions, plan the logistics of your expedition with a seriousness normally reserved for a NASA space launch—but all it takes is one little tumble, and *bam, I'm screwed.* Or one short excursion off trail to go to the bathroom, and *uh oh, where the hell am I?* Or a sudden freak weather event and *crash,* a tree falls on your tent. Or some other random act of God, and *rumble and roar,* you're careening down an avalanche chute. Nature's beauty often brings me to tears, but every now and then, she can also scare the shit out of me.

Did the PCT Missing slip off the trail and fall to their deaths? Did they get lost and die of exposure? Or did they, like me, injure themselves in an abysmal location? These thoughts troubled me, and I slept poorly. I ran through a few of the more horrifying outdoor mishaps I'd responded to and some of the disastrous expeditions I'd read about. Then I recalled stories of adventurers who, after becoming lost or wounded in the wild, were visited by shadowy apparitions. Unlike Tahquitz, these phantoms were benevolent beings who provided emotional support and lifesaving advice. Many famous explorers, including Ernest Shackleton during his doomed quest for the South Pole, have described encountering one of these spirits during a peak moment of peril. Scientists call an event like this a sensed presence experience (SPE), essentially an episode created by the human brain under extreme stress and/or during long periods of isolation. Others believe these hallucinations are guardian angels. But the distinction is irrelevant to the adventurer meeting one of these compassionate entities when his situation is most dire. In my tent, with my ankle throbbing, the idea of SPEs was reassuring. Perhaps one of them comforted Sylvia, Fowler, and O'Sullivan in their moment of greatest need, when—if—they died.

My own guardian angel, though, was made of flesh and blood. A solid woman who, if I wasn't off this friggin' mountain by 1500 hours on Sunday, would initiate a search and never give up until she found my sorry ass.

In the morning my ankle felt worse, but I was able to hobble out of the ravine to the top of the isthmus—a long, broad mesa between two drainages. From a high spot on the mesa, my phone showed one bar, enough to text Cathy that I was injured and needed to camp an extra day before hiking out. Neither of us wanted to call official Search and Rescue. For one, getting me out of this canyon would require a risky helicopter evacuation that might cost thousands of dollars. Second, and more importantly, when threatened, I kick like a mule—playing damsel in distress is not my forte—and if I could rescue myself, that's what I was going to do. If that meant I had to crawl out of this hellhole on my hands and knees, so be it.

While on the isthmus, I checked my GPS unit. I was 0.2 miles from a Vass coordinate, but the terrain was too rough for me to get there safely in my condition. Instead, I scanned the site with binoculars. Then I looked west across a deep gorge between me and a jagged row of granite spires. On the other side of that saw-toothed ridge was the PCT. I could not fathom how or why David could have reached my location from there.

The next day, I left my creek-side camp for the isthmus to check in with Cathy. She had called Jon King, who had graciously agreed to help. We formed a plan. In the late afternoon, once the temperatures had cooled, I would limp out as far as I could and spend the night. In the morning, before daybreak, Jon would hike to my location with extra water and assist me down the steepest part of the route.

My slow pace made conserving water a priority. To avoid using up all my water by hiking during the hottest part of the day, I waited until late afternoon before climbing out of the gully. My agonizing traverse back across the brushy bench was tedious and unnerving. By the time the setting sun blanketed the gorge in a rosy light, I had made enough progress to relax. At dusk, a female bobcat jumped on top of a rock fifty yards ahead of me. While surveying her territory, she twitched her tail with curiosity and contentment. I spied on her for a moment before clanging my trekking poles together. The bobcat glared at my insolence—*What are* you *doing here?*—before she dived into the brush. Shortly after, I reached a windy saddle, a low point between ridges. Here, at the top of the steepest descent, I camped for the night.

At dawn, I met Jon King in person for the first time. In his forties and sporting a rather civilized British accent, the mountaineer arrived looking tall, lean, and sturdy. He was also kind. To lighten my load, Jon insisted on wearing my pack on his back and his own smaller pack in front. On our way down, he shared stories of his own misadventures, including the time he succumbed to a strange parasite while working as a biologist in the Philippines. Jon and I had lots to talk about—which was a relief, because, at my debilitated pace, it took us five hours to descend the bouldered ridge and walk across the desert floor. Once we reached Cathy's car, I sat in the gravel next to her RAV4 and removed my boot. Angry bruises pooled in my calf, foot, and toes. Jon winced.

"That's not trivial" was his very British diagnosis.

## CHAPTER 18

# *Blue Eyes at the Yellow Deli*

———————————

**A**FTER MY DISASTROUS TREK, I SPENT TWO DAYS IN MY HOTEL ROOM WITH MY LEG propped up on pillows. My calf was bruised and swollen from toes to knee. Cathy offered to take me to urgent care, but I refused. As a nurse and a former medic, I should have known better, but denial often overrules common sense. A little ice. Some ibuprofen. Lots of elevation. I'd be fine.

My flight to Denver was in four days. I used the downtime to catch up on the notes I'd been taking over the course of our investigation. Cathy brought me dinner. While devouring our takeout deli sandwiches side by side, we rehashed all our theories about O'Sullivan, Sylvia, and Fowler with an assortment of files, maps, and notebooks splayed across my king-sized bed. My failure to reach the exact coordinates left a question unanswered. *Could* David be where Vass said he was?

In my opinion, Dr. Vass was full of shit and the family should let go of any angst that David might be there. But I did not force these convictions on anyone. It seemed best if people reached their own conclusions in their own time.

On the second night, Cathy asked what my plans were for the following day. I wanted to see Vista, the city where Chris Sylvia lived before he disappeared, and conduct more surveillance on the Twelve Tribes.

"I should go with you," Cathy insisted, glancing at my leg. "I'll drive."

Cathy walked and I limped down Main Street to the Yellow Deli, a two-story house painted creamy yellow. The lunch crowd consisted mainly of retirees dining at umbrella-shaded tables on a front patio with lush plants growing from massive pots. Once inside, the décor reminded me of medieval pubs I'd seen in movies—plank wood paneling, rustic tables, and exposed timber frame. An iron staircase spiraled up to the Yerba Mate lounge on the second floor where, as you'd expect to see in any coffee shop, a diverse group of twenty-somethings stared at their laptops in a darkened room.

We sat down on a hand-carved wooden bench and waited for a table.

"As far as cults go," Cathy said, "this one is pretty cool."

A male host wearing a Bluetooth headset came by to get us. I recognized him almost immediately. He was the same handsome waiter who had served us at Morning Star Ranch! The coincidence, for surely it was that, delighted me. "I know you!" I gasped with the warmth of an unexpected reunion. "We saw you in Valley Center a week ago."

The man's eyes lit up as he greeted me with equal familiarity, pleased by the serendipity of our meeting. He had a soft sandy-blond beard (like Kris Fowler's), and his hair was pulled back into a short ponytail. He introduced himself as Ahood. Today was Ahood's first shift working in Vista. He and his wife had moved there from Morning Star Ranch that very morning.

Ahood ushered Cathy and me to a lovely table on the second-floor balcony. Then he sat down to chat, answering our questions freely. "We aren't Christian, but we are believers," he clarified. He told us the Tribes moved him around a lot. In addition to the two operations in California, he had also lived and worked for the community in Tennessee, North Carolina, Virginia, and Colorado.

A week ago, at the café in Valley Center, Ahood had seemed distracted and didn't pay us much notice. This afternoon, his blue eyes attended to ours with a gentleman's charm. Cathy told him she was single, lived out of her car, and wanted a life apart from the mainstream.

"I got tired of living for no one but myself," he said, gazing intently at Cathy. "So I left everything behind in Washington and went to Tennessee."

Cathy sneaked me a glance, a question gleaming in her eyes. *Are you thinking what I'm thinking?* The Twelve Tribes recruited in California *and* in Washington. From Washington, they had whisked their recruit, Ahood, off to Tennessee with nothing but the clothes on his back. Would they do the same thing to a hiker the authorities were looking for?

Prior to his disappearance, Kris Fowler had shown a developing interest in organic farming. Several of his friends and family reported that he had asked about agricultural work at both a vineyard (picking grapes) and a cannabis farm (trimming marijuana). The Twelve Tribes owned ranches in western Washington and Canada that were well within hitchhiking range of the Northern Terminus. At these farms, a broke or lonely thru-hiker would be given shelter, food, and a job that included lessons on sustainable agriculture. Maybe the snowstorm convinced Kris that finishing the PCT was unattainable. Maybe no one heard from him after October 12 because he became an off-grid farmer in a cult.

We ran our theory by his stepmother. This scenario was more agreeable than the alternatives, but Sally Fowler didn't see it as a real possibility for her son. Sherpa may have been intrigued by the Tribes' lifestyle, but like Sally, Kris was no pushover. The Kris she knew would not allow his family to suffer this nightmare of not knowing. The man Sally raised since the age of ten loved his friends in Ohio and would not have intentionally missed his father's funeral.

I agreed. Kris Fowler was independent minded. For him, the novelty of the Twelve Tribes would wear off quickly. But what about David O'Sullivan? Could he have joined them? Cathy and I discussed the possibility. Jon King had seen Twelve Tribes pamphlets pinned to the bulletin board outside Nomad Ventures in Idyllwild. Like Ping-pong, the Japanese hiker, the Irishman may have been naive enough to let recruiters drive him from Idyllwild to Valley Center, where he'd recuperate for a night, but I believed David would soon insist on returning to the PCT. That left Chris Sylvia, the guy who placed *Siddhartha* in a hiker box and left his belongings behind on the trail. Of our three missing hikers, he was definitely the one most likely to join a cult.

> None of you can be my disciple who does not give up all his own possessions.
>
> —From a Twelve Tribes "Freepaper"

> You have renounced your home and your parents, renounced your birth and possessions, renounced your free will, renounced all friendship. This is what the teachings require.
>
> —A passage from *Siddhartha*

Despite my swollen, aching leg, I enjoyed my lunch with Cathy on the balcony of the Yellow Deli. While paying the bill, I bought more green bars to take home as souvenirs. Near the cashier, I noticed a sign welcoming all to a "lively" conversation on

Wednesday nights. "Disturbed? Dissatisfied?" the sign inquired. "Bring it to the table. Humanity is being stewed, lulled into a fatal and spiritual sleep." Underneath a hand-painted cartoon of a frog in a pot of boiling water, the sign proclaimed, "Something's gotta change before we are all cooked."

I read this poster in 2018. The headlines had been dreadful lately, and although I couldn't know it then, they were going to get so much worse. So, when I read the words "something's gotta change," it occurred to me that the Twelve Tribes' call for deliverance would appeal to many Americans, especially a nature-loving, anti-materialistic, off-grid thru-hiker.

The next day, I flew home. A week later, I was still limping and whenever I pressed on my ankle bone it made me nauseous, so I booked an appointment with an orthopedic physician. "Your fibula is fractured," he confirmed, and I needed surgery for it to heal correctly.

So much for talking my break into a sprain.

Ten days later, Dr. Bharat Desai performed an excellent reconstruction job using a titanium bar and five screws. I spent six weeks in a boot and a month on crutches, and, well, I could have done without the pain. Following Vass's bogus lead had ended up costing me six thousand dollars on top of what my insurance covered. But the psychological impact on the O'Sullivans was damaging in other ways. They remained concerned that David's body might be where the famous anthropologist said it was—until Jon King hiked to each coordinate and reported that there wasn't "a single piece of evidence up there."

# CHAPTER 19

# Signs

I
T HAD BEEN HARD ENOUGH FOR ME, AN EXPERIENCED HIKER, TO GET TO MY INTENDED destination—and I *knew* how to get there. David O'Sullivan had gone missing in the San Jacinto Mountains, and we had to wonder if that was because the Forest Service signs in the area were so confusing. Every year, people needed to be rescued after wandering off the trails. A few, like that PCT hiker John Donovan, who lost his way at Saddle Junction, had died in the process. But the government seemed to be doing absolutely nothing about a problem that was theirs to fix. Cathy and I were perturbed by this. We sent the USFS a detailed proposal with photographs of signs needing to be corrected or replaced. When that didn't move the needle, Cathy hiked deep into the backcountry to a perplexing intersection where the PCT crossed a dirt road near Fuller Ridge. She glanced over her shoulder to make sure no one was watching, pulled a stencil and brush out of her backpack, and painted "South" on the trail marker. Years later, in 2020, when the USFS still hadn't rectified the larger problem, an anonymous group hired a carpenter to construct wood signs in the government style engraved in government font and paid someone to hike in to post them at several troublesome locations.

Cathy had faith in signs (both the literal and the figurative) and their ability to guide us. Yet the directions offered by many of these "signs" often baffled her. One day, after searching under Fuller Ridge, she noticed the name DAVID carved into a log alongside a dirt road. The letters were fresh enough, but the rendering was crude, and the log was an inconvenient distance from the PCT. She didn't believe David O'Sullivan, who wasn't the vandalizing type, would have done it, though she had a handwriting expert do a comparison, to be sure. Even so, seeing David's name on a log gave her the chills. Was someone, or something, trying to send her a message?

It seemed possible to Cathy, who enjoys new age diversions like synchronicity, divine timing, guardian angels, and numerology and believes we can gain insights from playing around with these phenomena—if we pay close enough attention. There are signs everywhere providing guidance, she says, but we are all so busy and distracted that we often miss both the message and its meaning.

In a more prosaic fashion, professional searchers agree. In textbooks and resource guides, wilderness searchers are taught explicitly to look for "signs" that a missing hiker has traveled through an area. And trackers "cut for sign" by methodically and meticulously inspecting the environment for clues. The missing person is a "clue generator" who leaves behind "signs" that deliver "messages" to the "clue seeker." And, although these messages may be difficult to decipher, they can reduce the uncertainty surrounding a missing person's location or direction of travel. Ultimately, however, "the ability to find clues depends upon the sensitivity of the clue detectors," caution the authors of *Managing the Lost Person Incident*, a textbook for search management. "Much like the proverbial tree falling in the forest, a message that is not receivable or detectable by searchers does not constitute a clue." In other words, if you don't find it, or can't interpret it, it doesn't exist.

Like Cathy, Kris Fowler's stepmom was willing to entertain the idea of supernatural interventions.

"You get signs sometimes," Sally once told me. "I'm a common-sense, even-keeled person. I don't plan my life around that kind of thing. But…"

On her son's case, Sally received advice from nearly twenty-five clairvoyants of one type or another from across the country. Several visualized numbers resembling GPS coordinates. One psychic closed her eyes with a pen in her hand and drew a picture of a man wearing a beanie. At least two said Kris Fowler was dead after falling. Their visions ran the gamut. He was in a tent buried in snow. He was hidden within the trees. He was below a cliff. He was under a bridge. He was alive and being held against his will.

"It was a lot of bizarre stuff," Sally admitted, "but you start feeling a little lost. You'll take whatever help you can get."

None of the psychics any of us spoke to asked for financial compensation. One medium sent Sally a free box of crystals from her store and made a large donation to the search fund. Another trained search and rescue member living in Washington who claimed to have "the gift" spent hours of her own time searching for Kris. Though she never found him, the woman with the gift told Sally that Kris communicated with her through dreams. *A rookie mistake. What a dummy I am*, Kris reportedly told the dreaming woman, shaking his head at his own foolishness. *I hiked over two thousand miles all the way to Washington. And I made such a rookie mistake.*

In contrast to Sally's and Cathy's open-mindedness, I have zero faith in psychic ability. The dead are not trying to communicate with us. Clairvoyant visions and dreams might seem thought-provoking, but they do not locate missing people. Even so, my convictions are not an indictment of intuition. So, I'll hear what they have to say because listening to a psychic may trigger new insights in someone who knows the case well. And I appreciate how "messages" from dead loved ones provide comfort to the grieving.

One night, I even had a dream of my own in which Chris Sylvia had a fish tattoo. I woke up knowing I needed to ask his brother whether Chris had any tattoos. Yes, Josh confirmed, he had several. The accept, learn, and let go symbols on his torso. Plus a yin-yang koi, two fish, on his calf. My premonition surprised me. Then I realized I must have seen this information during my research—in fact, Chris's koi tattoo is displayed on one missing person database—and my subconscious used a dream to remind me.

My skepticism is so entrenched that I had never worked with a psychic until early 2017, back when television producers had pushed me to collaborate with Pam Coronado, a self-described "intuitive detective," on an unrelated case. During our investigation, I asked Pam to review photographs of known sex offenders living in an area of interest. From my photo lineup, she chose two men from dozens of faces. Later, the missing child's family recognized one of the two men Pam had chosen from my lineup. The father of the victim had worked on the sex offender's car! This tip did not solve the case, but it was a lead I would not have received otherwise and that made a distinct impression on me.

Pam Coronado didn't look at all like how I imagined a psychic would look. If you saw the Californian out walking her dog on a local trail, you might guess she was a physical therapist or a teacher. A trim redhead with an outdoorsy vibe, she could pass for forty but had recently crossed over fifty, like I had. Before 1996, Pam had lived a typical suburban life. Married. Mother of three. Two cats and a dog. A comfortable home in beachy Ventura County. Then a bizarre dream catapulted her into a darker world.

She was in the back seat of a car. Up front, behind the steering wheel, sat a man she didn't recognize. Dream logic told Pam she was married to the driver. In the front passenger seat was her dream husband's mistress. They had a knife. Instinct told her she was in great danger; they were going to kill her. All of a sudden, an angel appeared outside the car window, beckoning to Pam to follow her. Pam flew out the car window into the sky and toward the angel. From above, she glanced down and saw the car rambling down a dirt road. The angel led Pam to an area that looked like heaven. Pam woke up feeling a powerful reverence. The dream was vivid and disturbing. She wrote it all down as fast as she could, before she forgot any details.

Three days later, Pam was sitting at her kitchen table reading the newspaper when she saw the face of the man in her dream. According to the news article, the man's wife was missing, but Pam kept her dream to herself. *People will think I'm crazy.* From then on, however, she followed the case obsessively in secret. One night, the missing woman's mother cried on the news while begging for anyone with information to come forward and pleading for volunteers to help with an upcoming search.

Finally, Pam volunteered to help. If she couldn't tell people about her dream, she could at least join the search for the missing woman. As it happened, the man leading her search party was an old friend from high school. She felt confident that she could share her vision with him, and he wouldn't dismiss her as a lunatic. Pam pulled her friend aside to tell him about the dream and described the road she saw. They looked at the maps and highlighted a route matching Pam's description—Canada Larga Road. That day, a group of searchers found the victim, Sherri Dally, in a gully off a dirt road like the one Pam had seen in her dream. Later, the investigators learned that Dally's husband and his mistress had stabbed his wife in the chest five times before dumping her body alongside Canada Larga Road.

That incident changed the trajectory of Pam's life. A decade later, she was a well-known intuitive investigator who appeared on *The Dr. Phil Show* and costarred in a television series titled *Sensing Murder.* She established a nonprofit to help families of the missing and taught intuitive detection courses. As her stature in the clairvoyant community grew, Pam became the first female president of the International Remote Viewing Association (IRVA). According to its website, IRVA is a nonprofit organization of open-minded scientists, former military officers, and other individuals who promote the unbiased study of the "intelligence gathering tool" known as "remote viewing." Practitioners of remote viewing—or "psychic spies," as they were called during the Cold War—use extrasensory perception to visualize and then describe details about a target (such as a missile base or the location of a missing person) that is "inaccessible to normal senses due to distance, time, or shielding."

Remote viewing, clairvoyance, psychometry (gaining an impression of a victim by holding an object associated with them)—this was all folly to me, but Pam's professional approach to these quirky disciplines along with her apparent "hit" on the sex offender's photo impressed me enough that, in July 2018, I was curious to see how she'd react to Chris Sylvia's disappearance. What harm would it do me, or the case, to hear what she had to say?

"He has striking eyes." We sat at a small table inside my hotel room and Pam studied a photograph on my iPad, one of the last taken of Chris Sylvia. In this photo, Chris's brown hair was cropped super close to his head, his greenish-blue eyes sparkled with flecks of amber, and he seemed happy. Pam looked up from the iPad, and I stopped taking notes when her dog, a large and lovable Catahoula Leopard Dog named Boris, took a loud drink from my toilet and then jumped on my bed.

"He's not alive," Pam said, once we recovered from the distraction of Boris. "I see bones. And a cat. I keep seeing a big cat."

After her reading of Chris's photo, Pam and I drove to the PCT crossing at Chihuahua Valley Road and hiked the short distance to PCT mile 127.4, the scene of his disappearance. I was out of the boot by then, and although I feared I'd never be as strong a hiker as I was before the fracture, I had healed enough that I could walk a mile or two. Boris whined about his harness, but the rattlesnakes worried Pam too much for her to release him.

"I feel the presence of another male," she murmured when we reached the site where Chris's gear was found. "Did he have some sort of row or unfortunate exchange with another male?"

As a matter of fact, yes, he did, with his roommate, over the phone, but I'd never told Pam this or any other details about the case.

"He gets mouthy," she continued, meaning Chris. "The argument was petty. He had remorse afterwards. Like he started a fight he didn't want to finish."

I handed her a picture of the abandoned gear. While looking at it, Pam spoke in her own voice but assumed Chris's point of view. *"The dude has a gun and I've pissed him off. There's something wrong here. He's unstable. He doesn't like me."* Then she returned to her own perspective. "I don't think he harmed himself. He was scared, not suicidal. He came here [to the gear site] to get away from someone." We walked south from the gear site and a few steps later, as soon as we entered a sharp bend in the trail, Pam stopped in her tracks.

"Someone snuck up on him," she continued. "Someone he encountered before. He was spooked. He was being followed." Pam turned 180 degrees to face north. "Something happened behind me. To the southeast. No struggle. No shots, but a man with a gun came up this trail, and surprised him, then this man persuaded Chris to move to another location. Maybe to a car." Pam pointed to Chihuahua Valley Road, which was visible from our location.

Her theory made sense. Chris's gear was found on the north end of a blind corner on the trail. If you sat there to take a break, someone could hike from the south undetected until they were almost right up on you. I hadn't noticed this until Pam pointed it out. News reports stated the authorities had discovered no signs of violence at the gear site. But Pam's foul-play-at-another-location theory remained plausible. She also hit the nail on the head about

Chris having a petty argument with a male before he vanished. Then again, if she'd researched the case beforehand, she might have uncovered hints online that Chris Sylvia's last phone call to Min Kim had not gone well. Once Pam finished with her reading, we returned to my car and turned on the air conditioner. At 12:45, it was already hot. We were both sweating. I reached for my purse.

"That's not necessary," Pam said.

I paid her anyway. When I considered her time and gas money, her nominal reading fee seemed reasonable compared to the exorbitant amount the O'Sullivans had given to Dr. Vass.

Pam wasn't the only one who believed Chris may have fallen victim to foul play. But I didn't see it. To be fair, my conviction came from intuition as well. When I reviewed all I knew about the case, Pam's foul play theory didn't quite pass the so-called duck test—*if it looks like a duck, swims like a duck, and quacks like a duck, then it's probably a duck*—a form of abductive reasoning that applies common sense (otherwise known as intuition) to infer the most likely explanation for something unknown. For me, the clincher was the remoteness of the area, alongside the difficulty a murderer would have faced dragging a body out of that terrain without leaving behind evidence.

Plus, there was the book. If Chris placed *Siddhartha* in the hiker box before laying out his gear on the trail, it likely meant that he intended to rid himself of his belongings before he disappeared— something that backs up the theory that he was adopting, or at least considering, certain tenets of Buddhism. In addition to being widely known as pacifists, Buddhists also often reject their worldly possessions. So Chris, stripping himself of his material belongings? That's something a person does when he has a plan in mind. It is not something we conveniently and coincidently do right before we get murdered.

I expect some of you will disagree with my conclusion from the "duck test," while others will see lots of holes in Pam's readings.

And that's totally fair. No psychic is 100 percent accurate, is how Pam explains her failures. Clairvoyants cannot provide all the answers to families of the missing. There are psychics out there with good intentions, she warns, but many have no idea what they are doing. Per Pam's advice, if you are going to work with a clairvoyant, choose one with experience, favorable references, and a professional approach. She wants people to consider her as one of many investigative tools. She loves her work and sees it as a life calling, but she admits, over the course of twenty years, she's made some mistakes.

As if to prove her own point about the fallibility of psychic visions, a few weeks after she and I visited the site of Chris Sylvia's disappearance, Pam Coronado would make the most momentous miscalculation of her career.

## CHAPTER 20

# *Fire*

---

"**C**ATHY'S DETERMINATION TRAIN," AS PAM CALLED IT, WAS CONTAGIOUS. "I couldn't help but jump on for the ride."

The intuitive clairvoyant had worked many cases alongside dozens of cops, hundreds of searchers, and a few FBI agents, but she'd never met anyone, let alone a volunteer, quite like Cathy. What the retired pharmacy manager lacked in credentials or experience, she more than made up for in tenacity. In addition to the volunteer's spunk and steadfastness, other aspects of David O'Sullivan's case pulled at Pam's heartstrings. The Irishman was exactly one month older than her own daughter; plus, like David, she was also an avid hiker and international traveler. Pam couldn't imagine how awful it would be to have your kid vanish in another country.

A handful of psychics had given Cathy their thoughts on David's disappearance prior to Pam. Cathy filled me in on what these mediums had said, and we both felt they had provided us with nothing substantial to follow up on.

"Why don't you compare those earlier readings to what Pam has to say," I said, before introducing them via an email. Cathy brought an appropriate amount of skepticism to her dealings with psychics, so I didn't see any problem with this. Besides, I knew Pam was down to earth, had a good heart, and wouldn't charge Cathy any money. But I never expected the psychic to become so engrossed with David's case. Or the trouble that obsession would lead to.

"My first readings are the most accurate," Pam explained to Cathy during their first phone call, "because the more you learn about the case, the more [your own] logic makes noise." She asked Cathy not to provide her any details about David O'Sullivan, to avoid what psychics call "front loading."

Cathy was happy to oblige this request.

The psychic homed her second sight on David, verbalizing her vision out loud while Cathy took notes. Pam was seeing David put his backpack down and leave it behind. Maybe before taking a selfie. At this moment, David was happy, having no fear or anxiety, and pleased about reaching a goal, like a summit or the top of a strenuous climb at the edge of a cliff. Then Pam's vision changed dramatically in tone. David tumbled backward and slid down a slope at an awful speed.

"He's not alive," Pam concluded, before directing her mind's eye back up to the point on the trail from which David fell. She noticed rock steps. Conifers. A distinct vista. She mentally labeled the view "three purple mountains." Pines framed the vista. There was a distinct rock on her right. David fell near this boulder, Pam told Cathy. If they located it, they would find him.

"That mountain is *riddled* with boulders," Cathy sighed.

After the reading, Cathy sent Pam photos of the San Jacinto section of the PCT, hoping the psychic might recognize the trail, the view, and the boulder in her vision. When this process failed to turn up any matches, Pam agreed to meet Cathy in Idyllwild to get a feel for the area in person.

During their first hunt for the boulder, Pam offered up a disclaimer. "You aren't going to like what I'm going to say, but I have a problem with distances."

"You're right." Cathy said. "I don't like it."

Pam explained that gauging distances was one of many complications psychics face when looking for a missing person, such as a

hiker. Why? Because a mental image of the woods is difficult to interpret. Everything looks the same. Trees. Rocks. Dirt. Creeks. In contrast, whenever she did remote viewing of a city, there were house
numbers or unique buildings to see and describe. Compass bearings
were also a challenge. To determine direction in her visions, instead
of North, South, East, and West, Pam used an imaginary clock face.

"Seriously, Pam?" Cathy threw her arms up in the air. "Why do
dead people have to speak so cryptically? Come on! Give me some
GPS coordinates. No more of this 'there is a boulder to the right and
look for a view of three ridges framed by trees' nonsense."

"If we can just find that rock," Pam insisted, "I'll get that 'aha!'
moment we need to break the case."

The two soldiered on. Pam and Cathy didn't always see eye to
eye, but their common purpose united them. "She made me laugh
a lot," Pam later said of Cathy, "but she drives like a bat out of hell."
And Cathy's habit of ruling out leads based on logic concerned Pam
because valid scenarios are often dismissed by investigators making rational assumptions.

Cathy, on the other hand, cringed when Pam's dog—the slob-
bering and shedding Boris—jumped into her car. Admittedly,
Cathy is "not a pet person," but Boris was drawn to her despite
that and rarely left the volunteer's side as they hiked. The psychic's
foggy contradictions were equally exasperating. On their first hike
together, Pam experienced a distinct pull of déjà vu, indicating that
David went up the Devil's Slide Trail. But, the next day, Pam tried
some "pendulum dowsing"—a divination technique using a weight
on a string—and came to a different conclusion. She wrote names of
the San Jacinto trails on index cards, turned them upside down, and
held the pendulum over each one of them until the right card made
it swing in a circle. When she turned over the chosen card, it said
Suicide Rock, a trail that isn't used by PCT hikers.

*I'm so done.* Cathy rubbed her temples. *I can't deal with this. I have
to think logically.*

In July 2018, Pam returned to Idyllwild to search a specific area she couldn't stop thinking about. Cathy was out of the state, so the psychic had asked her friend Aanjelae Rhoads, an experienced hiker who does trail restoration work, to join her instead. Pam wanted to search the Seven Pines Trail, a strenuous route that practically no one used to access the PCT. When she applied for a hiking permit required by the USFS, the woman behind the desk scoffed, "Seven Pines Trail? Why would you go up that?" Pam decided it was best not to answer the government employee's question. But she had her reasons. She had seen the words "Little Bear Valley" in one of her visions. There was no "Little Bear Valley" in the San Jacinto wilderness, but on the map, she saw there was a "Little Round Valley," and the Seven Pines appeared to be the quickest way to it.

Pam won't deny it; clairvoyance isn't an exact science. Things get lost in translation all the time, which is why she believed she needed to be open-minded and flexible when it came to interpreting her visions. Perhaps the Little Bear Valley in her vision referred to Little Round Valley in real life. The area intrigued Pam for rational reasons as well. In May 2017, hikers reported seeing an unaccompanied blue backpack at a confusing intersection near Little Round Valley, where the Seven Pines Trail hits the PCT. Cathy had ruled out this tip months beforehand, concluding that a hiker must have left behind the backpack, temporarily, as he or she made a quick side trip off the PCT to bag San Jacinto Peak. Immune to Cathy's logic, Pam obsessed over Little Round Valley and insisted on visiting the site herself so she could do her own reading.

On July 24, Pam and Aanjelae left Ventura for Idyllwild. On their first day there, they drove up to the Seven Pines Trailhead to get a "feel" for it before they conducted their search the next day. Once they reached the trailhead, Pam felt sick to her stomach. She told Aanjelae her intuition was screaming, *Something's wrong.* The women debated over what they should do until they ultimately decided that "if something went sideways," they could handle it. Pam walked a short distance up the trail and stopped. David "materialized" in front of her with a stern look on his face. A heavy foreboding clouded the psychic's mood. *Maybe I'm picking up on his trauma.* She'd experienced this before. In her line of work, when someone intuitive feels the same intense emotions felt by the victim they're focusing on, these ominous sensations are viewed as a good thing. All her apprehensions only meant she was getting close. That she was on the right path. Encouraged, Pam was more determined than ever to reach Little Round Valley.

To avoid the inevitable midday heat, Pam and Aanjelae set out early the next morning. The vague apprehension Pam had felt yesterday persisted, but she was prepared. She had packed plenty of water, some food, a jacket, a headlamp, an emergency blanket. They encountered no one else on the trail, and the terrain was tiresome. They climbed over more blowdowns—large trees that had fallen over the trail—than she could count. Five hours in, they arrived at the section where the blue backpack had been seen. Pam performed a reading, but all that came up was more confusion, no strong sense one way or the other whether the backpack belonged to David. When they reached the path to Little Round Valley, a sign told them it was closed for maintenance. By then, it was after two. Time to head back to the car.

They turned around and headed back the way they'd come, Pam following Aanjelae's lead. Hiking with her head down, plowing through and lost in her thoughts, an hour and a half went by. Then, the women stopped in the middle of a wide-open space carpeted by pine needles. Pam later described it as a "twilight moment" when all of a sudden, it hit her. They were no longer on the trail. They couldn't follow their footprints out of the clearing because the pine needles hid them. *They had no idea where they were.*

They looked for a path out of the clearing but couldn't find one. Pam remembered crossing a drainage four times on the way up. When they found a wash, the women hiked down it, hoping it would lead them to the trail. They were baffled, but not afraid, and decided to keep trekking in hopes of finding their way. Once it got dark, they strapped on their headlamps. The moon was full, lighting up the conifers, bushes, and rocks in magical hues of blue. They continued down the wash until a sketchy drop-off blocked their way. While navigating around this obstacle, Pam stepped on a snake. It was a California kingsnake, which isn't poisonous, but stepping on a snake was enough for Pam to decide it wasn't safe for them to continue in the dark. It was better to make camp and wait for dawn.

They pulled out every item of clothing they'd brought with them and put it on. It wasn't that cold, but the mosquitoes were horrendous. They wrapped their emergency foil blankets around their bodies, which helped keep the bugs at bay. "I could make a commercial about these emergency blankets," Pam joked. They weren't scared. Not yet. Their predicament was part misadventure, part slumber party. They stayed up and chatted most of the night. Pam was certain they'd find their way out once the sun came up.

After the sun rose the next morning, the women climbed a ridge to get their bearings. At the top, they took in the view, but Pam didn't recognize the landscape. Tall pines, massive boulders, steep ridges. Everywhere she looked. She was surrounded by scenery, and it all looked the same. This dialed up the volume of her concern, but it wasn't the only thing. Temps were climbing. She had less than a liter of water. Her phone was dying. There was no way around it. Cathy wouldn't be happy, but they needed her help.

"We are lost," Pam texted. "Went up 7 pines and got off trail."

In Pennsylvania, Cathy glanced down at her phone. "Lost? Really?"

"Yes."

"OMG. Why are you on the Seven Pines Trail?" As Pam had predicted, Cathy was miffed. *That's a dangerous trail. They should have done more research. She should have come to me for advice.*

Using her phone's tracking system, Pam texted her GPS coordinates. But when Cathy placed them on a map, the coordinates put Pam near the Paradise Valley Café, a location twenty-five miles south. Cathy immediately elicited help from Morgan Clements, Sarah Francis, and me through our private Facebook group. Then she dispatched Jon King from his log home in Idyllwild. When she informed Jon that Pam's phone battery was nearly dead, the English mountaineer recalled all the other San Jacinto rescues he'd participated in and retorted, "When is that *not* the case?"

Meanwhile, the rest of us discussed how Pam could use her iPhone to send Cathy the exact coordinates of her location. Within minutes, Sarah Francis came up with an idea and texted it to Pam:

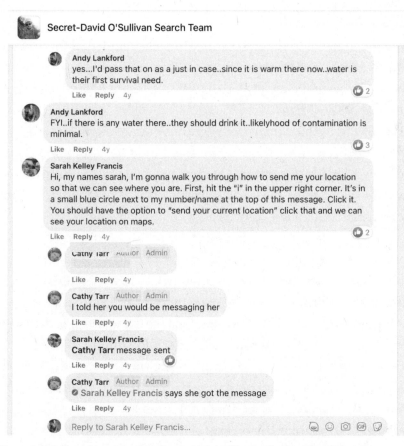

Screenshot of exchange on Facebook. Used with permission of participants.

As fate would have it, by the time Pam received this text, all the texting back and forth had drained her cell phone's battery down to the red. Aanjelae had a suggestion. Recently, she'd seen a TV show about sailors lost at sea. When their phone lost its charge, the men let it rest for a bit in the sun and the heat gave the phone enough juice for them to call for help.

"Okay," Pam agreed. What else was she going to do? She laid her phone in the sun and, like a miracle, it charged itself enough for her to get the proper coordinates and text them to Cathy.

Cathy sent the coordinates to Jon, and we all breathed a little bit easier. With the mountaineer en route to Pam's location, things were under control. All we had to do was wait. Aanjelae was so reassured that she even dozed off.

Unbeknownst to the duo, while Aanjelae napped, thousands of feet below them, a thirty-two-year-old man with a history of mental illness and several cans of WD-40 was igniting a half dozen brush fires with a BBQ lighter.

Unaware of the danger below, Pam became "super restless." To walk off her nervous energy while she waited for Jon to find them, she aimed for a break in the trees toward a view of a bluebird sky. But once she reached the vista, she saw something horrifying. Pam texted a picture of it to Cathy. "There's a fire! How far is it?"

*Not far enough*, Cathy thought when she saw the picture. An atomic bomb thunderhead of smoke billowed above the San Jacinto Mountains. Even worse—Morgan quickly discovered—this tremendous firestorm was less than ten miles from Pam's location.

Like most Californians, Pam was too familiar with forest fires. The year before, a deadly blaze had traveled a mile a minute as it scorched through neighborhoods near her home in Ventura County. Here in the San Jacintos, the wind was hitting Pam in the face, pushing the fire closer. If the massive fire was only ten miles away, it could possibly reach her in ten minutes. Pam's restlessness skyrocketed to panic.

"Where's Jon?" she texted.

After getting the call for help, Jon left his dog, Anabel, at home, before rushing out to find the lost women. Moments after he arrived on the scene, ash was raining down on them and Jon's phone was "going bananas" with frantic messages from his wife (who was up in San Jose for business) and neighbors about the mandatory evacuation order for all Idyllwild residents. A thunderous roar crashed across the sky above them.

"Great," Pam said, "it's going to rain!"

"That's fire thunder," Jon corrected her. Pyrocumulonimbus clouds send updrafts of scorched air from the fire into the upper levels of the atmosphere. These monstrous thunderheads create their own weather, which can include dry lighting, fire tornados, and nasty winds that shoot burning embers across the landscape. The massive plume billowing toward them was a heat dragon that roared thunder, breathed smoke, and spit fire. Jon cursed, remembering that Anabel was trapped inside his log home. "We have to get out of here!"

Over the last twenty-four hours, Pam had been rationing water, afraid of running out. Now, because of the nauseating effects of heat exhaustion, she couldn't hold down the fluids Jon gave her. She felt faint and was having trouble staying on her feet.

Jon urged her to keep moving. "Come on, Pam. We have to get off this mountain!"

A long four hours brought them back to the trailhead. When Pam at last spotted her car, she broke into tears. There was Gatorade inside it, and she was safe. Still woozy, she wanted to take a nap, but Jon insisted that she follow him to the highway.

When they reached pavement, Aanjelae turned right into the line of evacuation traffic, but if he was going to rescue Anabel, Jon had to turn left against the bumper-to-bumper line of cars going the opposite way. He watched all his neighbors driving by. *Holy shit, what do I do?* Leaving Anabel behind to be burned up in a forest fire wasn't an option, so he gunned it and shot across the road through a break in the traffic. He drove sixty miles per hour on a thirty-five miles per hour road, fast enough to catch up with a fire truck running full lights and siren. He followed the fire truck into the town everyone else was fleeing.

When Jon pulled into his driveway, he was relieved. His log home remained untouched by the blaze, and Anabel had slept through the whole ordeal. Desperate for a shower, the mountaineer rinsed off the smoke and sweat. By the time he toweled off, the winds had shifted, sending the fire in another direction. Jon hunkered down and rode it out.

Meanwhile, on their way out of town, the women stopped by their hotel. Pam didn't care about the stuff in her room, but she did want to pick up her computer. The scene at the evacuated lodge was apocalyptic. Fire hoses snaked down the parking lot, but no one was manning them. The Idyllwild Bunkhouse had a log cabin ambiance and the friendly proprietors used old-fashioned keys. *Thank God.* Otherwise, Pam wouldn't have been able to enter her room because the power had been shut off. The women grabbed their belongings, threw them in the car, and joined the long line of souls escaping the fire via Highway 243. Aanjelae pulled over several times so Pam, still suffering from heat exhaustion, could vomit off the side of the road.

The next day, Pam confessed to Cathy that a vague dread had overcome her while she was packing for the trip, the morning before she left her home in Ventura. The premonition bothered her so much she left Boris behind, because "something" told her not to bring him.

"Well," Cathy wanted to know, "why didn't that something tell you where the trail was at?"

"I've been lost before," Pam said when I spoke with her a few weeks later. "Most hikers have, but never like that. It was the weirdest thing, stepping into a flat acre of pine needles and suddenly having no clue where you were. Like you'd been struck dumb with amnesia." *What the heck is going on here?* Pam had wondered. *Is the mountain trying to get me?*

If you believe in the Tahquitz legend, the answer to Pam's question is yes. The San Jacinto Mountains are out to get us.

Pam is convinced she made a grave error the day she saw the vision of David on the Seven Pines Trail. When the lost hiker appeared before her with a stern expression on his face, he wasn't telling her his body was near; he was trying to warn her not to go.

"I knew when I saw him," Pam surmised, thinking back. "Something was wrong, but I thought I could plan and prepare my way through it."

Before it was out, the Cranston Fire torched 13,139 acres, injuring several firefighters, destroying five homes, and closing two highways. Seven thousand people evacuated their homes and one Idyllwild resident died from a heart attack triggered by his rush to escape. Caught in the act by eyewitnesses, the mentally ill arsonist was arrested; later, he was sentenced to twelve years.

During the two weeks it took for firefighters to contain the blaze, the fire forced some straggling PCT hikers off the trail, including a thru-hiking couple who had first met in March and were now engaged. Trail angels invited the couple to hole up at a ranch outside Idyllwild. The hikers, trail names Medic and Steel Magnolia, hung out at the ranch, waiting for the right opportunity to continue their trek north. But once the betrothed hikers returned to the trail, trouble followed, and a few weeks later, one of them was reported missing.

CHAPTER 21

# The King of Trail Trolls

**D**ESPITE WHAT WE SEE IN THE NEWS AND ON SOCIAL MEDIA, IT'S EXTREMELY RARE for a missing person case to go cold. According to the FBI's database, of the six hundred thousand or so missing person cases filed in the United States every year, over 99 percent of them are resolved. No one keeps proper track of how many people vanish from recreational areas on a national level, but during the busiest seasons, at least several times a week a hiker is reported overdue. Most of them are found alive, and according to search statistics, over 97 percent of lost hikers (alive or dead) are located within twenty-four hours. But for loved ones awaiting answers, knowing you're at the minority end of the statistical scale doesn't make things any easier.

In 2018, whenever appeals for help on Facebook connected Sally Fowler with anxious parents who hadn't heard from an adult child last seen on a trail, she counseled them as best she could. Cathy, Morgan, and I initiated cursory investigations into at least a half dozen of these cases. These efforts cut into Morgan's workday just as I had to juggle my response to fresh cases with my own responsibilities at home and at work. By then, I had caved, like most of us do, and created two Facebook groups—"Find Chris Sylvia PCT Missing Hiker" and "Missing from the Pacific Crest Trail."

Neither group brought in any case-solving leads, but the medium was useful in other ways. Whenever a mother posted in the PCT hiking groups that her child, who was trekking through a multiday cell service dead zone in the High Sierra, hadn't texted her lately, people would send her to my page, and I'd soothe her fears. When a thru-hiker hadn't communicated with a friend for a few weeks, I'd make a post sharing their identifying information, and hikers or trail angels would respond that they'd seen the individual that day, and they were fine.

This was the sort of fortunate outcome we assumed would be the result when Brandi Valenza, a bartender living in San Francisco, posted this on Facebook:

**Brandi Valenza ▶ Pacific Crest Trail Angels**
September 1, 2018 · 🌐

People on the PCT: My partner Jason Storm and I are looking for his stepmother, 📍 Kira Moon. She last posted on facebook from somewhere just north of bakersfield (we believe). She is most likely traveling NORTH with a man named Jim/Jay Cerilo (trail name Medic) whom she met near the start of the trail at the Southern Terminus.

We have not heard from her via phone since August 2nd, and her last post on facebook was August 11. Needless to say, we are extremely worried about her. If anyone has seen her recently, please let us know. And if you see her please have her get in touch with us (or please contact us directly.)

post updated with new flyer

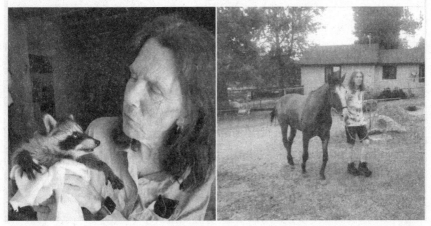

*Facebook post by Brandi Valenza. Used with permission of Brandi Valenza.*

Hikers and a few trail angels responded to the query. They had seen Kira Moon in California. She was okay and hanging out with the hiker going by "Medic." Some commenters implied Kira might be avoiding family on purpose because she seemed to be in no distress and was enjoying her life on the trail. A few people also accused Brandi and others who were trying to help of being meddlers. They lectured us to mind our own business.

In case we could be of any use, Cathy, Morgan, Sally, and I decided to look into the circumstances ourselves and joined the Facebook group created to locate Kira. We studied the facts and offered advice, but the conflicting reports about Kira Moon's state of mind made it easy to dismiss the incident as a case of family dysfunction that would resolve itself. Besides, all we were doing to find Sylvia, Fowler, and O'Sullivan already took up much of our free time. I enjoyed digging into a fresh case with my new friends, but there were occasions when I felt put upon because most of these "missing hiker" incidents were false alarms due to miscommunication. There seemed to be no end to them.

The best trail names make you chuckle. It's easy to imagine the misadventure that transformed Monica into "Snake Charmer," "Bear Bait," or "Toilet Spider." Or why Frank's trail buddies call him "Blood Beard," "Numb Nuts," or "Creaky Knees." During her first days on the PCT, Kira Moon became "Steel Magnolia," or "Steel" for short, because of the unique gray shoes she wore. But Kira was more magnolia than steel. Hikers and trail angels described the sixty-two-year-old as a gentle person who was "dangerously unprepared," "vulnerable," and "fragile." Alarmingly thin with long gray hair, Kira Moon was surviving on disability payments after injuring her back, and her little dog, a teacup Yorkie, had died recently. Embarking on a PCT thru-hike was Steel Magnolia's attempt to recover from her injury and her grief. She departed from Campo on March 18.

A week later, on March 25, another thru-hiker posted a photograph on his Instagram account, where he went by the handle @hiking_for_hope. In the photo, a man who identified himself as Jay Cerilo stands next to a Christmas tree in what looks like a hotel lobby. A black bandage is wrapped around his left knee, one arm is held tight to his side, and his left hand flops. Captioned "after stroke," the post kindles your compassion for the disabled hiker.

A few days after this image was posted, Steel Magnolia met Jay Cerilo on the PCT. The tall, muscled hiker appeared to have recovered from the stroke afflicting him in the Christmas photo. A fit man in his fifties, with a shaved head and chest tattoos, Jay had adopted the trail name "Medic" because, he said, he'd been a paramedic in the military. True to his moniker, Medic displayed caregiving tendencies. When Steel Magnolia couldn't hike more than five or eight miles a day, he slowed his pace to match hers and hauled some of her gear. When Steel was too sore to walk, other hikers observed Medic carrying her in his arms.

On @hiking_for_hope, Medic posted selfies with Steel Magnolia by his side. The new hiking partners looked happy in photographs, but their trekking style was slow and chaotic. They flip-flopped a lot, returning to southern destinations when every other thru-hiker marched north. Around July 1, Steel and Medic were still well south of the Sierra Nevada when they should have been farther north, approaching the Oregon border.

In Warner Springs, Medic discussed David O'Sullivan's disappearance with a group of fellow hikers, as if he knew a lot about the case. Search dogs had caught David's scent on Fuller Ridge, Medic said, but authorities failed to locate the body. Although this was false, one hiker took Medic's statements as fact and wrote about it in a blog, causing some confusion and upsetting David's parents.

In late July, the same wildfire that threatened Pam and Aanjelae had forced Steel and Medic off the PCT. A picture on Steel's Facebook page placed her on a ranch outside Idyllwild, a haven that had taken in animals fleeing from or wounded by the fire. In the photo, she held the reins of a burned horse, alive with white salve spread across its face. Steel's long, gray hair was now auburn, and she sported a trendier haircut. On @hiking_for_hope, there were images of Medic and Steel holding a baby raccoon wrapped in a towel, another victim of the wildfire. The age difference between the two companions was noticeable, but the PCT hikers looked content and healthy, and from afar their predicament seemed romantic—a new couple stranded by a wildfire, caring for animals.

In August 2018, they left the ranch and returned to the PCT. Hikers and trail angels alike noticed changes in how Medic treated Steel. The doting charmer had turned controlling and mean and some PCT hikers reported they had seen Steel with a black eye, although she insisted the bruise was only a "camping mishap." Not to mention, the more Medic talked, the more his stories didn't add up. One day, he said he was a former Army medic. Another day he was apparently a Navy diver. He claimed that he was wealthy, worked with computers, and owned a yacht, but he always used Steel's credit card to pay for hotel rooms. Sometimes he called himself Jim. Other times, his name was Jay or Will. He told one hiker he was recovering from cancer. Others heard the tall, tattooed hiker say he'd been hospitalized for a fractured rib. Or was it a punctured lung? There were so many versions of the hiker's backstory, it was hard to distinguish truth from fiction.

Whatever the reason, Medic had been injured at some point in the past. On @hiking_for_hope, there is a photograph of him in a hospital bed and another displaying a bloody laceration in his upper torso. Perhaps the two-inch slit was a puncture from a fall off the trail after a rattlesnake had spooked him, like Medic claimed. Or maybe, as it looked to me and my colleague, Dr. Kipper, the gash was a stab wound.

Medic could wrap all his stories up in a satin bow, but Dimitri Lenaerts, a young PCT hiker from Belgium that the couple met, wasn't buying them. One day, the Belgian hiker pulled Steel aside and asked her if Medic was telling the truth about his background. Steel insisted he was. Then on August 2, Steel Magnolia stopped communicating with her family.

In early September, a few days after Brandi Valenza posted her concerns about Steel's welfare on her Facebook, Steel messaged Valenza through Medic's phone. She was fine, she said, and she was back on the PCT in the Sierra. To prove it, she texted a photo of their campsite—a spot beside a picnic table shaded by huge trees with reddish bark.

Valenza showed these photos to a trail angel who noticed the trees looked wrong; the photos showed a campsite nestled under the coastal redwoods on California's Central Coast, not the giant sequoias in the Sierra. To Valenza, and everyone watching this unfold on Facebook, it was all very confusing. But Steel insisted she didn't need an intervention, while Valenza's instincts told her otherwise.

A few weeks later, on September 28, members of the Facebook group PCT Class of 2018 read this shocking post:

**PCT Class of 2018**
Thomas Phillip Moore · September 28, 2018 · 

I am sure many of you remember the story of ❷ Kira Moon the missing hiker. Along with the crazy rollercoaster ride of events that made no sense to anyone. Kira is in the hospital after being held hostage by the man "medic". He is in jail now being held on multiple charges including several federal warrants. Further research on this "medic" fellow shows a history of kidnapping, fraud, theft and violence.

This is the real "Medic" http://unsolvedmysteries.wikia.com/wiki/Tony_DeCompo

Many in this group accused her family of stalking Kira and called those that know Kira liars. We live in a dangerous world people and although I would like to believe that the trail is safe from this kind of thing its not.

UNSOLVEDMYSTERIES.WIKIA.COM
**Tony DeCompo**

                                                              114 comments

👍 Like                              📨 Send

An admin turned off commenting for this post.

*Facebook post by Thomas Phillip Moore. Used with permission of Thomas Phillip Moore.*

The poster added a link identifying who Medic really was. Medic's real name wasn't Jay or Jim or Will Cerilo. It was James William Parrillo, aka Tony DeCampo, aka Angelo Parrillo, aka Angelo Gambino, aka a dozen other names. "Many in this group accused [Kira's] family of stalking Kira and called those that know Kira liars," the poster cautioned us. "We live in a dangerous world, people, and although I would like to believe that the trail is safe from this kind of thing, it's not."

Once I learned Medic's true identity as James William Parrillo, I conducted my own research. Working with an internet sleuth who wants to remain anonymous, we logged nearly fifty social media accounts under dozens of names associated with James Parrillo. The amount of information the con man had posted about himself online was over the top. "He apparently has some ability to charm," the sleuth wrote to me in an email, "but he is not at all particularly intelligent or imaginative in covering his tracks." Indeed, a 1994 newspaper article detailing one of his most violent exploits was posted on Parrillo's own Flickr account. As if he was *proud* of it.

According to news reports and a 1996 episode of *Unsolved Mysteries*, in December 1993—twenty-five years before Steel met Medic on the PCT—a man in his twenties approached Valerie Earick outside a Florida truck stop. The young man appeared to be both deaf and mute. Using handwritten notes, he told her he was a Navy SEAL who'd been shot in the Gulf War. Earick was newly divorced, and the Navy SEAL was near her in age, twenty-eight. He was also tall, handsome, and charming. "Will you marry me?" he scribbled within hours of meeting her. Although Earick refused this marriage proposal, she was swept off her feet by the attention and allowed "Tony DeCampo" into her life.

Before long, DeCampo experienced a miraculous recovery. No longer deaf and now able to speak clearly, he allegedly began to deceive, defraud, and beat Valerie Earick until, on one occasion, blood ran from her ears. After months of this alleged manipulation and abuse, Earick escaped DeCampo by hiding on the floor of a hotel courtesy van driven to the police station by a sympathetic bellman. Ever since then, DeCampo/Parrillo had been on the run. "What he did to me," Earick told reporter Patti Rosenberg for an article titled "Searching for Mr. Wrong," "I couldn't live with him doing to someone else."

Police missed their chance to nab "DeCampo" during a 1994 encounter with him in Florida. When a cop in Fort Lauderdale noticed a strange man loitering around a hotel, James Parrillo ran. With cops in pursuit, Parrillo jumped into the bay, swam to the docks, and climbed aboard a $17 million yacht. Once aboard, he pointed a gun at the captain and his crew, hijacking the boat. To calm the crew, Parrillo told them they all needed to wait long enough for the fifty narcotic pills he had swallowed to do their job and end his life before the cops closed in. Four hours later, after Parrillo fired his gun at the police but missed hitting any of them, negotiators and a SWAT team persuaded Parrillo to release the crew unharmed. They were unsure why the "fifty Dilantin" Parrillo claimed to have ingested hadn't been enough for him to go unconscious, much less kill him.

Parrillo served a short time in jail for allegedly kidnapping the yacht crew before a sympathetic jury acquitted him. On more than one occasion, Parrillo has taken advantage of his uncanny ability to charm cops and courts, and best I can tell from court documents and news reports, no one connected the dots that Parrillo the boat hijacker was also DeCampo the alleged woman abuser.

Valerie Earick died of an illness in 2013 at fifty-one, while Parrillo appeared to be continuing his lying, conning, and victimizing ways. After several run-ins with the law, including a stint in prison for another kidnapping, the con man brought his schemes to the PCT in March 2018, which is around the time he met Steel.

On September 26, after months of Parrillo's degrading abuse, Steel escaped her tormentor by running to an urgent care center while Medic was distracted inside a grocery store. When the cops showed up, they arrested Medic on a misdemeanor warrant out of Santa Barbara. Kira went to the hospital where X-rays proved that if Medic had hit Steel as she alleged, he did it so violently that four of her ribs were broken. Despite this evidence of physical abuse, the authorities released Medic from the unrelated misdemeanor warrant with no further charges on October 5. That day, Sally Fowler thought it was in the public interest to warn hikers by posting warnings on the PCT Facebook groups, exposing everything we could prove about Parrillo's long history of violence and deception. Although Parrillo never faced charges for his alleged abuse of Kira Moon and Valerie Earick, court documents showed that he had been convicted and sentenced to twenty months for making threats against the president of the United States, a felony, in 1998. Just four years later, in 2002, he was sentenced to three years after being convicted of grand theft and kidnapping in California. We shared links to a timeline, with sources, compiled by Brandi Valenza, that linked Parrillo to these and other crimes, but a few contrarians criticized us for tarnishing an innocent man's reputation. Others expressed doubts that the hiker they knew as Medic was capable of such behavior. "He never seemed the type," one man wrote on Facebook, "not even close."

It's astounding to watch a con man's charisma override solid proof of his criminality. But for most of the PCT tramily, the gig was up. In 2020, *Backpacker* magazine vindicated our warnings in an article titled "Kidnapped on the Pacific Crest Trail" written by Bill Donahue. With help from Valenza and Moon, Donahue reported the inside story about how, for months, Steel Magnolia was so terrified of what Medic might do that she hid signs of the alleged abuse from other hikers and her family. Donahue's reporting also revealed seven other women who claimed that Parrillo had allegedly kidnapped and raped them. "The accusations that women have made against him to me and others," Donahue wrote, "are remarkably consistent. They depict him as a dangerous and fantastical liar who survives by scamming anyone he can."

Among Medic's many lies were the stories he told about David O'Sullivan. Via a text exchange through Brandi Valenza, I asked Kira/Steel about it.

"Did you remember his talking about the missing Irish hiker David O'Sullivan?"

"Yes, many times," Kira confirmed.

"What was he saying about him?"

"That he was at the bottom of a gorge at Walker Pass," and the authorities "didn't want to risk harm to agents [by] fishing him out."

At the end of our brief exchange, Kira added, "He threatened to throw me off a cliff."

There was no truth to Parrillo's stories about David. The account about a dog catching David's scent on Fuller Ridge, for example, was false. Walker Pass (mile 650) is too far north of Idyllwild for David to have hiked that far without being seen by other hikers. As to his motives, well, I'm not sure why Parrillo would tell one group of hikers that David's body was on Fuller Ridge and then tell Steel, in private, that David fell off Walker Pass. Parrillo's stories about David are unsettling. Perhaps he was using them to intimidate his hiking partner and alleged victim into submitting to his demands. The anonymous internet sleuth and I scoured Parrillo's many social media accounts, but we could find virtually nothing connecting him to any of the PCT Missing—except for one very weak yet disturbing lead. In an email David sent to his mother about the day he first arrived on the PCT, the Irishman mentioned he had met a "Jim" who was "a former Marine" while on the bus transporting him to mile 0 at Campo.

On October 31, 2018, only a month after Steel escaped his clutches, Parrillo was back on the PCT, hanging out near Mount Laguna and Warner Springs, telling people his name was "Paul." But thanks to the viral warnings on Facebook, the hiking community was on high alert. With his cover blown, Parrillo left the PCT. Temporarily.

Kira's recovery from her traumatic experience was short-lived. On February 7, 2019, eleven months after she met Medic, Steel Magnolia died in a kitchen fire inside her sister's Bay Area mobile home. Both Kira's family and the authorities believe the cause was an electrical accident and in no way suspicious. But Brandi Valenza still blames Parrillo. "He made sure she had nothing to come back to," Valenza told me. "Kira lost her apartment because of him. If he hadn't have spent all of her money, she wouldn't have been living in that trailer with her sister."

Later that spring, I received reports that Parrillo had meandered over to the Arizona Trail (AZT), taking advantage of trail angels, telling tales, and cozying up to middle-aged women. After I warned hikers on Facebook, a deputy called me. Through my Facebook group Missing on the PCT, I had been outspoken about Parrillo for nearly a year. Interested parties, like journalists and potential victims, often messaged me to share information about Parrillo's whereabouts. At first, the deputy dismissed the concerns of the hiking community as "drama" and "maybe this guy just has bad luck everywhere he goes." I impressed upon him that news reports and court records proved this was much more than "drama. This guy is a serial kidnaping con man, for real, who preys upon hikers."

I believe my conversation with this deputy, combined with the pressure people in the AZT Facebook group were putting on local agencies, motivated law enforcement to act. After receiving reports that Parrillo was befriending a middle-aged woman in southern Arizona, the cops persuaded him to leave their state. From there, he went east to the Continental Divide Trail. But a young female hiker who knew Kira Moon recognized him. She put up an impassioned warning on YouTube, pushing Parrillo off yet another trail. From there, he headed west, to California's Lost Coast Trail. Again and again, social media posts and YouTube videos targeting the hiking community shined a bright spotlight on Parrillo's movements, forcing the felon to bounce.

Two years later, I was contacted by a couple who met a hiker hanging out near Sycamore Falls, a suburban park north of Los Angeles. The magnetic man claimed to be former Navy. He was bald because he'd been undergoing chemotherapy, or so he said, and a ride to the PCT would help him out. On May 14, 2021, the sympathetic couple gave the cancer-afflicted hiker food, and some cash, before driving him to Soledad Canyon (PCT mile 444). From there, a man matching James Parrillo's description got out of their car and ventured off into the wilderness.

## PART FOUR
# WITNESS AND CLUE

# CHAPTER 22

# *Greenwater*

---

A SHES TUMBLED DOWN LIKE SNOWFLAKES, WHITENING THE HOODS OF OUR CARS and landing in our hair. Cathy and I were staying in Winthrop, a frontier town west of Washington's Okanogan-Wenatchee National Forest. It was August 2018. Three weeks had passed since we'd helped Pam escape the Cranston blaze in Southern California, and now two more wildfires, the Crescent and the McLeod, were burning in the North Cascades, forcing the USFS to close long sections of the PCT just as the northbound thru-hikers were trickling in. Smoke hung low and heavy in the valley, agitating our lungs while simultaneously obscuring the mountain scenery. When we stopped at Methow Valley Ranger Station to ask about trail closures, the woman behind the front desk relayed some disturbing news. An older PCT hiker had died inside his Winthrop hotel room the night before. The Forest Service employee said the man's death appeared to be from natural causes, but my nursing background detected another suspect. Trekking through that smoke would have surely exacerbated any underlying heart conditions a middle-aged thru-hiker might have.

Cathy also had an underlying condition. When relistening to the interviews I recorded during the first half of 2018, it's pretty evident that she often stops midsentence to cough. "I keep trying things, but I'm facing roadblocks, like, 'What do you mean you can't get a cadaver dog in there?' Then I got sick on Christmas Day! [*cough*] I was mentally overwhelmed, and it became too much. I needed to get away so I could relax. I went to my daughter's [*cough*] and spent time with my grandchildren. People tell me, 'If I get lost that you're the one I want looking for me,' but I haven't found anybody! [*cough*] I'm not an expert at this. I can't find these missing hikers. All I did is create a lot of noise."

By July, the vicious cold Cathy had caught in December had not let go. Her symptoms—chills, headache, hacking cough, shortness of breath—appeared to be from a wicked flu strain going around, but as soon as she'd start thinking she was over it, the crappy symptoms returned. One coughing attack was so severe it caused her to vomit. That's when she saw a doctor and learned the pathogen tormenting her was not a cold virus. Nor was it influenza. Cathy was diagnosed with Legionnaire's disease, a rare and occasionally lethal form of bacterial pneumonia. Unlike most flu and cold viruses, Legionnaire's isn't contagious from person to person. You catch it by breathing in contaminated water aerosolized by misters or air-conditioner units. At first, Cathy blamed the air conditioner inside the Hemet hotel room where she slept while searching for David O'Sullivan. Later, after another doctor diagnosed her son with the same disease, she decided a mister outside a restaurant in Tempe, Arizona, had sickened them.

What weighed heaviest on Cathy's mind was not her ailment. It was her failure to find David O'Sullivan. For nearly two years, David's case had consumed her waking hours, and for what? She was no closer to having answers than when she started, and the Cranston Fire had torched half her search area. Thousands of miles away, on the other side of a massive continent and then a large ocean, Carmel O'Sullivan had anguished over this most recent development. "Oh no, was [David] burned up?" she asked Cathy in an email. "Are we never going to find him?"

Cathy's mounting frustration evoked existential questions. "Is the universe against us?" she wondered out loud. "Look what happened to Pam. Are we not supposed to find him?" And yet, even in the face of worsening odds, the volunteer's concern for Carmel O'Sullivan pushed her to keep searching. When asked, her reason was simple and consistent.

"I've started something that I can't walk away from."

I understood the pressure Cathy was under, as did the others who were risking their lives and sacrificing their free time to find the PCT Missing, and this camaraderie bonded us. "It's not Cathy's fault," Pam said when I asked the psychic how our friend was coping, "but she'll take it that way. She carries this burden because she's gotten so close to the family. She's having to learn something I learned earlier in my career. You can only take on so much responsibility." There will always be unsolved cases where everyone works so hard but the missing person remains lost.

"You aren't in control of whether someone gets found or not," Pam explained. "There are all these factors going on that have nothing to do with you."

By the time we met up in Washington, a round of antibiotics had improved Cathy's pneumonia, and my ankle fracture was healing, but we were still too weak to venture far into mountainous terrain. Weeks earlier, Kittitas County had sent a local SAR team to follow up on the unresolved tip reported by the trail runner in 2017 by searching for signs of Kris Fowler along the section of trail Cathy failed to reach via the Mineral Creek route last fall. This time, they combed the right area, but they found nothing more than irrelevant trash—an empty vodka bottle, men's underwear, and a sock filled with what appeared to be human feces.

Appreciative of this diligent search performed by Kittitas County officials, we scratched the trail runner lead off our list and focused our efforts elsewhere. Cathy gave me a tour of Ravensong's Hiker Hut in Mazama, a short drive from Winthrop, and we paid a visit to the local outfitter, Goat's Beard Mountain Supplies. Kris had mailed his last resupply box to this shop, but no one had been able to find it. When a thru-hiker mails himself a resupply package to a private business along the trail, the box enters an honor system. The packages are rarely tracked, and the procedure is casual, but a Goat's Beard employee assured us they would never throw away a thru-hiker's resupply package before the end of the year because they recognized how much late-arriving thru-hikers relied on the items in those boxes. A resupply package Kris had addressed to Snoqualmie Pass was gone, too. And so was the unknown item he mailed from the post office in Packwood. Sally elicited help from the postmaster general during her attempt to track down all the resupply packages Kris had mailed according to a list he'd made and left with his father, but none of them could be located.

The absence of Kris's resupply packages implied he may have picked them up, supporting what I call the Off Grid Theory. Perhaps Kris Fowler gave up on trying to fix his phone charger, went off the cell service grid, and continued his hike north, retrieving his packages in Snoqualmie and Mazama along the way. By sustaining himself on the food and cash from his resupply boxes, Sherpa could avoid leaving behind a paper trail via his credit card. And several witness sightings supported the Off Grid Theory. A bartender who may have seen Kris in Greenwater on October 14. A construction contractor who believed he gave the thru-hiker a ride to Stevens Pass on October 22. And a clerk in Mazama who sold a candy bar to a guy matching Kris's description that same day.

Cathy and I conducted two in-depth interviews of the contractor in person. After checking the calendar on his computer, and watching his reaction to videos of Kris, we both decided that the hiker he picked up wasn't the one we were looking for. I planned to interview the Greenwater bartender in a week. But for now, we were focusing on the clerk in Mazama. From the outfitter next door,

Cathy and I walked into the adjacent general store, a trendy outpost with a hip selection of snacks and souvenirs. I grabbed a snack to purchase and asked a cashier if she knew the clerk who believed he saw Sherpa. He no longer works here, she replied, and had left town recently.

Back at Cathy's hotel room, we called the clerk using a number Sally had given us. When he took the call, I put him on speaker and placed my phone on the bed.

The Mazama clerk was weary of telling his story. Footage from security cameras contradicted his memory, and he felt weird and confused about the whole thing.

"You aren't alone with these feelings," I said. Others who believed they'd seen Kris had been doubted as well and, in some cases, proven wrong. We weren't judging him. "We are only trying to make sense of it all."

The clerk mentioned that he saw a missing person flyer for Kris on November 1, 2016, and recognized the face. *Wow,* he'd thought, *that's the guy I talked to.* He remembered the hiker purchasing coffee and a candy bar, either a Snickers or a Butterfinger (which would make sense because Sally says Butterfinger was one of Kris's favorites). Although the store was busy, the hiker was quiet and kept to himself. He had sandy-blond hair and a scruffy beard. When the clerk asked for his trail name, the Kris look-a-like said "Sherpa."

The clerk reported his sighting to the police and a few weeks later, during Sally's 2016 trip to Washington, he invited Kris's stepmom to his home in Winthrop. "You may be the last person to be near my son," she said. "I just want to be near you." Sally hugged the clerk and cried while he told her everything he remembered from the encounter.

The clerk didn't view himself as someone who sported false memories, but the store owners could not find a receipt to match his recollection of selling coffee and a candy bar to a hiker on October

22. After the cops reviewed four days of security tapes and found no evidence of Kris being in the store during that time period, the clerk, who was in his fifties, accepted that he could be wrong about the date and other facts. "But the human part of me," he maintained, "is ninety percent positive I saw Sherpa and talked to him."

The clerk seemed mature, honest, and forthcoming. I detected no hint of attention-seeking behavior. At the end of the interview, he warned us: the Air Quality Index outside in Winthrop was 250 and rising. Breathing this air ranked "Very Unhealthy." That's why he'd skipped town for clean skies on the coast.

"You have to leave," I told Cathy as soon as I hung up. "This isn't good for your lungs. They are still healing."

You wouldn't know it by those August wildfires, but the PCT in Washington State is the wettest five hundred miles of the trail. A constant barrage of storms fills to the brim hundreds of frigid lakes and thousands of roaring creeks in the North Cascades. In the low-elevation forests, all that moisture keeps the mushrooms plentiful, the ferns huge, and the undergrowth lush. Above timberline, blizzards maintain seven hundred perennial snowfields and glaciers that hug the treacherous slopes. These chilly storms last well into summer, inspiring locals to joke about freezing their asses off while hiking the North Cascades in "Juneuary." As is often the case in grand locales, what nourishes the sublime scenery tortures the nature lover, with weather conditions ranging from miserable to cataclysmic.

What does a thru-hiker do when caught between nature's wrath and glory? To escape a cold storm, most will descend in altitude and head to the nearest road to catch a ride to the nearest town, where they can dry off, warm up, get a hot meal. At Chinook Pass, a two-day hike north of where Kris Fowler was last seen, a twenty-five-mile hitch down a snaky highway—State Route

410—will bring a wet hiker to Greenwater, a tiny village along a river at the base of a daunting mountain range that includes Mount Rainier. In Greenwater, the first place a hiker would likely seek shelter is the Naches Tavern, a local pub that has been serving a mix of loggers, hikers, bikers, skiers, mushroom hunters, and tourists since 1919.

A century after the tavern first opened, I was the only customer when I sat at the bar at eleven a.m. in August 2018. A bumper sticker stuck to the ceiling instructed me to VISUALIZE MOVING YOUR YUPPIE ASS BACK TO BELLEVUE, but I preferred my current scenery—a dusty saloon with a moldy couch, a stone fireplace, and well-spiced chili on the menu. The bartender, the reason for my visit, had a shiny ring encircling one nostril and more tattoos than I could count. Her icy blonde hair was cut edgy and short and she was drop-dead gorgeous, in a I'm-for-damn-sure-not-from-Bellevue kind of way.

The bartender told me that she'd met a hiker she believed to be Kris Fowler on October 14, 2016. Or was it the thirteenth? She couldn't be sure. Around noon, on a cold, wet day, a dirty but attractive hiker walked in, sat at her bar, and asked for a glass of water. The tavern was empty, giving her time to chat him up. The bartender, a former street kid, knew how to read people. The hiker looked like he needed a "psychological boost," but he seemed too proud to ask for help. His mood aroused her compassion. She offered him a free sandwich, but he turned her down, sticking with his glass of water. When she asked him about the trail, he perked up. Yes, he was hiking the PCT, he said, "but I'm behind."

"What's your name?"

"My name's Kris, but everyone calls me 'Sherpa.'"

The bartender told the hiker that trail names reminded her of when she lived on the street, where people called her "Blue" but "my real name is Liz." Business picked up after one o'clock. Juggling customers, the bartender lost track of time. Around three p.m., she looked for the hiker, but he was already gone.

Blue described the hiker's eyes as "piercing." She said he made eye contact and saw her "as a human being," which saddened me to hear because it implied that most of her customers didn't.

Two months later, she walked by a missing person flyer, recognized Sherpa's face, and her "heart dropped." The bartender returned to work and told her boss. On December 20, 2016, he called the police.

Now Sherpa had been missing for a year and a half, and I was at the same bar asking the same bartender the same questions Sergeant Briscoe had asked her.

"What do *you* think happened?" I wanted to know after getting past all the preliminaries.

"Too many hikers come here unaware," she replied. "There are hazards in these woods. Lions. Bears. Berries that look edible but aren't."

I brought up the bear hunter's false statement about seeing Kris on Blowout Mountain on October 22.

She frowned, agitated. "Why do people do that?" A second later, my ulterior motive for mentioning the false testimony of another witness registered. "I know in my gut I saw him. So much so, it hurts." When she said this, the bartender teared up and placed a hand on her heart.

I took a sip from my Arnold Palmer. When it comes to criminal cases, studies have shown that over 50 percent of wrongful convictions are due to mistaken eyewitness accounts. Which raises some concerns. Should missing person investigators consider how strongly a witness feels about their sighting? Or should we pay attention only to the facts, like how the details of the bartender's story never changed, even after multiple interviews by multiple people?

Before I could settle the bill, the bartender posed her own question.

"Did he go McCandless?" She wondered, referring to the young man who abandoned his possessions, burned his money, disowned his family, took a new name, and voluntarily disappeared *Into the Wild*.

I shrugged. In my opinion, Kris Fowler did not "go McCandless." Neither did David O'Sullivan. But when a reluctant witness finally agreed to tell me what he knew, I could no longer dismiss the possibility that Chris Sylvia may have.

CHAPTER 23

# Voluntary

---

**A** METAL FENCE GUARDED THE BUDDHIST TEMPLE FROM THE OUTSIDE WORLD, but—lucky for me—the iron gate remained unlocked. Taking that for an invitation, I pushed it open just enough to squeeze through.

Some have described the Buddhist temple on Chihuahua Valley Road as creepy. To me, the monastery seemed alluring, if forlorn. I rang the meditation bell and its plaintive moan echoed through the untended gardens and across a stack of cheap plastic chairs collecting dust inside a cinderblock building (formerly a gathering hall). According to a pamphlet I pulled from a plastic box on a post, the Lieu Quan Retreat Monastery was built in 2000 and each of the massive sculptures lording over the grounds represented a major event in the Buddha's life. The reclining Buddha symbolizing Siddhārtha Gautama (the actual Buddha who founded the Buddhist religion 2,500 years ago, not Hesse's character) lying on his deathbed was as tall and long as a semi-trailer. Meanwhile, a statue depicting when "the prince Siddhartha" reached enlightenment while sitting in a lotus position under a Bodhi tree was as colossal as an elephant. I placed my palm on the fat Buddha's marbled thigh. It was glacier white, smooth and cool. The only evidence

that anyone had ever come here to worship were the rotting tan-
gerines and scorched sticks of incense someone had placed at the
Buddha's feet.

Here at the temple, as I traced what might have been his last
footsteps, I couldn't stop thinking about a puzzling fact lingering
around Chris Sylvia's case. Before he went off grid, there were two
days of unaccounted-for time. Chris left Anza on February 12. He
called Min Kim four days later, on February 16. San Diego County
would not release the GPS coordinates of Chris's last cell phone
ping, but I assumed he called from a spot not far from where he
abandoned his gear. This timeline gave Chris four and a half days
to hike a section of trail that should only take two. How had Chris
spent those extra forty-eight hours? *I've found this awesome temple!
Pick me up there.* From what Chris told Min in his last phone call,
some of that time was spent visiting this monastery. Had there been
a divine intervention to prolong his stay?

When I called Chris's mother, she shared with me the kind of
sad details another parent might tuck away in a drawer, never to
think about them again. Nancy Warman struggled with substance
abuse and was currently homeless. Her son's disappearance had
tormented her over the years. During the early days of the search,
an official informed her that they had still not recovered the phone
Chris borrowed from Elizabeth Henle. He speculated that Chris
may have wandered off trail to track down a cell signal. Nancy
accepted this possibility, but she also believed her son could have
been a victim of foul play. There were so many plausible theories.
Nancy understood that any one of them could have happened.

Chris did not have an easy childhood. In addition to his older
brother, Joshua, Chris had three younger half-siblings. His father
had died from an overdose of heroin and vodka when he was
young, and a friend described his family life as a "steam pot boiling
over" that required "a lot for them to keep their heads together."

When Chris was a teenager, Nancy did a stint in jail. The day she was released, she came home to find her son unconscious on the floor with a belt around his neck. Nancy called 911, and Chris spent a month in a mental health facility where the treatment he received helped. "When he came back," Nancy recalled, "he was more of a stand-up guy."

Friends and schoolmates described Chris in a similar way. He could be overly sensitive and belligerent when drinking, and he suffered from depression at times, but Chris was a stand-up guy. Someone who remembered if he owed you money. A true-blue friend who backed you up even if you were in the wrong. A "vagabond spirit" who tried to make the best of an unpleasant situation by making you laugh when you were down. The guy at the party who "set the vibe on positive."

Chris lacked the funds to purchase fancy gear, but he loved the outdoors and graduated quickly from being a novice to an intermediate hiker by backpacking sections of the Appalachian Trail (AT) with Min Kim. One trip, from Maryland to Luray Caverns, Virginia, lasted two weeks. The AT tested his tolerance for rain, but he and Min survived the misadventure in good humor. To Chris, nature was "a free way to have fun." He often ran ahead of the group, occasionally going off trail, and sometimes bushwhacking with a machete deep into the bush to discover a unique place to show his friends.

Min Kim did not respond to my first attempts at contact, but I must have passed some sort of test when I found Chris's copy of *Siddhartha*, because after that, Chris's best friend agreed to talk to me.

"I can sound like a really big asshole sometimes," Min confessed when we finally spoke over the phone, "though I'm trying not to be." The best friends had been butting heads a lot after Chris lost his job. Min was paying his friend's share of the rent and bringing home leftover food from the restaurant where he worked for Chris to eat. Then, four days after Min dropped him off at the trailhead,

Chris called, wanting a ride home. Min felt burdened by his friend's financial and emotional needs, and he let it show.

When Min arrived at the Buddhist temple, Chris was nowhere to be seen. "Chris is strong-willed but emotionally sensitive," Min explained. "He gets quickly turned off by shit." He wondered whether the tone of the call had pissed Chris off so much that he changed his plans and continued hiking to Campo per the original plan. It didn't seem out of character for him not to call Min to tell him that. It wasn't until days later, when no one was answering the cell phone Chris had borrowed from Elizabeth, that Min began to worry. On February 24, he reported his friend missing.

For Min, the investigation was all a blur. Although others may not have seen it, he was overwhelmed by worry, regret, and a lot of guilt. He understood that the detectives were only "doing what detectives are supposed to do," by ruling him out as a suspect. He spoke with a television reporter, who verified with the authorities that Min was cooperating fully. At that time, he didn't want to speculate publicly about what might have happened to his best friend. "All we can really do is hope he is okay," he said on the air, "and try to remember as many positive moments as we can."

A month later, Min wanted an update on the investigation. Plus, some of the backpacking gear the police collected from the scene belonged to him, not Chris. Replacing it would cost more than Min could afford. He also wanted to know which items Chris left behind. But the detectives refused to release any information about the gear to anyone. Not to Min. Not to Chris's mother. Not to the press. Not to this writer. When Min and I discussed this years later, he didn't understand why the authorities couldn't tell us what they found in Chris's pack.

"I simply want to know what was there," Min said. Then, maybe, he could figure out what happened.

"I have no idea what happened," said Tory Strader, Chris's ex-girlfriend from Maryland, when I asked her what she thought about his disappearance. "Some of me thinks that he's living out on a beach somewhere. Doing whatever he wants to do."

Strader had started dating Chris when she was twenty, and they spent "every single day together for about two years." She vividly remembers a moment when the two were sitting together on the couch and she'd suggested they move to upstate New York. Chris loved the idea of going somewhere new, so they packed their belongings into one backpack each and hopped on a Greyhound bus the next morning. "We didn't have any maps or anything. We just kind of went for it....Whatever you have on your back, you can make it work and you can meet people and you can survive off that."

They got engaged at some point, but eventually went their separate ways. Chris was heartbroken, but they kept in contact. The last time Tory Strader heard from him was in February 2015, the day before he left on his hike, when he texted her, "Hey, how have you been? Love you."

"Hey," Strader replied, "how are you?" but she never received a response.

During the late 1960s, a search and scent dog expert from Canada, William "Bill" Syrotuck, came up with an innovative idea: by compiling data on lost hiker behavior, statistical probabilities could be applied to search operations that would "facilitate prediction, with some reasonable degree of accuracy, as to the most likely location a missing individual will be found." Although a few old-school searchers dismissed Syrotuck as "nuts," in 1971 the National Park Service developed a prototype training course built around Syrotuck's ideas, thus forming the basis of modern search theory, an operational approach applying probability theory to search planning that can be taught and replicated.

In 1976, with help from his wife, Jean Anne Syrotuck, an American nurse who studied hypothermia, Syrotuck examined hundreds of resolved lost hiker cases and recorded his findings in a book, *Analysis of Lost Person Behavior.* He determined that 75 percent of lost persons were found within a 3.75-mile radius of their point last seen. Among the 229 cases he analyzed were 100 hunters, 44 hikers, 46 children, and 5 "despondents." Syrotuck concluded this final category of the missing, people contemplating suicide, did not go into thick underbrush. But he admitted there were limitations to any deduction derived from only five cases. However, from a larger study, a younger search expert, Dr. Robert Koester, came to a similar conclusion. Despondent hikers are only seeking enough room and privacy to contemplate the act. They are not inclined to achieve that solitude by crawling through impenetrable vegetation.

When looking for missing and potentially suicidal subjects, my experience with the NPS taught me to check areas of scenic or personal significance that were out of view of the public. The Buddhist temple was meaningful to Chris, making it a high-probability location. I spent over an hour peering into every corner of the gated compound, checking under all the trees, all along both sides of the fence line, and even the field across the street.

After searching the monastery, I drove five miles to where the PCT crosses Chihuahua Valley Road. From there, I hiked the trail north and took a short side trail to Combs Peak—a 6,193-foot mountain visible from the gear site. On the way to the peak, my cell phone pinged with new email messages. The reception in the area was excellent; Chris could easily have called Min from this spot. At the top of Combs Peak, I found a summit register stuffed into a rusty can. Chris had not signed it. Before returning the log to the can, I wrote an entry, dedicating my climb to the memory of the PCT Missing: Chris Sylvia, Kris Fowler, and David O'Sullivan.

From Combs Peak, I hiked south, back to the gear site at mile 127.

In 2003, a wildfire caused by dry lightning burned over the PCT near Mike's Place. What had once been a lush oak woodland was now a skeleton forest of bare trunks poking out from impenetrable brush. I peered under these dead oaks, hoping I would not find Chris. Not here. Not among these heat-cracked boulders. Not leaning against a tree scorched black by fire. The mental image alone was hard to bear. My feelings reminded me of something Pam told Cathy. From the psychic's perspective, when the missing (who are deceased) know a searcher doesn't want to find them, they stay hidden. Sometimes, according to Pam, this happens because the deceased are embarrassed to be found and don't want their families to see them that way.

When I'd had enough of this morbid duty for one day, I headed over to Mike's Place to tell Josh McCoy about the novel and the pair of camouflage pants Chris had placed in the hiker box. I hated to give any consideration to the theory that Chris took his own life, but perhaps he didn't intentionally leave those things behind because he was adopting Buddhist principles. Perhaps he left them behind because he knew he wouldn't need them anymore.

McCoy raised his eyebrows, unconvinced. "If he did it here, he would have been found!" The trail angel was adamant. "The ravens. The birds. There would be signs. They would have found him." McCoy's logic applied to other theories as well. If Chris Sylvia fell or got lost while searching for a cell signal, if a mountain lion attacked him while going to the bathroom, if he hurt himself within two miles of mile 127, searchers and their dogs should have located his body.

"I think Chris might be alive," Cathy had said after reading *Siddhartha* in 2018, and I got goosebumps. Like the way I'd felt while searching for Gabriel Parker in 1995, I didn't want to believe Chris had killed himself, and my reasoning wasn't entirely the result of a personal bias. In 2006, when he was only nineteen, Chris did something so unusual, it would cause anyone investigating his case to think twice.

In 2006, Min Kim's brother died by suicide. At the time, Chris was living with his grandmother in Costa Rica. Thinking it might do their surviving son good to see the tropics and hang out with his best friend, Min's parents booked Min a flight to Costa Rica and gave him some spending money.

According to Min, Chris got along well with his paternal grandma, but his step-grandfather was a "hard ass American dude" who wanted Chris to join a missionary. Min thought he and Chris had made their intentions clear; they were going to use the money provided by Min's parents to travel and "chill out" as Min processed his brother's death. He assumed the grandparents were cool with it. With packs strapped on their backs, the nineteen-year-olds embarked on an extended excursion across the country. While lounging on beaches and hiking through rain forests filled with sloths and howler monkeys, they fantasized about starting an expat business in Costa Rica: a farm with a café and a hostel. They'd call it Casa Verde, the Green House. It would be a laid-back place. Min would be the chef and Chris would cater to the tourists.

Three weeks into their Costa Rican chillout, the young men walked into a small-town convenience store.

"Hey!" the clerk called out to them and pointed to the newspaper he was reading. Both their pictures were on the front page. "You guys are missing!"

Min looked at Chris. "Are we missing?"

They burst out laughing. Chris hadn't contacted his grandmother since they'd left her home, but it wasn't like they were hiding or anything. At nineteen—still boys, really—they didn't even have cell phones and were incapable of comprehending a worried grandmother's point of view. To them, it was comical.

It was less funny a few days later when two Costa Rican detectives tracked them down, hauled Min and Chris down to the station, and made them call Chris's grandmother. By then, they'd been "missing" for twenty-six days.

A Spanish-speaking private investigator helped me locate a Costa Rican newspaper article corroborating much of Min's version of events. "It was a weird situation," Min said. "So much more dramatic than it was supposed to be." He described Chris as a guy who hated the government, didn't want a smartphone, and refused to assimilate into a "normal" American lifestyle, but Chris also liked people. His attitude "was more about finding a niche," Min believed, "not about disappearing or escaping."

I asked Min for his opinion. Could he see his best friend walking away from everything and starting a new life?

He hesitated, gathering his thoughts. "At first, I instinctually thought he killed himself." But Min worried that his own personal family tragedy could have skewed his perspective on Chris's state of mind. Now, after having more time to think about it, "I equally believe any possibility."

I emailed the same question to Joshua Sylvia. He believed his brother might intentionally disappear for weeks, maybe months, at a time. "Chris was not your everyday assimilated citizen," Joshua explained. "My brother was often rebellious of standard norms." Perhaps he didn't want to "rely on me or anyone else anymore." He may have "said 'fuck you' to the world and decided to find his own path."

Chris's mother, Nancy, told me her son's passport and Social Security card were the only items among those recovered that the authorities gave to her. But lacking a passport had not stopped the Man in Brazil—the Canadian with the uncanny resemblance to Kris Fowler—from crossing international borders.

As much as I'd wanted to find a definitive answer by ruling out voluntary disappearance in this case, I couldn't. If a mentally ill fugitive could travel from Canada to South America with no money or identification, then Chris Sylvia could too.

# CHAPTER 24

# *Unus Testis*

---

IN LATE 2017, DURING THE EARLY DAYS OF CATHY'S SEARCH FOR DAVID O'SULLIVAN, a reporter called her with a tip: "I have a picture of David from Hillbilly."

Cathy knew Hillbilly as a trail angel living near the PCT in Cabazon who had mentioned to authorities that back in April 2017 he may have given the missing hiker a ride to town from the PCT crossing at I-10. Cathy had interviewed Hillbilly and several hikers he had given a ride to on the day in question and ruled out the sighting based on what she heard, but now there was a photo.

"Whoa," she said to the reporter, "that witness never told me or David's family he had a picture!"

"I'll email it to you."

The reporter sent her a photo of a young man who resembled the guy she was looking for. Cathy forwarded the image to his older brother, Niall, for confirmation.

"It looks like David," Niall agreed, "but it's not."

Cathy called Hillbilly to tell him the news. "I sent the family your picture, and they say it looks like David, but it isn't."

"What picture?"

"You gave a picture to a reporter today."

"No, I didn't."

*Okay, enough of this.* Someone must be lying to her. Cathy called the reporter back and asked for the real name and phone number of the "Hillbilly" who gave him the photograph. As it turned out, no one was lying. There were *two* trail angels in Southern California going by the moniker "Hillbilly" who believed they gave a ride to David O'Sullivan. But neither of them had. What were the odds?

Three additional witnesses contacted Cathy's team to say they had seen a hiker who looked like David staying at a hiker hostel in Wrightwood, California (PCT mile 360). All three described the hiker as a man in his twenties with an Irish accent who was "nerdy but not goofy." Ill with a stomach bug, the hiker recovered at the hostel in Wrightwood for several days and complained that he needed to call his mother but couldn't because he was having trouble charging his "device."

This all sounded like David, but the Wrightwood sighting posed a time frame problem. One witness thought the "super sick" hiker stayed for a week in May or June while another said it was in late April. Also, the witnesses were partiers who admitted that they were high much of the time. To believe these people saw David O'Sullivan, you had to believe David made no credit card purchases and contacted no friends or family for at least three weeks after he left Idyllwild. When Cathy traveled to Wrightwood to investigate further, she found no evidence that O'Sullivan had ever been there.

Witness sightings are funny things. Sifting for kernels of truth hidden within the chaff of false reports bedevils nearly every investigator when a case goes public. Even after speaking with dozens of witnesses in the years that followed their disappearances, I concluded that no matter how "certain" witnesses were that they had encountered either Sylvia, Fowler, or O'Sullivan, most of them had not actually seen one of the PCT Missing.

Despite this conclusion, a few of these uncorroborated reports continue to haunt me to this day. Especially the bartender sighting of Kris in the Naches Tavern. But Cathy is more skeptical. All the hard evidence—the phone pings and credit card charges—indicate something happened to Kris Fowler within two days, and before he reached civilization via the road at Chinook Pass. And she doubts the bartender's story because Blue said the "Sherpa" she met refused her offer for something to eat and, according to Cathy, "no thru-hiker turns down a free sandwich."

Sally, who talked to the bartender over the phone, is more open-minded about all the Sherpa sightings. She believes Blue could have seen her son at the tavern on October 14. "Her story has never changed," Sally says, "and I believe Kris got farther north than people think. Not because he was some super hiker but because of his determination and his ability to get what he wanted."

But acceptance of the sighting of Kris by the bartender in Greenwater overwhelms anyone attempting to contain a search area for Fowler. If he made it to the tavern, lots of things could have happened. Maybe he met a friendly tourist or a commuting local and bummed a ride to Seattle or anywhere else he wanted to go. Maybe he skipped ahead and got in trouble closer to the Northern Terminus. Or he could have accepted hospitality from someone nefarious and fell victim to foul play far from the PCT. If the bartender truly met a hiker who said, "I'm Kris but everyone calls me Sherpa," then the boundaries of your search area become so immense you don't even know where to start. Kris Fowler could be *anywhere*.

Until a case is solved, even the weakest, most bewildering sightings will mess with your head.

On October 31, 2016, the night Sally joined the club no one wants to be in, Seattle's Fox 13 aired Fowler's story on the evening news. Before moving on to the next topic, the anchor instructed anyone with information on the missing hiker's whereabouts to call the

Yakima County Sheriff's Office. The next day, a search team found human tracks on the PCT north of Chinook Pass, where the trail crosses Highway 410. The tracks headed south and appeared to be ten days old.

It's likely these tracks were made by the southbound (SOBO) PCT hiker who posted the following on Sally's Facebook group: "When I got off at White Pass (heading SOBO), [Sherpa] had signed the trail register a few days before I got there but I never saw him on the trail north of there." The south-bounder described the weather conditions. On October 12, it was cold and clear, but the next day, it began to rain at five a.m. and didn't stop. Temperatures dropped and snow accumulated at the higher elevations. By the time he reached the trail register, the SOBO hiker's hands were so cold he could barely sign it.

On November 1, two weeks after weather conditions forced the SOBO hiker off the trail, the bear hunter called the Yakima County Sheriff's Office to tell Sergeant Briscoe that he and a friend had met a hiker matching Kris Fowler's description near Blowout Mountain on the morning of October 22. That date didn't fit the timeline for Sherpa's trek, but the bear hunter claimed to be an expert on the area and lectured a female searcher to stay clear of the woods there.

Later that winter, when someone discovered human remains that might belong to Kris, the bear hunter messaged Sally right away and asked her for more details. The bones ending up belonging to someone else but the bear hunter's interest in them still left Sally feeling unsettled.

Police reports show that, in July 2017, a sheriff's deputy met up with the bear hunter on Blowout Mountain along with two human remains detection (HRD) K9s and their handlers. The deputy drew a map of the bear hunter's description of the sighting, using stick figures to represent the hunters' positions on the trail relative to Kris Fowler's. The cadaver dogs worked the scene and detected nothing. The hunter let the deputy know he and his friend were both "straight-and-narrow" and had never been arrested. He offered to come back to the scene to help or answer questions, anytime.

After Morgan sent his ten-page report to Sergeant Briscoe— the one proving the bear hunter was in Seattle, at a Huskies game, on October 22—deputies interviewed the bear hunter again. Once caught in his discrepancies, he told them he must have seen the hiker on October 23 instead of October 22, but Morgan disproved this claim as well. The hunter and his family were at a friend's home that evening, watching another football game on TV. Which brings us to his second false statement: that when he saw a hiker matching Kris Fowler's description, he was with a friend.

But this friend not only denied being on the PCT on October 22, 2016, he denied knowing anything at all about the sighting until the bear hunter had called him a few days earlier, on November 11, 2017, to let him know the cops wanted to interview him about the incident. A deputy met the bear hunter's friend at a Starbucks, where he signed a written statement testifying that he was not hunting with the bear hunter during the weekend of October 22 in 2016 and adding that he knew "nothing about the missing hiker until he told me about it this past Friday."

The bear hunter sighting vexed Sally. Why would someone lie like this? For months, she pushed Briscoe to do more follow-up. In April 2018, deputies met with the bear hunter again, this time at a Baskin-Robbins, where he admitted to them that he'd made another mistake. His friend wasn't with him when he saw the hiker, the bear hunter said, but once he realized this, he didn't know what to do. To avoid getting into trouble, he decided to "just let it roll." These discrepancies didn't change what he saw, the bear hunter insisted. He did see a hiker who looked like Kris on the trail in October 2016. When a deputy casually implied the bear hunter may have shot Fowler by accident, the subject emphatically denied it and agreed to take a lie detector test.

By the time deputies recontacted him to schedule that polygraph, the hunter had lawyered up, as any innocent person should do if they feel they are being investigated by the police. In lieu of a law enforcement–administered test, his attorney scheduled a private polygraph at the bear hunter's expense. The private exam consisted of three questions. Did he lie when he said he saw a hiker in October 2016? Did he lie when he said he was alone when he saw the hiker? Did he harm the hiker he met in the Cascades in October 2016? The bear hunter answered no to all three questions and passed.

"I'm so angry at him," Sally seethed. Dozens of professional and volunteer searchers had spent hundreds of hours searching hazardous areas north of Blowout Mountain because of this sighting—hundreds of hours with *nothing* to show for it.

"The bear hunter is asked a total of three questions by an examiner provided by his own attorney," Morgan said. "An answer he gives to that polygraph is contrary to what he told Briscoe." Despite how much time and effort the bear hunter's sighting has wasted, Morgan believed charging him with making a false report would do little to ease Sally's mind.

The bear hunter wasn't the only witness who changed his story. In September 2017, almost a year after the bear hunter incident, the southbound hiker with the freezing hands confessed that his initial statement was inaccurate. He *had* seen a hiker on October 13. He was camping at Two Lakes (nine miles south of Chinook Pass) when he unzipped his tent one morning and glimpsed a tall, bearded hiker with a large backpack heading north. The south-bounder had met Kris earlier that year. He would recognize Sherpa if he saw him, but that morning he only saw the hiker from the rear and was too far away to identify him.

"I was a mess," the SOBO hiker explained while apologizing to Sally for changing his story. "I was frost-bitten. I thought I was going to die. I was not myself. I was not in a good place mentally. I blacked it out."

The southbound hiker's inconsistent statements frustrated Sally's amateur searchers; nevertheless, they remained polite on social media. He "is our friend," one member posted. "I'd like it if zero negativity is sent his way."

Cathy believed that anyone examining this case should dismiss much of what the south-bounder said about seeing or not seeing a hiker on that section. The real takeaway from this statement was its account of how bad the weather was on October 13, the day after Kris Fowler was last seen.

It's also worth noting that Kris and David, whose cases have been more visible in the media and on Facebook, have been "seen" by many people, while only one person came forward to say she saw Chris Sylvia. According to this witness, she saw a Chris look-a-like salute the patrons in a beach town doughnut shop north of San Diego in 2015. Amplified by social media, emotional fervor around a missing person case can stir up false leads. I observed this firsthand years later, when a volunteer searcher shared some of his poetic ruminations in Sally's Facebook group:

"Whispers in the trees," he wrote. "Echo from the stream. Secrets hover tantalizing, floating on the breeze. Vision comes to me. Nothing's as it seems. Shivering in darkness I awaken from the dream."

After this post, two new witnesses came forward to say they had seen the missing hiker. The first claimed she met Kris Fowler on the Goat Rocks section of the PCT in September 2016. The second believed she and her son met Kris (also in 2016) on a vague date in a vague location in an area far off the trail north of Chinook Pass.

We quickly ruled out this second sighting, but the first witness was unshakable. She was hiking on the Goat Rocks when she met a hiker who was "tall, young, and moving fast." She added that she'd even asked him for his trail name and he replied "Sherpa."

Morgan studied this woman's personal Facebook page and found a post she had made telling her Facebook friends that it "took her breath away" when she realized the hiker she met had gone missing. Even though the post dated back to February 2019, the woman hadn't notified Sally until five months later. "I'll never forget him," she wrote to Sally. "My heart goes out to you, and always will."

"I didn't think he made it to the Goat Rocks until October," Sally messaged back.

"No, Sally, he did," the witness insisted, correcting the mother who knew her son's case backward and forward. "I have my 2016 calendar and can go back and check it....I know with 100 percent certainty that it was him."

The woman checked her notes. The date she "saw" Kris Fowler on the Goat Rocks was September 25, 2016.

Sally asked Amber Johnson, Kris's hiking partner, to review her own journal to corroborate the timeline. "We were definitely together in Portland on September 24 and 25," Amber replied. Despite her "100 percent certainty," there was no way the other witness could've seen Kris Fowler on the Goat Rocks that day.

In a message thread about these sightings among me, Sally, Morgan, and Cathy, I wrote: "Most of these people are conflating real memories with made-up ones. We all do this to some extent. The '100 percent' comment is a clue that they've become so psychologically committed to the story that they are prone to inventing memories to make it fit."

"Agreed!" Morgan said.

"Ugh," groaned Cathy, "like when someone new comes on and acts like it's day one in the investigation."

"Riiiggghtt," Sally responded, "and you don't want to be rude in case they are the magic missing link, but damn."

For three years, Sally's hopes swelled whenever someone said they saw her son. She tracked down every witness and listened to their story. It was a way for her to feel close to Kris in his absence,

to focus on something concrete she could check out. But false
sightings aren't helpful, they're distracting—and they sometimes
pull resources away from following legitimate leads. A search in
King County was called off because of the sighting in Mazama.
And Yakima County suspended at least one search based on the
bear hunter's story. When Sally told officers she was creating a
GoFundMe and posting a $10,000 reward, officials warned her this
would encourage false sightings. But, "Hell," Sally said, "I had that
before we had raised ten bucks."

None of the sightings I studied gave me any indication that
these witnesses came forward with a financial agenda. Instead, I
sensed subconscious, psychological motivations. Today, Cathy and
I are steady proponents of *Unus testis, nullus testis*—in other words,
one witness is no witness. "I personally don't believe one sighting
unless there is a picture or signature to back it up," Cathy main-
tains. "I didn't used to be this way, but then I saw all these knuckle-
heads who wanted to be part of a case when they had nothing."

Even when it came to the bear hunter, I couldn't wrap my head
around him being responsible for Kris Fowler's disappearance. It
was more likely that he saw Sherpa's face on the Fox 13 news report
and conflated that with an older memory of meeting a PCT hiker on
the trail years before. Caught up in the moment, and perhaps wanting to be helpful, the hunter called in his sighting right away, without checking his own calendar or contemplating the accuracy of
his memory. His solicitous manner toward law enforcement, along
with his eagerness to communicate with Sally, hinted at a possible motive to continuing the ruse. Becoming an integral part of a
search effort gives one a sense of belonging. Advising women about
dangers on the trail inflates one's sense of one's masculinity. Having a deputy meet you in the woods to take notes and diagram a
map about what you and your friend "saw" makes you feel important. At some point, the hunter realized his mistake, but instead of
admitting it, he chose to "let it roll."

Even so, Sally can't stop herself from imagining her worst-case scenario—that her son was killed in a hunting accident and then his body was buried in a shallow grave or fed to wild animals. And that's perhaps the most egregious wrong committed by the bear hunter's false testimony: he put a horrible image into the mind of a grieving parent—one that is nearly impossible to shake without evidence to the contrary.

CHAPTER 25

# Smoke and Feathers

---

**D**URING THE SUMMER OF 2018, THE WASHINGTON FIRES RAGED ON, SMOTHERING most of Washington State with thick, toxic air. After interviewing the bartender in Greenwater, I camped overnight near Blowout Mountain and hiked to the spot where the bear hunter said he'd seen Sherpa. Then, to escape the smoke, I headed south to California, while Cathy went east to Montana. We were both focused on driving when Sally messaged us via Facebook.

She had recently received a promising tip. A northbound PCT hiker looking for a campsite had stumbled upon some abandoned gear "in a strange place" under a rock alcove near Spectacle Lake, a popular destination along the PCT north of I-90 in an area with scenery that is so captivating it's called "The Enchantments." The gear was located roughly 118 trail miles north of Kris Fowler's LKP and appeared to have been out there for a year or more. The hiker sent Sally several photos of what he found: a blue tarp, a sleeping bag, a foil emergency blanket, some dehydrated meals, and a sleeping pad. An excellent witness, he also sent a screenshot of a map with GPS coordinates showing the location. Sally immediately forwarded all of this to her A-team: me, Morgan, and Cathy.

Morgan observed that the gear was found in an area matching the trail runner's report from 2017, and the sleeping bag and the tarp were the same color as the ones Kris carried. This information fueled Sally's hopes. Could it be the lead that brought her son home? "I sent Kris an emergency silver blanket," Sally messaged back. "I'm shaking."

"Space blankets are pretty common," Morgan cautioned her.

"Those items will need to be bagged for evidence," Cathy wrote as soon as she joined the message group. "I can go up Friday, but the authorities will want these items."

"These items" were in the area that Cathy had failed to reach via the Mineral Creek route in October 2017. Back then, snow had hampered her search and forced her to turn around. Today, she worried searchers wouldn't be able to hike the route because of the forest fires.

Because it was his day off, Sergeant Briscoe had yet to respond to Sally's texts about the new lead. After I crossed the Oregon border into California, I pulled over to review Sally's message thread. Morgan, Sally, and I studied the higher-resolution pictures that the hiker had sent over. Morgan and Sally focused their efforts on the freeze-dried meals and the bottle of travel-sized mouthwash seen among the items, while I zoomed in on the sleeping bag and the inflatable Therm-a-Rest pad. On the sleeping bag, I spotted black straps. "That's not a typical thru-hiker sleeping bag," I typed. Looking closer, I noticed another interesting detail. "There are four slashes in the Thermarest that look man-made to me."

Cathy told us that she'd drive back the next day. "It's beautiful here [in Montana], but I was just driving, no destination anyhow." She turned her car around and headed back to smoky Washington.

"This is the closest we have been to anything," Sally wrote, filled with hope. "It's what I've been praying for. I know the bed roll throws a wrench in it all, but the rest of it is uncanny. When I saw that mouthwash and it was the exact same kind I sent him, I gasped. *Let this be it.*"

After Sally went to bed that night, Cathy reached out to Morgan and me in a new private thread and asked our opinions. "What do you two think about all this?"

Morgan ran through everything that matched and everything that didn't before he concluded, "This is the best lead yet."

Cathy was less enthusiastic, but she wanted to stay positive for Sally. "I'll grab some PCT hikers if just to make Sally feel better and send them up there."

Even though he was hopeful, Morgan expressed concern for Sally. If this wasn't Kris's gear, it was "going to be a huge letdown."

"I agree," Cathy concurred. "A HUGE letdown."

"I'm worried this isn't Kris's gear," I chimed in. The sleeping bag wasn't right. The Therm-a-Rest sleeping pad was damaged, explaining why a random hiker would leave it behind. And the gear was cheap, the type of stuff I'd seen novice backpackers discard in the wilderness because they are too lazy to carry it out. I knew we needed to be realistic about this new lead and not take any chances.

"Spare your lungs," I advised Cathy, "and focus on finding someone else to go up."

The next day, Corporal Ellis Nale with the Kittitas Sheriff's Office sent in a team and they were as optimistic about this lead as Sally was. These professionals had searched many times for Kris and wanted this clue to be the one that finally solved the case.

We all spent a long day on pins and needles, waiting for word from Nale's team, until Sally finally texted us.

"It's not him."

"Sorry, Sally," Morgan replied. "I initially thought this could be it."

"Dang it," Cathy wrote.

"Thank you all for everything and hanging in there with me the past few days," Sally handled her disappointment gracefully, "*and* the past twenty-two months. I appreciate you so much."

Right then, I felt it again. Like when Gabriel Parker's father thanked me after I failed to find his son at the Grand Canyon, Sally's words filled me with regret. We hadn't found Kris. We didn't *deserve* to be thanked. And I was beginning to wonder if our efforts were helping at all, like maybe we were only making it harder for Sally and the other mothers to let go. But even if that were true, even if we *were* doing more harm than good, we couldn't stop. Not then. Perhaps not ever. No way on God's green earth could we abandon Sally and her mission to find Kris.

"You need some downtime, Sally . . . some rest," Cathy suggested.

This was one of many times we observed Sally suffer from what therapists who work with families of the missing call "a hope hangover." Chasing lead after lead after lead, year after year after year, fatigues and demoralizes. This is something the armchair spectators who typed "never give up" on Sally's Facebook page failed to comprehend. Even if the false lead keeps you on a temporary high, once the other shoe drops, your hopes fall to the ground, smashed to bits.

"I feel bad," Morgan wrote. "I feel like I raised her hopes on this one."

"You were only trying to help, Morgan," Cathy consoled him.

"It seemed so promising at first," I added.

"Unfortunately," he concluded, this was "a book that currently does not have a happy ending."

Morgan's defeat broke my heart more than Sally's disappointment. "The happy ending is you guys. You, Sally, Cathy, all the nice people who are helping."

"The best final chapter would be these hikers being found," Morgan conceded, "but I guess the reality that sometimes they aren't [found] is equally important."

"Yes, the reality," I wrote. "And how we face it."

But does facing reality require us to give up? My experiences with such dilemmas are not trivial, yet the answers still elude me.

When do you advise a terminally ill patient to consider palliative care? When do you use your service weapon to put a wheezing fawn out of its misery? When do you stop rescuing an addict from his own behaviors? When do you flee the front line and let the wildfire burn? When do you terminate CPR? When do you tell a mother you're going to stop searching for her child?

Undeterred by her harrowing experience on the Seven Pines Trail, Pam Coronado returned to the San Jacinto Mountains several more times to search with Cathy. Still committed to finding David O'Sullivan, the women sweated in the heat, scoured the woods, scrambled up unstable scree, and searched cliff bottoms until their middle-aged bodies bruised and bled and ached. One day, an unidentified beast in the woods growled at them. Another time, a rock tumbled down a scree slope and pinned Cathy's leg. Pam feared her new friend had broken a bone, but Cathy was able to push herself free while Boris the hound gallantly scrambled down to "rescue" the woman he so irritated.

When the treacherous terrain became too much for them, the women got creative. In a Hail Mary attempt to locate the elusive boulder Pam had seen in her first vision, they persuaded Jon King to hike the entire San Jacinto section of the PCT with a GoPro attached to his head. They viewed the footage and noticed at least one rock that resembled the boulder in Pam's vision, plus a sneaky switchback that could lure an unwary hiker off the trail. Unfortunately, those who searched around these same sites afterward didn't find anything.

When Pam's pendulum reading first picked out the trail to Suicide Rock, it didn't make sense to Cathy, until she went back to the map and saw ways it could feasibly happen. Suicide Rock was a granite outcropping below a high-altitude section of the PCT. Perhaps David got lost while using one of several drainages leading to Suicide Rock as an avenue to escape the snow.

Ever resilient, Cathy carried a pack of angel cards in her suitcase. A simplified and decidedly more optimistic version of tarot, "Angel Prayer Oracle Cards" provide sunny guidance and cheerful inspiration. On the morning she and Pam set out to search near Suicide Rock, Cathy pulled a card from the deck and turned it over. The oracle for the day was "Signs from Heaven," with the card depicting a young woman sleeping in bed beneath a shower of white feathers floating down from the sky. In an instruction book that came with the cards, Kyle Gray, the creator of the deck, indicated that a sign from heaven arrives during times of great need. When "seeing the same numbers, finding feathers, or receiving visits from loved ones in your dreams," the angels are letting us know that we "never walk this path alone." On Gray's webpage, "the hottest name in spirituality" expanded upon the meaning of this card while offering this cautionary advice: "Try not to rely on the signs to prove anything. Instead, take them as gentle reminders that you aren't alone, and all is well."

A few hours after Cathy pulled the "Signs from Heaven" card, she and Pam were on the Suicide Rock Trail, hiking toward Marion Creek, when a break in the trees opened to a view. "That's it!" Pam cried. "I see the three ridges!" She'd visualized three purple mountains in her first reading, and the three ridges now called to her like a beacon. The women hiked on to Marion Creek, where Pam filled up her water bottles. Alas, Pam's hopes were soon dashed. "I'm not feeling anything here," the psychic said. "Let's go back."

On the hike back to the vista, a distinct sensation tickled the back of Cathy's brain. Someone or something was following her. This invisible "thing" hovered in the air above and behind her, to the right. The perception was more unsettling than creepy, like the time, when she was a child, she felt something watching her from behind, and when she turned around, she saw a house cat.

"It's David," Pam assured her.

Cathy didn't know what to believe, but the sensation of being watched from above while she hiked was certainly odd. She remembered the angel card from earlier that morning. "Signs from heaven," Cathy chanted, "signs from heaven," five times in a row. Out of the blue, a fluffy white feather—like the ones on the angel card—floated down from the sky and landed on the trail in front of her.

Inspired, the two women stared at the feather for a bit before splitting up, searching different parts of the trail ahead. They pushed through brush, entered cave-like alcoves under large boulders, and wandered along the bottom of scree slopes where someone might land if they fell. The vegetation was thick. Seven hikers walked by and none of them noticed Cathy watching them from her own spot.

By the time she reconnected with Pam, Cathy was all scratched up. "I can't find anything."

"We have to go now," Pam said, urging her friend off the trail. It was getting late. On their hike out, the psychic entertained the idea that maybe David's mother wasn't ready for her son to be found. Pam advised Cathy to "tell her she has to release whatever it is she's holding on to."

Through an email, Cathy relayed Pam's advice "to release whatever it is she's holding on to" and Carmel, who was Catholic and had a shrine of candles for David in her home, took it especially hard.

"Is she saying it's my fault if he doesn't get found?" she asked. "My knees are so sore from praying."

CHAPTER 26

# *Magical Thinking*

"**T**HIS WINTER," SALLY PROMISED HERSELF, "I NEED TO GET SOME SLEEP." IT WAS November 2018, and Kris had been missing for two years. After dedicating so much of her time to finding out what happened to her son, Sally was more than ready to move on to the next phase of grief "and not have to deal with these crazy people anymore."

The current "crazy people" Sally had to "deal with" were some disgruntled members of her Facebook group who disagreed with Sally's choice to withdraw the open-ended $10,000 she had offered in return for information leading to Kris's whereabouts. This small clique of amateur searchers was now "bitching" on social media, Monday morning quarterbacking how Sally and another mother of a missing hiker were using their GoFundMe accounts.

"I did a response," Sally said, referring to an unshared Facebook post she had written, "then I walked around the house." A particularly petulant member of her Facebook group wanted Sally and the mother of another missing hiker to show a reckoning of their GoFundMe accounts. Sally understood why, but she still felt violated. "It's not like I'm going to take that money and go to Fiji. He's so mad when the reward is taken way," she said, referring to her troll-like critic. "It's all about the money. *Go get a job.* I'd like to thump him." Much to her credit, Sally's grace and professionalism prevailed. Not wanting to become a part of a "shit show," she deleted her drafted response to the hecklers and moved on.

Around this same time, a friend commented that she couldn't believe how much time Sally spent advising other parents of missing hikers.

"I've gotten so good at it," Sally replied. "It doesn't take me that long and people did it for me."

However generous she was with her time, the truth of the matter was this: every moment of precious energy Sally spent wrangling trolls and helping other families was a moment stolen from the search for her own son. "It's like you open a door and that leads to another door to another situation, and next thing you know I'm on Facebook messaging for twelve hours straight on my phone or iPad and it takes on a life of its own, especially for Morgan, who can dig deeper than anybody. I'm so glad to have you guys [me, Cathy, and Morgan] on my side. I wish we could all solve our situation, take a break from it, and figure out how to bottle it and help other people."

"We'll just pace ourselves," I encouraged her. "One thing at a time."

Sally sighed. "I need to step away from [this] every now and then. It's a full-time job, and I already have a full-time job. You get discouraged. New people come in [wanting to help], but it is exhausting answering the same questions."

"Let them show you their stamina first," I suggested, thinking about the newbies. "Let them display what they can do."

Later that same day, Sally shared with me her fantasy about what a "traditional memorial" for Kris would look like when we found him. "I want to take some of him back out there to one of these beautiful places and meet all of you. They'll have to fly my fat ass up there in a helicopter so I can bring a cooler of liquor, but that would bring me lots of peace." After a few moments, she changed the subject.

"I've been talking to Gavin's stepmom."

Among the people Sally had been advising recently were relatives of Gavin Johnston, a twenty-year-old devout Catholic from Everett, Washington. In 2018, Johnston told his family he was going to hike the PCT to "become closer with God" before he parked his vehicle at Stevens Pass (PCT mile 2474) on October 16 and hiked south. By that point, snow already dotted the ground and more was on the way. A novice hiker, Johnston had purchased his gear at Cabela's, and he'd left his maps behind in the car. His family reported him missing within days. The authorities conducted a few searches, some by air, until the blizzards shut them down.

There was a sense Johnston may have disappeared on purpose. Sally instructed his stepmom to "get the laptop. Get in his storage unit. Whatever you have to do." But like other families of the recently missing that Sally had helped, Johnston's stepmom "dragged her feet" on implementing this advice, because, as Sally explained, "When you are in the moment, you think, 'I'm not going to have to do all that, he's going to show up any minute. He's going to show up today.' And you don't want your family business out there."

Eight months later, in June 2019, a backpacker noticed a smell of decomposition coming from a blue tent set up near the shore of Glacier Lake (PCT mile 2460). Search and rescue discovered Johnston's body tucked inside. He was lying in a fetal position, a rosary cradled in one palm. Stuffed inside his wallet was a handwritten note dated "11/10/18." The tone was curiously pragmatic, but there were no details of Johnston's experience or what happened to him. No explanations for how he ended up there.

The medical examiner's report listed "accidental hypothermia" as the cause of death. If the date on his note is correct, Johnston lived alone in the wilderness for at least twenty-five days. He was alive when SAR conducted their flyovers. His car was within fourteen PCT miles from his campsite. From his tent at Glacier Lake, a side trail would have brought him to a highway in three hours. And we'll never know why he didn't hike out.

I'm the kind of person who wants to run toward a problem and fix it. "Do no harm," we tell medics and doctors, "but do *something!*"

Grief, however—grief doesn't need a fixer. Grief needs a witness. I learned this from David Kessler, the author of *Finding Meaning: The Sixth Stage of Grief*, while attending his grief course for therapists and health-care workers. I ruminated on this idea as I reflected on our failure to find the PCT Missing, a failure that frustrated me to the point that I was seeking alternative strategies to help their families.

People in Sally Fowler's position eventually reach a stage when they must make a brutal decision—should they keep exhausting themselves by pursuing every lead, no matter how flimsy, or should they stop following leads altogether? At what point do you cease setting aside your own life to search for answers that you may never find? During Kessler's course, I raised my hand and asked him for recommendations on how to help a family in this situation.

"Hollywood movies tell them persistence pays off," Kessler replied, and this results in "magical thinking" that doggedly chasing every lead is what brings a missing loved one home. Kessler suggested that someone (like a counselor or a park ranger in charge of a search) should sit down with the family member and go through the reality of how cold missing person cases are resolved. More often than not, it's by accident.

In 1999, Professor Pauline Boss pioneered the term "ambiguous loss" to describe the "frozen grief" induced by "not knowing if a loved one is absent or present, dead or alive." Dr. Boss was a family therapist with decades of experience dealing with families caught in an external situation (like when a loved one is missing) that makes "letting go" impossible. She had worked with the families of those missing from the New York 9/11 attacks and with survivors of terrorism in Kosovo whose loved ones went missing because of ethnic cleansing. Boss's theories on ambiguous loss also applied to families of people suffering from severe Alzheimer's, because when a loved one's personality changes and they forget who you are, they seem both present and absent—alive and dead, at the same time.

"The overall goal is learning to live well despite the lack of closure," Boss wrote in her book *Loss, Trauma, and Resilience: Therapeutic Work with Ambiguous Loss*. Boss's advice on dealing with ambiguous loss is as practical as it is profound. Some families, especially those of us from secular Western cultures, value mastery of fate over predestination. This causes us to suffer more when facing problems that we can't solve. But giving in to helplessness isn't healthy either. To live within this paradox, we must walk a tightrope between our desire to feel in control and our need to endure that which we cannot master. To cope within a chaotic and mysterious world, to truly "solve" the unsolvable case, we may, on occasion, need to let go of our yearning to fix it.

"We're trained to cure, not just witness. But witness we must," Boss instructed therapists and other healers. "A person's story of loss, you see, is not real in the social sense until someone is willing to hear it."

In December 2018, I received a distracting email from Cathy. "Vass and Dostie are still working missing person cases," she complained, "and someone needs to put an end to it, one way or another."

In three months, I would undergo a second surgery to remove the titanium plate holding my fibula together—the result of that ill-fated chain of events initiated by Dr. Arpad Vass's initial involvement in the O'Sullivan case. Cathy, however, was getting a headache each and every time a friend relayed new stories of Dr. Vass "finding bodies." This friend, who aspired to become a search dog handler, had maintained contact with Paul Dostie after meeting him during the David O'Sullivan search in January, and Cathy feared she had been "brainwashed." In a recent email, this friend had even bragged, "Arpad just found four bodies in Florida."

"Who do the bodies belong to?" Cathy wanted to know.

The friend couldn't remember, but promised that she'd ask Paul the following day.

Cathy knew in her gut that those names would never come.

Prodded by Cathy, I ran Vass and Dostie through the search engines to see what they'd been up to since we last saw them. I was unable to track down any names for the four bodies Cathy's friend claimed had been found by Vass in Florida, but a lot of other information popped up instead, and it was shocking.

When the O'Sullivans hired Vass in January 2018, the patent for an invention he was then calling "the INQUISITOR" was pending. Six months later, in July 2018, the US Patent Office approved a patent for the INQUISITOR, and a new website surfaced. "There will soon come a day when criminals will not be able to hide a human body," boasted the anonymous author of www.forensicrecoveryservices .org, because Dr. Arpad Vass's INQUISITOR, a "grave-detection machine," can "detect a single drop of blood over twenty years old." How the INQUISITOR worked was "a closely guarded secret," but Dr. Vass's machine could supposedly locate your "great-great-great-grandfather's grave" among "20,000 headstones" with "85% accuracy," using your fingernail clippings. And a new feature had the ability to measure the mass of bones from the air, with a range "up to thirty miles." These incredible services could be had for a mere $1,000 "engagement fee," on top of the $300 per hour paid to Dr. Vass. If you wanted to bring along a "grave-detection dog," it would cost you an extra $150 per hour. Plus all their travel expenses. "If there is no reward available either through a GoFundMe page or from personal funds," the website warned, "then we have no alternative but to charge fees upfront."

*Wow.* As outlandish as all this sounded to me, several law enforcement agencies had engaged Vass on their cases. I was stunned to find a photo published in an Alabama newspaper of Dr. Vass leaning on a conference table in front of a team of investigators, including the sheriff, a captain with the State Bureau of Investigation, and the district attorney. According to the article, the county sheriff had recruited a "world-renowned scientist and body locator" to help search for twenty-four-year-old Jessica Hamby, a suspected murder victim who was missing. Farther north, in Virginia, another police chief had requested Dr. Vass's assistance in finding the body of three-month-old Arieanna Day, another suspected victim of foul play. Day had been missing since September 11, 2018. According to news reports, including one televised on WDBJ7, investigators used Dr. Vass's services, and "samples had been recovered." No further information about those samples was disclosed, and the infant was still missing, but, according to the police chief, Vass's "ground-breaking" instrument was "like a bloodhound on steroids."

*Lord,* I thought when I read this, *cops can be so stupid.* And I used to *be* one.

With help from a college roommate, I contacted a PhD specializing in the forensic use of LiDAR (light detection and ranging) with the UTK Forensic Anthropology Department, where Dr. Vass had once worked. In an email, this PhD expressed her concerns about what she called the "super sniffer" and how it was being used on cases. "Most of us in this field believe that [Vass] is making claims he cannot possibly back up with science."

When I asked Dr. Monte Miller of Forensic DNA Experts to review the claims made on forensicrecoveryservices.org, Miller came to a similar conclusion. Regarding the use of DNA from fingernails to find the bodies of family members, Dr. Miller stated there was "no way to properly apply a resonant frequency paradigm between this machine, DNA, fingernail clippings, bones, and buried bodies.... This would not work with bodies 30 feet away, and certainly not at 30 miles in distance." He also noted that fingernail DNA is problematic in several ways, one being that we often have other people's DNA on or underneath our nails.

To counter the assertion that any device could detect a single drop of blood left at a crime scene twenty years earlier, Miller explained that "a drop of blood on the ground and in the elements is likely to have undergone a complete breakdown of all of its constituent parts. In twenty years, there is nothing left to detect," and added that this could be "a simple way to explain false readings when a body is not located."

*Gross.* I felt sick about the whole thing. *Those poor, desperate families. I should have worked harder to persuade the O'Sullivans not to use him.* It seemed rational that, in the public interest, I now had a duty to warn prosecutors, detectives, and families about the unreliability of Dr. Vass's grave-finding device, but when my tips to media outlets went unnoticed, the only recourse I could come up with was to debunk the grave-detection machine in a detailed blog. If a family or a law enforcement officer took the time to Google Vass before hiring him, they'd see my findings and, hopefully, reconsider.

I was not the only person concerned about the potential fallout from using the grave-detection machine on death-scene investigations and the impacts that it might have on families of the missing and in the courts. In 2019, a former high-ranking special agent for the federal government shared with me an email in which Paul Dostie boasted to loved ones of the missing that by "using the helicopter," Arpad had gotten "a hit on the DNA frequency, Caucasian Bone, and Zirconium" of a missing cannabis farmer named Chris Giauque.

I called the missing man's father, Bob Giauque, and he explained that Dostie's mention of zirconium referred to the metal rod surgeons had placed in his son's back to repair a child-hood injury. In 2003, when he was thirty-six, Chris Giauque dis-appeared in Humboldt County, California, and was presumed to have been murdered. Giauque's profession, the violence-prone can-nabis industry, had put him at risk, but his father, Bob, described the marijuana-use advocate as "totally nonviolent and generous." In his eighties, Bob Giauque, who had offered as much as $400,000 to anyone who found his son, was approached by Dostie in 2018. In an email to Giauque, Dostie wrote, "Dr. Vass has a device that can detect a specific person alive or deceased from a great distance. Buried is not a problem."

Giauque said he never paid the duo, but he did mail them a few toenail clippings and some metal, as requested. After Dr. Vass flew over a search area of interest a few weeks later, Dostie sent Bob Giauque an email with coordinates to a site in Humboldt County and informed the missing man's father that "we were able to locate Chris's burial site" from a helicopter with an accuracy of "50 to 100 feet," but the Sheriff's Office wouldn't accept their "data," and the grave was on the private "property of a grower" so there was "noth-ing more" they could do.

Three years later, in 2021, investigative journalist Rene Ebersole participated in a weeklong forensics course for law enforcement officers and crime scene investigators organized by the National Forensic Academy (NFA) in Tennessee. Her resulting story, one that seemed diligently researched and fairly reported to me, was published by the Marshall Project—a well-regarded nonprofit news organization covering the US criminal justice system. In an article titled "He Teaches Police 'Witching' to Find Corpses. Experts Are Alarmed," Ebersole revealed that Vass, an instructor for the NFA, was teaching crime scene investigators how to dowse for bones using *L*-shaped metal rods.

On forensicrecoveryservices.org, Vass described Ebersole's arti-cle as "fake news," and clarified that the machine he now called the

"QUANTUM OSCILLATOR" did "not operate on the same technology as dowsing—it uses resonance frequencies to locate the target." He also explained that he had experienced "failures in trying to precisely pinpoint deceased individuals" and speculated that these outcomes might be due to "environmental interferences, signal bounce, [and] frequency overlap," but he remained steadfast in his belief that his "QUANTUM OSCILLATOR machine" will, one day, "find everyone who has gone missing."

Vass supporters kept the faith as well, displaying a cultlike loyalty to the forensic anthropologist and his machine that was so fierce, I gave them a nickname—"the believers"—and my attempts to warn people about the unreliability of the grave-detection machine had them frothing at the mouth. In text messages, one believer called me "an idiot" who was "butt hurt." Another chastised me in public Facebook posts, reminding me that Dr. Vass was "the expert."

Others who expressed a rational skepticism about the grave-detection machine on social media were also rebuked with irrational debates filled with ad hominem arguments. One generous woman who had volunteered to help the mother of a teenager missing in California ended up so severely gaslighted by proponents of the grave-detection machine that she needed therapy. When this source contacted me, hearing what I had to say made it clear. *She* wasn't crazy; *they* were.

Not long after I posted my blog questioning the science behind the device, a new website appeared, www.searchandrescuescams .com, with a bizarre narrative that strained to convince the reader that Dr. Arpad Vass was a wonderful man "who is revolutionizing the world" with his "incredible machine." Meanwhile, according to this website, the truly "fraudulent" scammers were Cathy Tarr, who "relies on psychics," and Andrea Lankford, an "arrogant and self-serving park ranger" who "wallows in a quagmire of ignorance and stupidity."

My unfortunate involvement in all this preposterousness definitely felt like I was "wallowing in a quagmire of ignorance," but not in the way the writer of this blog meant it.

This victim-blaming diatribe infuriated Cathy. I didn't exactly love it either, but I still suggested that we ignore the three-ring circus and focus on the task at hand.

Once Cathy got over her initial state of being pissed off by everything Vass and the believers had done, she became immune to "all that noise." She remained the optimistically realistic woman who showed up to fix things. But one day, while searching for David O'Sullivan on that lovely, dreadful mountain, after hours of crawling into shadowy alcoves in the granite and inspecting the insides of hollowed-out trees, the volunteer realized something that made her shiver. Cathy had never seen a human cadaver before and had no idea how she'd react if she found one. Her goal was to end the O'Sullivans' torment by locating David's body, but if she came upon him in the forest, by now, he would be nothing more than scattered bones. This dawning awareness took her by surprise, and momentarily reduced her to tears. Taking a deep breath, Cathy brushed herself off and resumed her quest to peer into every nook and cranny of the San Jacinto wilderness that her eyes or drones could reach.

CHAPTER 27

# *The Bone Finders*

---

O N MAY 27, 2019, THERESA STURKIE—THE WIFE OF A MISSING MAN—RECEIVED A peculiar email under the subject line: Dr. Vass's Scent Tracking Machine.

"When I read the tragic story of your husband's disappearance," the sender addressed Theresa, "I thought you might be interested in the following information."

The "tragic story" referred to an article published the day before in the *San Diego Tribune*, in which Theresa had made an appeal for volunteers "and other specialized equipment" to search for her husband, John Sturkie, who was last seen in the San Jacinto Mountains months prior. The author of this message had a suggestion for Mrs. Sturkie: she should consider using the "cutting-edge forensic science" developed by Dr. Arpad Vass to find her husband's body.

Theresa ignored him; the email looked like spam anyway. By then, her husband had been missing for nearly five months. She had grown accustomed to strangers sending her worthless advice.

In contrast to those unhelpful distractions, the on-the-ground efforts of someone else had become *very* useful to Theresa. According to the same article, an amateur searcher had "made numerous trips to the mountain" with Sturkie's wife and coordinated two group searches using volunteers. Despite these efforts, the fifty-five-year-old father of four was still missing, but, with this person's help, Theresa Sturkie discovered a clue the authorities had missed.

On Friday, January 4, 2019, John Sturkie left his home in Oceanside, California, to take a solo trip to "the mountains." It was normal for Sturkie, a seasoned hunter and hiking enthusiast, to spend a weekend alone in the woods. It was not normal, however, for the electrician not to come home by the third day. When he failed to show up for work on Monday, Theresa called her local police department and told them that her husband was overdue. But the officers she spoke with didn't react the way Theresa expected them to. They seemed to believe that John was a full-grown adult who was out on some kind of bender, perhaps avoiding his family on purpose.

Their nonchalant attitude forced Theresa to conduct her own investigation and provide her own proof that her husband was indeed missing. She pulled credit card and bank statements with relative ease, and these documents showed no financial activity by John after January 4; then, she hit a wall with T-Mobile, who said that it needed a subpoena before it could provide her the tracking data from her husband's cell phone. Theresa appealed to the Oceanside PD for help—Sturkie had been missing for a month by this time—and her local police department pulled the data from his cell phone and discovered that the Android had last pinged in the San Jacinto Mountains on January 5 at 6:42 p.m. Using that location and date as a reference, an investigator sifted through a 911 database and found a relevant call.

On January 5, three men were off-roading on Black Mountain Road when they met Sturkie near Fuller Ridge. A winter storm was dumping impressive amounts of snow, and Sturkie's Toyota Tundra kept getting bogged down in the muck. The men offered to give the electrician a ride down the mountain, but Sturkie insisted that he didn't need any help, even though they were expecting the weather to get worse. Once the men returned to an area with cell service, they called 911 and expressed their concerns for Sturkie's welfare. They gave the operator Sturkie's name, his license plate number, and last known location. The 911 operator forwarded this information to officials with Riverside County and the California Highway Patrol, but because Sturkie himself wasn't requesting assistance, the response was called off by Riverside County.

Many weeks later, once the recovered 911 call placed Sturkie's last known position inside the boundaries of Riverside County, law enforcement finally initiated a search and flew over the snow-covered mountain several times without finding anything.

"He's probably not up there," a Riverside County investigator warned Theresa.

Frustrated by the whole endeavor, especially the failure to respond to the initial 911 call regarding her husband's welfare, Theresa turned to Jon King for assistance, and the mountaineer introduced her to Cathy. For two years now, Cathy and Jon had collaborated, off and on, while searching for David O'Sullivan, and they were developing a reputation for being *the* people to go to if your loved one went missing in the San Jacintos. Unlike the Riverside investigator who doubted Sturkie was "up there," Jon believed Sturkie's truck was stuck somewhere on the farthest, most rugged end of Black Mountain Road. On March 15, he hiked through the deep snow, and as expected, he found Sturkie's Toyota approximately twelve miles from the pavement, half-buried in snow, with one tire wedged between two rocks. Jon searched for signs of Sturkie's direction of travel, but because two months had passed, any tracks the stranded motorist may have left behind had been covered by fresher snow. Jon informed Riverside County about the truck, and they sent up a team a few days later. Lamentably, the professionals looking for Sturkie uncovered no more clues, and so, on April 11, they suspended their effort to find him.

The unofficial search carried on. Cathy interviewed the men who'd last seen Sturkie, while Morgan and I studied the cell phone location data that Morgan had retrieved from Sturkie's Google account. Interpreting this information challenged us. At the base of One Horse Ridge, a rocky knoll off Black Mountain Road with a view of the desert and Interstate 10, a half dozen GPS pings were scattered about a small parking area, as if Sturkie had paced around for an hour trying to decide what to do. There were more pings along the PCT as it paralleled Black Mountain Road between One Horse Ridge and Sturkie's truck. The timing of these pings along with their locations gave conflicting information regarding Sturkie's direction of travel.

Cathy proposed a theory. Stranded on the mountain in bad weather, John Sturkie either turned off his phone to save power or the battery died shortly after 6:42 p.m., the time of the last ping. He slept in the car, using the heater to keep warm. In the morning, the stranded motorist woke up and saw more snow on the ground. Realizing the only way off the mountain was to walk, Sturkie packed up a few items in a small backpack, locked the truck, and headed off on foot.

But which direction did he go? Back the way he came, down Black Mountain Road, was the easiest and perhaps the safest choice. However, from the truck, the PCT was a faster route to the desert. Sturkie loved the outdoors, was a downhill skier, and had been to the San Jacintos before. He would know that, if you were on foot, descending elevation via the PCT was a quicker escape from the deep snow and freezing temps.

Sturkie disappeared into the same vast and treacherous terrain Cathy had been searching for David O'Sullivan. Even so, she hesitated to join forces with Theresa. "I don't want to be the lead on this case," she told me. "I don't have the energy." Still, Theresa needed Cathy's help, and as soon as Carmel O'Sullivan offered to pay for search expenses using funds from David's GoFundMe, Cathy caved.

That spring, on the day she first drove Theresa up Black Mountain Road, Cathy felt a nagging sense of déjà vu, "like, 'oh my God, not again.' I hate that road. It's ridiculous." Damage from winter storms had worsened a route that was crummy even under the best circumstances. At least three times, the women had to get out of the car to move rocks, shovel dirt, or drag tree limbs out of the way. Each time they did this, Theresa, a devout Catholic, pulled out a container of holy water and flick, flick, flicked it around. When Cathy gave her a look, Theresa shrugged and said, "It can't hurt." Near the top of the mountain, Cathy tried to plow her RAV4 through a snowbank and got stuck. *Oh shit, we are never going to get out of here*, Cathy fretted until three PCT hikers came out of nowhere and asked, "You need some help?"

"Why, yes, we do." Cathy shoved a bunch of boards and branches under the back wheel and instructed the hikers to push, hard, until the SUV shucked free.

Cathy's eclectic philosophies on the afterlife are fuzzier than the biblical tenets behind Theresa's Catholicism. A firm faith in God's plan combined with her stoic personality allowed Theresa to approach the search for her husband in a businesslike manner. Her calm demeanor raised some suspicions, but Cathy knew any speculation about the tall redhead murdering her taller electrician husband for insurance money was hogwash. The 911 call confirmed that Sturkie was last seen alone on a mountain and refusing assistance, while his truck was pinned between rocks and covered with snow. The most brilliant spouse slayer in the West couldn't stage all that successfully. Besides, when it came to killing people, the San Jacinto Mountains required no assistance.

At home, grief lay thick but unspoken among members of the family. The Sturkies had four children, including one from a previous marriage. Theresa believed her kids were coping with the ambiguous loss of their father. But Cathy, whose mother had died when she was ten, knew better. Moments would come—in the days, weeks, months, and even years to follow—when they would feel awful about this. While Sturkie was missing, his youngest daughter turned sixteen and his son graduated from high school. Cathy knew how much Sturkie's kids would later dwell on their dad's absence at milestone events like birthdays and weddings.

And, before long, Theresa's mask of strength wore off, too. Cathy saw it the first day they reached Sturkie's truck, when Theresa broke down and started calling out John's name.

"I know it was the stupidest thing ever," Theresa admitted years later. "I knew he wouldn't answer." But she did it anyway. "John! John!" Theresa yelled, over and over, but the only response was her own pitiful voice—*John! John!*—echoing back to her.

Wanting to give Theresa the space she needed, Cathy climbed up a hill to check out an overhang in the rocks that could provide shelter, but nothing was there.

The women returned a few weeks later. This time, they had over sixty volunteer searchers with them and the keys to Sturkie's truck. Before Cathy could unlock the door, a volunteer called her over her two-way radio. Someone had spotted a sock in a shallow drainage less than a hundred feet away. Cathy and Theresa walked down the dirt road to inspect it.

"It's not John's," Theresa said.

A wife would recognize what socks her husband wore, Cathy thought, so she left the clue as she found it and they walked back to the truck.

The battery was dead, compelling Theresa to use the manual backup key. She opened the door and gestured inside. "There you go."

Like a greyhound at the gate, Cathy wanted permission to search that truck, but she felt awkward. John was Theresa's husband. The truck belonged to her.

"No, Cathy," Theresa insisted, "you should go through it."

It was weird sitting in the driver's seat. The first thing Cathy wanted to know was the brand of water bottles that Sturkie carried. They were Kirkland. Then, she picked up a container of vitamins, brand name "Live." *How ironic.* She reached her hand under the front seat. Among some papers, her fingers touched fabric. She pulled it out. In her hand was a sock that looked *exactly* like the one she had just seen a short time ago.

"Theresa, I found a match to that sock."

"No way!"

The sock's location—east of the truck—suggested a direction of travel.

"Okay," Cathy declared. "We have a new search area for the day." She instructed Theresa to pull everything out of John's truck and photograph it. Then, she redirected the volunteers to search between the truck and the northbound PCT while she went back to examine the errant sock. There was a dime-sized stain in the foot that looked like blood. *Odd. Why would Sturkie's sock be lying in a shallow drainage on the side of the road? Why would it have blood on it?* People suffering from severe hypothermia were known to disrobe when they felt a flush of heat before they died. Paradoxical undressing was the clinical term. Then again, the volunteers hadn't found anything but the sock.

"He was using it as a glove," someone suggested, and bingo, Cathy knew this had to be true. The drop of blood was right where your knuckles would be if you wore this sock on your hand to keep warm. One fender of the truck had a fist-shaped dent. Cathy imagined Sturkie either hurt his hand in his attempts to dig out the truck, or he punched his beloved Toyota in frustration. Once Sturkie decided to hike out on foot, he tossed the sock, soaking wet, into the brush because it was no longer keeping his hand warm.

The group failed to find Sturkie that day, but once Cathy better understood Sturkie's direction of travel, the search was significantly easier to plan. According to Dr. Koester's statistical analysis in *Lost Person Behavior*, there was a 75 percent chance of finding a stranded motorist within 2.8 miles of his abandoned vehicle. And the team wasn't about to give up.

In addition to updating the Sheriff's Office about the sock, Theresa tried to guilt trip them into doing something.

"We're going to go up again," she warned the cops. "I want to let you know you may have to rescue us."

Cathy, Theresa, and their band of volunteers returned days later to search between the truck and the PCT, focusing near a tricky switchback at mile 193 and along a ravine headed in the same direction. They found some candy wrappers and a discarded phone battery, but nothing that definitively tied to Sturkie.

At last, Sturkie's story in the *San Diego Tribune* combined with Theresa's guilt-tripping finally pushed Riverside County law enforcement to do something. On June 29, the sheriff sent in fifty people to search where Cathy's volunteers had found the sock. "I think they were worried two middle-aged women were going to find him before they did," Theresa reflected later. Within hours, a ground searcher spotted a boot in a manzanita bush. From there, searchers walked down a drainage and found Sturkie's body about two miles from the truck. He had his wallet and cell phone with him, and the location suggested he had either wandered off the PCT or was navigating down the ravine, where he likely died from hypothermia.

GPS tracks showed that two of Cathy's volunteers had walked within thirty feet of the body. Instead of frustrating her, this near miss boosted Cathy's confidence. Her theory about what happened had been correct. Her search plans would have found him, eventually. The Sheriff's Office located Sturkie *because* of the clue she'd uncovered. Plus, the government had more resources. Like helicopters, for example.

"We needed a drone," Cathy told Theresa when the widow expressed her desire to join future search efforts for other missing hikers. "If we had gotten something in the air, we would have found him."

Theresa refused to announce publicly that her husband's body had been located until Carmel O'Sullivan and Sally Fowler knew. From her own experience, she understood the complex emotions felt by families of the missing, especially when they heard someone else's loved one had been found before their own.

*Wow.* It impressed Cathy how much Theresa thought of other people while in the depth of her own grief.

"This isn't official," Cathy told both mothers. "Don't let this out. But I want you to know." Like Theresa, Cathy had anticipated the impact this news would have on Carmel and Sally. The mothers cried for more than one reason. A body had been found. John Sturkie was dead, and this was not a happy conclusion. However, one family was able to bury their loved one, and the Sturkies could move forward to another stage of mourning.

On the other hand, the families of Sylvia, Fowler, and O'Sullivan remained stuck in an agonizing purgatory because their men were still lost. And when you're a long-term, card-carrying member of "The Club No One Wants to Be In," it often feels unfair. Why does one family get resolution and the opportunity to bury their loved one, while yours is left to suffer? A human emotion—jealousy—bubbles up, but you don't "tap into that" because you are so grateful this other family has the answers you desperately want. Yet, you are also devastated by the loss because it reminds you that, even once you find the answers you seek, you will likely still suffer. Seeing this grief, this finality, up close—it can really take a toll on you. And all these painful, tangled, messy feelings are too much for the mother of a missing child to take in all at once.

"I'm better now," Carmel emailed Cathy a few days later. "I'm okay."

"I'm really sorry," Cathy replied, "that this wasn't the better news you wanted."

Nearly three hundred people attended John Sturkie's memorial. The traditional Catholic Latin Mass funeral was "heavy and serious stuff" to Cathy's new age sensibilities, but she followed along as everyone kneeled and took the sacrament. A cousin placed antlers and a jar of dirt from a favorite hunting area on top of a memorial table near John's casket. Thanks to their efforts, Theresa was able to put her husband to rest, and for that, Cathy was grateful. The Sturkies were no longer asking themselves, *What happened to John?* They would miss him, but at least they could move forward after mourning him properly.

"You never realize what a gift a funeral is," Theresa mused, "until you cannot find your loved one."

Six months after John Sturkie was laid to rest, on a cold December day in 2019, Morgan Clements was in his Missouri home, staring at his computer. He clicked on an image file, moved his cursor to the upper-left-hand corner of his screen, and zoomed in. Once the items on the photographed ground were in proper focus, he scanned the entire image (left to right, top to bottom) with his eyes, as thoroughly as possible, as if it were his loved one who was missing. Some images required ten minutes or more to search, and, on this particular case, he had reviewed at least one hundred high-resolution photos before something in file PM_JTNP_P2_Z3_F2 (435) caught his attention: a stark white branch lying in the desert next to a large boulder. Morgan zoomed in a bit more. The white stick had a knob at each end.

It looked like a bone.

Unbeknownst to Morgan, while he was image squinting at home, two PhDs with the School of Aviation and Transportation Technology at Purdue University in Indiana were researching the possibility of using drone imagery to find human remains. William T. Weldon and Joseph Hupy realized the potential of what was at stake here ("small pixel sizes in aerial imagery allow for discovery of even minute signs of a missing person"), but there was a big problem: "the number of images and the size of the data sets gathered in modern SAR missions make traditional manual image interpretation methods increasingly difficult." They noted that a "computer-assisted interpretation method" had been developed and was sold commercially, but it wasn't clear how well it worked. To examine the effectiveness of this application, the researchers designed a study that pitted the software against human squinters in a simulated scenario involving 1,075 images. When they analyzed their data and then published their results in an article entitled "Investigating Methods for Integrating Unmanned Aerial Systems on Search and Rescue Operations," Weldon and Hupy came to a surprising conclusion. Not only did humans find more clues and more "bodies" than the software; they did it *faster*.

Later, Weldon provided me with an explanation of why, to date, no one has been able to create software that can effectively search for human remains in aerial photos. Creating such a program requires a process software engineers call "deep learning"—but it takes a lot of time for a machine to catch up with the human mind. For example, a machine must review tens of thousands of images before it will "learn" something as basic as how to distinguish a dog from a cat (or a chihuahua face from a blueberry muffin), a task any motivated six-year-old can learn within minutes.

As for Morgan's take on the results of the Purdue study? "The human brain is especially adept at recognizing patterns of importance. . . . Can you teach software to use intuition? Nope. Does software know to look specifically at the bottom of fall zones, or in shaded areas where a human might have sought shelter?"

Nonetheless, Morgan's faith in the talents of mortal squinters rubbed up against a serious flaw that the Purdue researchers had discovered in their human-based system. It didn't take long for people to burn out, and few tasks were as lonely, frustrating, or headache-inducing as squinting at thousands of aerial images, looking for clues and cadavers. Indeed, by December 2019, Morgan had spent two years searching the lion's share of 5,451 aerial photographs of the David O'Sullivan search area, and the mapmaker's wife, Julie, often heard him cursing at his computer while he reviewed images late into the evening. Whenever Morgan spotted a potential bone or backpack or tent that might belong to David, his hopes soared—only to have them crash and burn once ground searchers hiked in and discovered the "bone" was a tree branch, the "backpack" was a rock, and the "tent" was a tarp abandoned by illegal marijuana cultivators. By the time Morgan found the white stick with knobs on each end, he had reviewed approximately four thousand aerial images without finding anyone at all.

On July 13, 2018—seventeen months before Morgan spotted something peculiar in image file PM_JTNP_P2_Z3_F2 (435)—Paul Miller decided to take a morning walk inside Joshua Tree National Park. As the Canadian left his hotel room, he reassured his wife that he'd be back before it was time to check out. He brought along a hydration backpack and a camera bag but left his cell phone behind. When he did not return to the hotel by noon, his wife reported him missing. Within hours, park rangers found Miller's car at a trailhead and initiated a search. In the following weeks, hundreds of people, six search dogs, and a helicopter crew spent six thousand hours scouring the park, but Miller was still nowhere to be found.

Sixteen months later, the case had gone cold when Miller's family persuaded the NPS to make a rare exception to their rules by issuing a permit allowing Western States Aerial Search (WSAS), a nonprofit based in Utah, to conduct a drone search for Paul Miller inside the park. Over one weekend, Greg Nuckolls's team captured

6,700 images of the terrain surrounding the trail Miller had hiked. But weeks later, only 15 percent of those images had been reviewed. Desperate for more squinters, Nuckolls sought assistance from Cathy.

When Cathy posted Nuckolls's plea for help on our private Facebook group, Morgan complained in the comments. "Why should we commit to more mindless image scanning? Especially if there are no ground searchers willing to follow up on leads?"

Gloria Boyd volunteered to do the onerous task of creating a spreadsheet of file names and GPS coordinates associated with each photograph WSAS had captured. Reluctantly, Morgan agreed to scan a few random images from the thousands Gloria had listed. One hundred photos into his review, he spotted that white thing with a knob on each end.

On December 15, Morgan sent that image over to Sarah Francis in Texas. Sarah pulled up photographs of the same area that the drone had captured from different angles and quickly found more white things that looked like bones. She also spotted a round object resembling a metal rim of a car tire. Shadows and fuzzy resolutions challenged her ability to interpret what she was seeing. Sarah sent Morgan a screenshot of the thing she thought looked like a tire rim.

"It's not a tire rim," Morgan texted back. "It's a hydration backpack propped up by the shoulder straps in a way that makes it look round and hollow, like a wheel."

*Paul Miller had a hydration pack with him!*

Morgan and Sarah would have been more excited, but experience told them the "hydration pack" could be a rock. The "bones" might belong to a cow. A week earlier, they had sent coordinates to the Joshua Tree rangers of an item they found that resembled a spine in the rocks, but when the rangers hiked in, nothing was there.

Morgan relayed the GPS coordinates to the park rangers once again, but this time, when the rangers hiked in, they found a human skull, a femur, more bones, and a hydration backpack leaning up against a boulder. Days later, the coroner determined that the bones did indeed belong to Paul Miller. Rangers presumed Miller died quickly, perhaps from heat stroke or heart attack, because there was still food and water in his pack. According to GPS tracking, professional searchers had walked within thirty meters of Miller's body without seeing it.

What searchers had missed on the ground, Morgan saw from his chair in Missouri while squinting at a photo that had been taken from the air. Two years earlier, UAS pilot Gene Robinson had told Cathy she could find a missing hiker using drones, and it turned out he was right after all.

"Why should we commit to more mindless image scanning?" had been Morgan's lament. "Because it works" was his vindication.

If Cathy and I lived in Missouri, we would have driven over to Morgan's house, gathered around his backyard firepit, and popped open a few well-earned bottles of beer. But our little band of amateurs worked remotely from one another and lived in separate states. Instead of taking a break to celebrate his victory, Morgan returned to his computer and clicked on another case file. He moved his cursor to the upper left corner and zoomed in once more. From there, he began to scan—left to right, top to bottom—the next image among thousands, looking for a clue that could end another family's torment of not knowing.

# CHAPTER 28

# *From the Mud*

A MBER JOHNSON WAS TWENTY-SEVEN, WITH LONG DARK BRAIDS, AND CUTE AS A button, but the skillful strumming of her ukulele may have been what most captivated the small audience of male backpackers gathering around her one summer day in 2016. A cello player who took up the ukulele in part for its portability, Amber carried the instrument in a backpack that was such a lurid purple she'd earned the trail name Ultra Violet, and thus her small, stringed companion had followed her all the way from the Mexico border to this High Sierra camp in central California. Among the bearded, dirty, hungry-looking men watching the show, she noticed a tall blond man in his thirties. *What a stereotypical thru-hiker,* Ultra Violet thought when she caught him looking at her, but Sherpa's soulful eyes and playful personality quickly won her over, and they started hiking together, off and on.

Within weeks, they were north of the Sierra, in the town beneath Mount Shasta, where they left the trail to bag the famous fourteener. To climb Shasta in August, you must slog up loose talus that occasionally slides underfoot and careens down the steep slope. Over the last century, at least fifty hopefuls have died on their way up to the summit, but these two thru-hikers, who now had 1,500 miles on their odometers, were confident in their abilities. Knowing they'd need to go at their own pace, Ultra Violet and Sherpa decided to temporarily part ways and climb the mountain separately.

Ultra Violet grew up in Colorado's Rocky Mountains, and she was eager to get an early start, which helped her make it to the summit on August 28. Sherpa, on the other hand, liked to sleep in. He made it halfway before fog obscured the route and he lost the trail. Afraid he'd fall while walking the wrong direction, Sherpa called 911 for advice, but the service was poor, and the call dropped. Sherpa set up camp, waited for conditions to improve, and safely descended the mountain the next day.

The couple reconnected in town. Ultra Violet half-heartedly busked tourists for tips with her ukulele before the pair returned to the PCT and continued north. One day, as they made their way through Oregon, Sherpa announced that he planned to celebrate the completion of his thru-hike by getting a new tattoo. One that would remind him of the freedom he experienced on the trail: a dragonfly.

Before long, Sherpa and Ultra Violet climbed out of the Columbia River Gorge and entered Washington's Cascade Range, winter snapping at their heels. Once the cold, wet weather stole the fun out of it, Ultra Violet decided that she'd had enough; she was leaving the PCT and going home. She urged Sherpa to come with her, but he still wanted to finish his thru-hike.

Amber set off on the morning of October 6. Snow had fallen overnight but the parting was casual; Amber doesn't even remember them exchanging the word "goodbye" since she was certain she'd see him soon. After he finished the PCT, Sherpa would hitch to Colorado to spend the holidays with Ultra Violet and her family.

A month later, instead of Kris traveling to the Rockies to rendezvous with her, Amber returned to the Cascades to help Sally Fowler look for her lost son. On the flight out, Amber was optimistic. Kris might be hurt in a way that required surgery or intravenous fluids, but she believed they'd find him soon, and he'd be okay. She even imagined a scene that involved her visiting him in a hospital room and had tucked a special dress in her luggage to wear for the occasion.

Upon arriving in Packwood, Amber finally met Sherpa's stepmom in person. To Amber, Sally Fowler seemed like "a force of nature." Formidable and relentless, yet warm and caring, the woman never gave up—and Sally's search for her missing son was an all-hands-on-deck operation. In Sally's hotel room, the coffee maker was kept full and hot. Maps were laid out on the table and the phones buzzed constantly. Back then, people still talked about finding Sherpa alive, but during the week she spent with Sally, reality hit Amber in a bad way. The mountains were white. It was getting colder by the day. Her friend had been missing for three weeks. Suddenly, she felt a pang as she realized: Sherpa was never getting a dragonfly tattoo, and she would not be wearing that cute dress.

Amber couldn't stop crying. "It's quite heavy," she confessed to Sally, referring to guilt she carried for not persuading Sherpa to leave the trail when she did.

"Come on," Sally hugged the younger woman. "It's obviously not your fault. You know Kris. When did he ever do anything anyone else told him to do?"

In the following months, Amber wanted to do more to help. She patiently responded to every one of Sally's texts, but the Facebook activity around Sherpa's case was too intense for her to handle. She kept her distance.

"I completely shut down," Amber said years later. "I didn't want to talk anymore."

As the third anniversary of Sherpa's disappearance neared, Sally contemplated closing the Bring Kris Fowler/Sherpa Home Facebook group. Maintaining a diplomatic and responsive presence on social media was a second career. Each time a new lead came in,

Sally's stress level shot up while her job performance took a nose-dive. So far, her boss had maintained an aura of sympathy, but how long would it last? Not to mention, despite all the hard work, the hassles, and the headaches, nothing had led her to Kris.

Then, in August 2019, the earth spit something back out.

Like Sally and her volunteers, members of the Yakima County search team were also struggling to let go of Kris Fowler's case. "Briscoe and I have talked on the phone for hours," Sally said. "He's avidly working on this. He went back to square one. He reread all the notes and revisited all the scenarios. He obtained Kris's phone records and went back through every call. He went through all the clues and leads, put a timeline together, and presented the whole case to a PhD in Search and Rescue. They spoke at length about it and the expert called this case a head scratcher. Briscoe's a good career lawman. My family will be eternally grateful for all the time he has put into trying to find Kris."

Working under the leadership of Sergeant Briscoe was Yakima SAR officer Wayne Frudd and his team of seventy-five trained volunteers. Frudd estimates that he alone hiked over 125 miles looking for the missing thru-hiker while following up on numerous leads. During the summer of 2019, a relative of Fowler who wishes to remain anonymous passed along an intuitive hunch inspired by a dream she had about Kris. Frudd studied the lead and the location, near a unique crook in the trail eighteen trail miles north of White Pass, and it "made perfect sense." Accompanied by two volunteers, Frudd hiked in, stayed overnight, and searched for days near the trail's intersection with Laughingwater Creek, the same drainage Morgan Clements flew out to search in 2017. The men were scouring both sides of the PCT looking for clues when Ron Buermann spotted a piece of fabric in the mud on the outer edge of a wilderness campsite, thirty-five steps from the trail and straddling the boundary between Mount Rainier National Park and William O. Douglas Wilderness. Buermann pulled the fabric from the muck and out came a ditty bag—a little sack that backpackers use to carry their toiletries. Inside the beige ditty bag with orange trim, a specialized product sold at REI, was a tube of tent sealer, a travel-sized toothbrush with toothpaste, and a plastic baggie filled with pink powder.

Nearly three years had passed since Kris had gone missing, and over that time Frudd had begun to trust Sally (and her close-knit team of civilian sleuths). "We don't hold our status as professional SAR as so sacred," Frudd later said while explaining his philosophies on collaborating with nongovernmental searchers. Once a case goes cold, "I need fresh eyes. I'm willing to think outside the box and listen to their ideas." Briscoe echoed a similar sentiment when he told Sally, "Hey, I'm as willing as you are to look under every rock." Men of their word, Frudd and Briscoe sent Sally photographs of the toiletry kit that Buermann had uncovered and the items inside it.

Sally forwarded these images to Amber, who couldn't recall any specifics about the toiletries Kris carried, though she had seen him dump red electrolyte powder into his canteen. To Sally, a grocery supplier, the lot numbers visible on the items in the toiletry bag picture provided a wellspring of information. With Morgan's help, she discovered that the ditty bag was made between 2015 and 2016, and the items inside of it had expiration dates that lined up with Kris's timeline, which meant that it was certainly possible that the ditty bag belonged to Kris.

While Sally and Morgan worked the lot numbers, I sent a photograph of the wet and dirty toothbrush to my forensic expert, Dr. Monte Miller. Could fingerprints or DNA from the toothbrush be used to identify its owner?

Fingerprints weren't Miller's expertise, but he said lifting prints from items subjected to time, soil, and elements was "a definite no." Collecting saliva DNA from a toothbrush was possible if it remained dry, sealed, and protected from sunlight, but using DNA to identify Kris as the owner of the toothbrush would be particularly complicated. Kris was an only child, and both of his biological parents were deceased. From a genetic perspective, his biological aunt was his closest living relative. Using an aunt's DNA to make an identification requires an "avuncular test," otherwise known as an "Aunt/Uncle DNA test." The accuracy of an avuncular test is suspect even when you have a pristine source of DNA. One look at the photo and it was obvious; the soiled and soggy toothbrush would not be able to provide us with an adequate sample.

Still, finding the ditty bag was a compelling clue in and of itself, and Sally's hopes had been raised. She asked Cathy to coordinate a search concentrating on the area where it was found, praying that the answers she'd sought for so long might be waiting somewhere nearby.

A day before this search, during the long drive from Tacoma to Packwood, Sally Fowler nearly threw up. A close friend, Marcia O'Rourke, had traveled with her from Ohio to provide emotional and logistical support and now the women were following behind me in their rental car. I spotted a roadside pullout by a lake and pulled in so we could use the restroom and take a quick break from the road. Marcia grabbed a smoke while Sally leaned back against their SUV to take in the view, a gloomy reservoir shadowed by fog and surrounded by conifers.

Sally's baby blues are big, round, and expressive. They remind me of Jennifer Aniston's eyes because they often radiate wonder, mischief, and humor. But when I met her gaze that afternoon, as she considered the densely forested mountains reflected in the dark waters of the lake, her eyes revealed her distress, and her lips trembled.

"Is this bringing up bad memories?"

Sally nodded, so close to tears she couldn't speak.

"I'm sorry." I hugged her tight and let her cry, not knowing what else to say.

The evening before, Sally had seemed cheerful when she met the small group of searchers assembling in the lobby of our hotel. We were a motley crew. In addition to Cathy and me, there was David Wolfe, the tattooed local hiker who nearly hit that elk the night he drove Sally to Packwood in 2016, as well as Mackenzie Pollard, a spirited young PCT section hiker with strawberry blonde hair. Rounding out the group was a pale-skinned, spectacled hunter named Aaron Samuel Wheeler, a Washington native whose painstaking searches for Kris had been inspired by the "leave no man behind" ethos drilled into him from a stint in the Navy.

On the front of Sally's camouflage T-shirt, a rhinestone-studded message of LOVE sparkled at the group as we moved our gathering to a firepit on the patio outside the hotel. While the rest of us attacked a box of calorie-laden gourmet "Killer Brownies" that she'd brought with her from Ohio, Sally excused herself to go buy us a round of drinks. "I can't find my son," she said, "but I can definitely find a bar."

Even though it was the first time I'd met Sally in person, I knew it was okay to laugh. By that point, we'd been speaking on the phone several times a month for nearly two years. We had discussed many thorny topics. I considered her a friend, we trusted one another, and I knew she came from a family who viewed humor in the face of tragedy as not only appropriate, but necessary.

We drank wine and ate appetizers for dinner. Then we graduated to cocktails while Sally danced in her seat to the tune of "Mustang Sally," which played from my phone. It may not have been evident that evening, but I knew that veiled behind this fun-loving persona were three years of unrelenting uncertainty that had put the woman from Ohio on a constant verge of mental collapse. Believing it would be therapeutic for her to return to Washington and participate in our search, Cathy and I had encouraged Sally to make this trip. That first night, meeting us in person had been a pleasant distraction. But sure enough, by the next morning, raw emotions were bubbling back up to the surface. As we hugged by the lake, Sally wept and I grew worried.

*Maybe all of this has been a massive mistake.*

Restless to get back on the road, Sally pulled herself together and we continued the winding drive onward to Packwood. Our first stop was the hotel where Kris had stayed two nights with the elderly couple before he disappeared. On the porch of the cute historic inn with the wooden bears out front, Marilyn Linder greeted us wearing a black-and-white flowered muumuu. Inside, her husband, David, wheeled over to us on a motorized chair wearing a blue T-shirt and the orange "Bring Home Sherpa" ball cap that Sally had sent him. David Linder was a big guy with a Santa Claus charisma, but his entire left leg was gone; the year prior, it had been surgically amputated because of a medical condition. This shocked Sally for a moment, but David's gracious demeanor was encouraging. This man's joy for Jesus would not be crushed by a missing limb.

Before we left, Sally asked David to say a prayer. We sat around David's motorized chair and held hands, letting his words wash over us.

"I'm praying for the eyes of the searchers," he murmured, "so that they find something and give Sally answers, oh Lord. Help them, oh Lord. Praying for their safety, oh Lord. Praying for Kris. Praying for our minds to stay open to the impossibility. The impossibility that he could still be alive."

Once we recovered from David's emotional prayer, we headed over to a pizza restaurant across the street, where Theresa Sturkie was waiting for us. During the long months that John Sturkie had been missing, Sally had given Theresa moral support and sage advice over the phone. Today, the widow from Oceanside, California, wanted to pay it forward by flying up to join the search effort for Kris. Our food arrived, and then two hunters, Andrea and Josh

Kirkman, walked in. Andrea had organized the group search that brought Cathy into the case back in August 2017. Now, years later, the young couple had driven six hours to meet Sally in person. Josh handed Sally a bright orange "Bring Home Sherpa" ball cap that had been signed by over a dozen volunteer searchers, including Cathy Tarr. While we ate, Josh showed me a map on his phone covering a large section of the Cascades. Nearly a hundred digital pins designated the areas that he and his wife had already searched.

In the parking lot, the Kirkmans said their goodbyes, and then the five of us who remained (Sally, Marcia, Theresa, Cathy, and me) drove on to White Pass—Kris Fowler's last known point. At the PCT trailhead, a summer flush of frogs had recently emerged from the slimy bottom of Leech Lake, a nearby pond, and now thousands of these tiny amphibians hopped around the parking lot like a biblical plague. An adorable nuisance. We watched our steps to avoid squashing them.

Once we stepped onto the trail, Sally's cell phone "blew up" with messages. There was service here. Kris had stood in the same spot, Sally believed, texting Amber and trying to call his dad before he entered the cell service dead zone in the forest.

Out of shape but determined to trek the PCT, Sally had done a fine job of dressing for the hike. She wore a sturdy new pair of leather boots with red shoelaces (which resembled the iconic hiking boot on the cover of *Wild*), and her Army green pants had so many functional pockets, I was downright envious. Meanwhile, Sally's safety-conscious shirt was hunter orange. Printed on the front, above the words "Bring Sherpa Home," was an artistic selfie of Kris, one that he had taken under a wide-angle canopy of trees. Before we headed up the trail, a bystander took our photograph. In it, five women stood shoulder to shoulder on the PCT, all of us donning an orange "Bring Sherpa Home" T-shirt.

As we soldiered on, we encountered some southbound PCT hikers who recognized Sally and knew about Sherpa. Before

October 2016, Sally hadn't understood why these weirdos would want to spend five filthy months hiking 2,650 dirty miles. Today, she wanted to hug every smelly thru-hiker who crossed her path.

After Mike Fowler died of lung cancer in 2017, there was a funeral service for him in Ohio. But his sister had reserved a portion of Mike's ashes, and these pulverized bone fragments were now bouncing around inside his ex-wife's fanny pack. Sally came to a spot on the trail that suited her and stopped. She reached into her pack and pulled out a miniature silver urn decorated with an American flag. We circled around to hear her speak.

"Mike was a man's man. A gregarious guy who loved Kris. We were divorced, but he was my friend. We had a love for one another. A different kind of love. Kris kept us in communication, and we cared. Mike knew before I knew. It's what did him in. The stress." She unscrewed the cap on the urn. Emotions flooded in and her voice quivered, "I'm gonna put you right here, buddy." She tipped the urn and ashes poured out. A fortuitous breeze took them north, the same direction Sherpa hiked on October 12, 2016.

"That was Kris!" Sally later exclaimed, referring to the wind, "all the way." She stuffed Mike's urn back into her pack. We gathered in a circle and held hands while Theresa led us in a prayer with pleas for help from Raphael and Tobias, two patron saints of travelers and happy meetings.

Back at the trailhead, Sally glanced at her phone. It was 5:43 p.m., the same time of Kris's last cell phone ping. A new text came through. A hiker had found something blue south of Chinook Pass, near the PCT, and Sally allowed herself to hope once more.

Tomorrow, the volunteers might find him.

## CHAPTER 29

# *Accept. Learn. Let Go.*

A SERPENTINE DRIVE UP HIGHWAY 410 LED SALLY AND HER FRIEND MARCIA through the forests at the base of Mount Rainier to Chinook Pass. When the women from Ohio topped 5,400 feet and turned the corner at the pass, the woods thinned out, revealing a fairy-tale view. Shrouded in mist, majestic conifers stood sentinel over yellow, white, and purple wildflowers exploding from vibrant green meadows. This palette fit for Monet shimmered in the reflections of jade-toned lakes. Several walking paths, including the PCT, meandered through the eye candy until they disappeared over undulating ridges. Interrupting all the grandeur was a score of garish orange T-shirts worn by the volunteers gathering in a trailhead parking lot.

"Oh my God," Marcia gasped. "Those are the people."

Rallied by Sally's Facebook posts, a diverse group of over twenty hikers from six states, most of them strangers, were already there waiting, ready to help her search for her son. Among them was a PCT "celebrity" named Cory Chance. The heavy-set hiker, trail name "Second Chance," had been vlogging his PCT adventure since February and his YouTube videos had amassed over a hundred thousand views. Other PCT hikers, like Pope and Smokey, were there as well, and it didn't matter how long it had been since they'd showered or that they wore Superman pajama pants and smelled like their names; Sally hugged them like they were family.

Cathy gave Sally enough time to greet everyone before corralling the group. She briefed the volunteers on safety and how to handle any clues they found. Then, Wayne Frudd, the Yakima County officer who led the team that found the ditty bag, echoed Cathy's speech before warning us that this was *not* an official search, implying that we needed to make a good impression by conducting ourselves cautiously and professionally. Cathy divided us up into teams, while Aaron Wheeler handed out two-way radios set to the same frequency. We split into our squads and hiked south, deeper into the backcountry, each headed to our designated search areas. Today's focus was to search along the PCT between Chinook Pass and the site where the Yakima SAR team had found the ditty bag, near the headwaters of Laughingwater Creek.

Once the ground searchers deployed, Sally and Marcia drove from Chinook Pass to a remote helipad. Cathy had chartered a helicopter to aid in the endeavor, which was generously paid for by Marcia. Sally acted "calm and cool" as she approached the aircraft, but inside, her nerves tingled. She'd never been in a helicopter before. *God, if this thing goes down*, she thought as it lifted off the ground, *there's not a damn thing I can do about it.*

Cathy's voice came through Sally's headset. "We don't expect you to search."

But Sally couldn't help herself. As the helicopter lifted into the air, she scanned the landscape below for signs of Kris. The terrain was speckled with an array of stunning features, from humongous mountains and valleys cut by ancient glaciers, down to the gigantic trees and sparkling lakes. All of it was "absolutely breathtakingly gorgeous," and it went on and on and on. *No wonder we haven't found him yet.*

While Sally took in a bird's-eye view of our search area, I was on the ground leading a team of volunteers through the woods.

The searchers assigned to me were men and women, young and old. They were fit hikers, but most had never conducted a line search. I gave them a quick tutorial on how to spread out in a single line, half of the team on each side of the trail, and directed them to walk forward while maintaining a distance between each searcher of no more than twenty-five feet. Once we were in position, the team walked slowly, eyes to the ground, searching for clues, while I stayed in the center of their line and issued instructions that kept them in a straight row, moving as one entity. The volunteers learned quickly, took their duty seriously, and worked well together. I was proud to lead them as we performed a methodical search across miles of challenging terrain. When Sally's helicopter flew above us, we waved. She could pick us out by our orange shirts and hats.

Watching us work moved Sally in a surreal way. As she gazed down from the helicopter, she couldn't help but be grateful for the people below, walking in a line through the forest, hoping to help her find the answers she'd been seeking for years. In addition to the volunteers, hundreds of oblivious hikers were out having fun that day. Sally's thoughts bounced back and forth.

*Oh my God, it's so vast.*

*How can we ever find him?*

*Damn, there are so many hikers down there, it looks like Disneyland.*

*Why hasn't someone stumbled upon him yet?*

*Surely somebody will go take a pee behind the right tree someday, and then . . .*

When she'd first visited Washington in November 2016, after Kris's disappearance, Sally wasn't encouraged to participate in the official search operation. She never saw a command post and didn't get to meet the professionals looking for her son and thank them. She got the distinct impression that "they didn't want me there."

In my opinion, this was an unintentional but grave oversight on the part of the authorities. On extended operations, search managers should plan for ways to allow family members to take part. The simple act of contributing to the search effort gives someone a tiny sense of agency over this horrible thing that's happening to them. Visiting the command post, meeting a few searchers in person, seeing the concern and professionalism in their faces—hugging them, thanking them, crying with them—these experiences connect the family to the larger humanity encompassing their personal tragedy.

After that first traumatic trip to Washington, Sally avoided the state where she'd experienced so much pain. Nearly three years later, she felt ready to return so she could join this renewed effort to find Kris. Acting as an operations chief, Cathy had organized a safe and effective search that ruled out acres of land. My team found a pair of women's shoes, collected lots of plastic water bottles, and spotted a pine marten in a tree. Despite our efforts, by the end of our day, we were still no closer to solving the case of Kris Fowler.

That afternoon, when we returned to the trailhead, John Anders, a local mountaineer, had set up to feed our small army of searchers. Anders had been mourning the recent death of his outdoorsy mother; after he learned about Sally and her grief, he felt connected to her and wanted to lend his support. Four of the sturdiest hikers—including Colin Hurley, the friend who started the PCT with Kris in 2016, and David Wolfe, the local who gave Sally a ride to Packwood—were still out on the trail. These kind men and one woman spent four days in the backcountry combing the remote area where Briscoe's man discovered the toiletry bag. They found a massive elk skull with antlers but little else.

We were starting to wonder if the ditty bag was really left by Kris, or if it was just one more dead-end lead left behind by a random, absent-minded backpacker.

On Sunday, Morgan and I changed tactics and instead followed up on the blue item mentioned in the text Sally had received on

Friday at White Pass. A hiker had sent us photos of the tarp he had retrieved from near the summit of Naches Peak. When it comes to abandoned gear found in the wilderness, cheap blue tarps are ubiquitous. But Morgan and I have a hard time letting a lead go, and for Sally's sake, we followed this tip to the end. From Missouri, Morgan studied the photographs on his computer while I viewed them simultaneously on my cell phone. Because of the style of ropes tied to it, we were already thinking this tarp was a random item left behind by a tired peak bagger, which meant it most likely was unrelated to Kris's case.

The night after we spread Mike Fowler's ashes on the trail, Sally, Cathy, Marcia, Theresa, and I had met at a picnic table on the grounds of our hotel. Too fatigued to go out for dinner, our food choices were sparse: rum and cokes, potato chips, trail mix, and more of the Killer Brownies made in Dayton, Ohio. Sally later described the evening as "good women. Good conversation." The morning when Sally cried by the lake, I had become anxious for her, but my concerns lifted as I enjoyed the company of this generous and supportive group of women—all of us brought together by tragedy and bonded by our journey through it—and I relaxed. We shared war stories about the more complicated characters associated with our searches, like all the narcissists who hijacked our missions to suit their own agendas. The rum kicked in, and we laughed, a lot. In the past, when she started to enjoy herself after Kris disappeared, Sally had felt guilty. From here on out, she would no longer apologize for the times she was happy.

But two days later, on Sunday, Sally had to do the thing she had been dreading for years: fly back to Ohio for a *second* time without finding her son. It hit her once Mount Rainier appeared outside her window. Sally later said, "It was awful leaving without him again." Then, she broke down and "had an ugly cry," but she was more aware of what she was dealing with. And what she saw during her helicopter flight above the search area had shifted her perspective on the difficulties surrounding her son's case.

"I'm a visual person," Sally explained, "so it made more sense to me [why Kris couldn't be found] once I'd seen it from the air." Leaving Washington without finding Kris was nearly as painful as it had been three years ago, but now there was more acceptance, more understanding of why things happened the way they did, and good memories were slowly balancing out all the bad ones.

You could say a trail angel earns her wings once a thru-hiker gives her a trail name. Sally earned the name "Trail Mom," a nod to her yearly safety warnings on the "PCT Class of" Facebook groups, which she still writes for bands of new hikers. These posts are titled "Tips from a Mother: Sally Fowler's Advice to Pacific Crest Trail Thru-hikers," and they always include the edict: "And one more thing, call your mom."

On the day of the search at Chinook Pass, a gentleman in a floppy hat walked up to Sally and said, "I want to thank you for everything you've done for the hiker community."

"I can't take credit for that. It's a group effort."

"Well, you're right about that, but it wouldn't be manifesting in the way it is without you. You have every right to be proud of all the changes you've made."

The guy was older, a quiet type who didn't fancy being in the group photos. He told her that he'd been hiking his whole life and because of Sally's Facebook posts, his hiking buddies were now talking more about safety and prevention. "I think you're the catalyst for it," he added, and Sally wept—but in a good way.

Though she still didn't have all the answers she sought, Sally was thankful that she was surrounded by her "amazing new friends," memorializing her ambiguous loss with the volunteer searchers who loved her, and whom she loved back. Being there in person made all the difference.

"It was magical" is how she summed up her second trip to Washington. "It was worth a million dollars."

Six months after our trip to Washington, doctors discovered three tumors in Cathy's breast. A surgery to remove the malignancies was scheduled for September 11, 2020. Cathy had returned to Pennsylvania to be near a sister who could help her recover from the procedure when something unimaginable happened. On August 23, the sister Cathy was relying on to care for her after surgery was attacked by a mentally deranged man.

The man had been stalking Cathy's teenage niece for months, forcing her mother, Karen Short, to file a restraining order against him. But a piece of paper doesn't stop an ex-boyfriend from breaking into your home armed with a dagger and a baseball bat. In a terrifying blitz, the ex-boyfriend stabbed, beat, and bit Cathy's sister, her niece, and a family friend, casting blood all over the house. The family friend fought off the ex-boyfriend, who fled the scene only to be captured by authorities the next day. The suspect had slashed Karen Short's throat so deeply, she spent time in the ICU and needed multiple surgeries to repair the damage. Miraculously, they all survived, though the male friend and Cathy's sister were hospitalized for days.

Cleaning up the crime scene fell upon Cathy. "It was a horrific attack, as you can tell from looking at all of this," she led a reporter through her sister's blood-spattered apartment. "I want you to see this because it shouldn't have happened."

Three weeks later, while recovering from her own surgery, Cathy watched over her sister's care, pushed prosecutors to do their job, and searched for a new, safe place for her family to live. The pandemic complicated everything.

A few weeks later, in October, I met up with Cathy in Idyllwild, California. I'd seen the optimistic realist bulldoze her way through setbacks before. But this was different. Cancer. Violence. Surgery. Attempted murder. How could anyone going through all that have anything left over for helping other people? Doctors had prescribed a new medication to keep Cathy's cancer at bay, but she was sore from the operation, and a haze of weariness muffled her spunk and positivity.

During our visit, Cathy showed me a story in the *Idyllwild Crier*, a local newspaper that the proprietors had provided in our rooms at the Idyllwild Bunkhouse. Over the last year, four people had gone missing while in or near the San Jacinto Mountains, and the local authorities couldn't find them. I proposed we scout the last known points for two of those cases. For the heck of it. Perhaps the expedition would take Cathy's mind off all her troubles back in Pennsylvania.

People described Rosario "Chata" Garcia as the life of the party, but during the summer of 2020, they had noticed some changes. The loving grandmother was forgetting things that had happened only five minutes earlier, and while visiting out-of-town family, Garcia left her hotel room and couldn't find her way back. "She was in the parking lot," her daughter, Maggie Garcia Zavala, told reporters. "She didn't know what she was doing there...and she was crying."

Married for fifty years to a Vietnam veteran, Garcia loved to dance and made friends everywhere she went. Like many of us, the seventy-three-year-old from Hemet, California, was feeling cooped up and isolated during the pandemic lockdowns. On July 7, 2020, a few days after the incident at the hotel, Garcia drove off in her silver 2016 Nissan Sentra to visit a friend. When she didn't return home that night, her family reported her missing. Two days later, a hiker came across Garcia's silver Sentra high-centered on a rock on the rugged dirt road to the Sawmill Trailhead, twenty miles east of Idyllwild. Garcia's car keys and purse were gone. Riverside County sent ATVs, aircraft, and bloodhounds to look for her. They searched for several days to no avail.

The inability of the Sheriff's Office to find their matriarch devastated Garcia's family. They posted flyers, pleaded for help on Facebook, and conducted a few searches on their own. "I just want answers," Garcia's daughter implored. "I want to make sure that she's okay."

Garcia had been missing three months when Cathy and I walked up the dirt road to the Sawmill Trailhead. The desert terrain—boulders, cactus, and brush—was a suitable environment to conduct a grid search by drone. Some people believed that Garcia was a victim of foul play. An elderly woman who walked with a cane could not drive her car that far up a rugged dirt road, they reasoned. But Cathy and I placed little faith in that theory. Garcia went missing in July, when the daytime temperatures were extreme. And she was exhibiting symptoms of dementia, a condition prone to make people wander from home. I had looked up the relevant statistics in Dr. Robert Koester's book, *Lost Person Behavior*. According to Koester, when a dementia subject leaves a road into a wilderness setting, they move straight ahead "until they get stuck" in "brush or briars or drainages" and do not travel far.

*She's here*, we both thought as we walked back to our cars. *We can find her.*

As I had hoped, our scouting expedition revitalized Cathy. A month later, she returned to Garcia's LKP with Pam Coronado. Pam scratched up the sides of her new SUV before they reached the rock where Garcia had high-centered her car. Cathy pinned the coordinates on the Gaia app on her phone. The women fanned out, searching on foot, battling cactus the entire time—but by the time the sun was starting to set, they hadn't found any clues and knew they had to call it a day. Pam felt awful. Someone's mother was lost out there, all alone.

"Her family probably believes no one cares," Cathy sighed. "I want to help them."

And she had an idea on how to do it.

Western States Aerial Search had perfected its technique while helping Cathy search for John Sturkie and David O'Sullivan. This terrain was ideal for drone searching, and Greg Nuckolls's team was composed of the right guys for the job. Since they would be searching within the boundaries of the San Bernardino National Forest, but not inside a designated wilderness area, WSAS could fly their drones there, legally. Still, she had seen how searches conducted by well-intentioned amateurs raised a family's expectations too high. Considering how her efforts might negatively impact Garcia's family, Cathy decided to conduct this search behind the scenes. That way, if she failed, no one would know—and, more importantly, no one would get hurt.

Cathy was itching to search right away, but the WSAS drone pilots weren't available until January 2021. WSAS works entirely on a volunteer basis. All the pilots have day jobs and live in Utah, hundreds of miles away. Cathy booked them an Airbnb and paid for their travel expenses with money donated to her cause.

On a Thursday, the WSAS team drove eleven hours to Southern California. All weekend, the pilots spent their days flying their drones in lawnmower grids over designated search zones surrounding the road where Garcia's car was found. At night, Theresa Sturkie cooked meals at the Airbnb that Cathy had rented while the drone pilots downloaded thousands of high-quality images onto their laptops. One pilot had to work Monday morning, so they left Sunday afternoon and didn't get home until late.

That evening, Cathy sent us a link to the image files, and Morgan jumped in. He took a moment to silently ask Mrs. Garcia to guide him to the right image before performing a cursory search of the thumbnails to see which photos "spoke" to him. The quality of the WSAS photographs pleased Morgan; he could see and identify items as small as a rusted tin can and individual blades of agave. After scanning over a hundred images, he spotted something out of place. A black-and-white striped blob, a purse maybe, and some fabric that looked like blue jeans. It was after midnight in Missouri when Morgan posted a photo to our private Facebook group.

"Possible blue clothing," Morgan noted, "next to striped purse, on sloped ground."

Cathy woke up early the next morning. As soon as she saw the photo Morgan posted, she texted me: "Almost positive we found Garcia." Then she called Greg Nuckolls. Using the coordinates from the image with the clothing, Greg found more photographs of the same area. What we saw in those images, taken from a different angle, removed all doubt. Working together, WSAS and Cathy's team had found human remains within five hundred feet of where Garcia had abandoned her car.

A few hours later, Cathy led a convoy of law enforcement officers to the site. It had snowed overnight, and the dirt road was now wet and sloppy. A deputy driving the lead car got stuck in the muck. Cathy pressured the officer to dig out his vehicle and keep going. She didn't want the Garcias suffering another day of not knowing, but the snow was too deep. Officials delayed the recovery operation until conditions improved.

Once Riverside County was able to retrieve the remains, the coroner confirmed the bones belonged to Rosario Garcia. They found no evidence of foul play. After studying the case, I developed a theory: Perhaps, Garcia's dementia confused her to the point that she drove out to the desert and up a dirt road, until her car got stuck. Out of habit, she grabbed her purse and car keys before getting out of her car. Then she walked down the road to a sharp curve, but instead of rounding the corner, she walked straight off the road and down a ravine until the heat, or the brush, stopped her.

Receiving news that your loved one's body has been found is never a good thing. However, if Cathy hadn't taken the case, Garcia's family wouldn't have known what happened to their fun-loving matriarch; they might still be searching for her to this day. On Facebook, Laura Atencia, Garcia's daughter-in-law, described Cathy as "the angel" who brought their beloved Chata home.

"What the county couldn't do," Atencia wrote, "Cathy did in three days."

A spokesperson with the Riverside County Sheriff's Office was less moved. In a news report on the case, he briefly mentioned to reporters that "trekkers" had located the remains.

In reality, Cathy's search for Rosario Garcia was a well-coordinated mission involving hundreds of hours, a dozen experienced volunteers, funding from a benefactor, and specialized equipment worth thousands of dollars.

"We are constantly training and improving our technique," Greg Nuckolls said of WSAS. "We're passionate about the work. Our goal is to get the absolute best images possible so that folks like Morgan will be able to identify what they are seeing."

Heartened by the mission's success, Cathy still believes—even now—that the strategy she and WSAS used to find Rosario Garcia is a repeatable process. "When official SAR groups lack the means or the funding for a well-coordinated drone mission with reliable image searchers, we can help."

But for this technique to work on a larger scale, people like Cathy need more help than they're getting. We need machine learning geniuses to design an artificial intelligence program that cooperates effectively with human squinters. We need squads of trained drone pilots, skilled image squinters, and ground searchers fit enough to respond to backcountry leads. We need government agencies to be flexible and permit these operations on public lands. Then, perhaps, thousands of aerial images can be scanned for the right clues within hours. Then, perhaps, the technique that Cathy, Morgan, and Western States Aerial Search have proven works will become so doable that SAR agencies and nonprofits around the world will use it to resolve dozens of cold missing hiker cases a year, allowing more families to bring their loved ones home.

In 2018, Cathy had entreated the universe, "I haven't found anyone. You need to show me a sign, or I'm done!" Two years later, the universe responded. And yet, despite all her search efforts focused on finding Sylvia, Fowler, and O'Sullivan, the answers about what exactly happened to the PCT Missing evaded us still.

Cathy attributed this paradox to what she called divine timing. "We haven't found them yet because we need to learn things. If we found David right away, we wouldn't know about some of the scams out there and be able to warn families about them. We would not have learned about [the inadequacies of] the Sheriff's Office and how initial investigations can go wrong. We wouldn't have learned about [the hazards in] the San Jacintos and what prevention measures needed to be done there. Divine timing means once we've learned everything we need to know, then we will find them."

"Do you see some sort of greater purpose at hand?" I asked.

"Yes, definitely a greater purpose here. If you look at everything that went wrong—oh my goodness—it was all so we could help other people in the future."

# *Afterword*

Initially, I had planned to travel to Maryland to meet Chris Sylvia's mother, Nancy Warman, in person, during the spring of 2020. I wanted to show her Chris's paperback, *Siddhartha,* and share with her everything that I'd learned while investigating her son's case. Unfortunately, coronavirus forced me to delay the trip. Six months later, in September, Chris's grandmother called to tell me her daughter, Nancy, had died from side effects related to her struggle with alcoholism, a condition that worsened after Chris's disappearance.

Crestfallen by this news, I texted Sally. Twenty-two years after my futile search for Gabriel Parker at the Grand Canyon, I had promised Chris's mother that I'd get her some answers, but she died before I could provide them.

"It's okay," Sally comforted me. "Now, she knows."

A few weeks later, I posted photos of Chris's tattoo on Twitter and asked Chinese speakers for an accurate translation.

*Author's rendering of Chris Sylvia's tattoos.*

According to his brother, Chris believed the symbols on his torso meant "accept, learn, and let go." Yet, English speakers requesting Asian-language tattoos sometimes make humiliating mistakes. Three Chinese translators gave me a more nuanced interpretation. They said the symbol for "accept" means *to receive/get.* "Learn" is more appropriately interpreted as *to wake up from sleep/consciousness.* And "let go" is *to give up/release.* When I asked translator Brenda Gong to put all that in context, she concluded the advice delivered by Chris Sylvia's tattoo is "to intentionally give up."

Gong's translation startled me. Even for this skeptic, it felt like a sign that I should heed—but one I would never fully comprehend. For decades, I'd carried with me a lot of regret after I gave up on finding Gabriel Parker; in the past few years, I'd picked up the case of the PCT Missing and added it to the load. For me, these cases, like the meaning behind Chris's tattoo, were an unsolvable riddle— a Zen Buddhist koan designed to "break the mind" as we grapple with ambiguity and paradox in our lives.

"Accept, learn, let go" isn't an answer.

It's a fundamental question.

*Why do we, as human beings, keep struggling so hard and so often to search for answers that we know we may never find?*

Three years after Kris Fowler went missing, Amber Johnson got a new tattoo on the inside of her wrist—a dragonfly with teal and lavender wings. This was Ultra Violet's vision of the ink that Sherpa said he planned to get to celebrate the completion of his PCT thru-hike. Today, whenever Amber looks at her arm, she remembers Sherpa as he was on the trail. Happy and free. Climbing rock formations. Doing yoga in the forest. Closing his eyes to enjoy the gentle kiss of the sun on his skin.

Amber sent Sally a photo of her dragonfly tattoo along with the story behind it. When Sally shared this on Facebook, Zuckerberg's shrewd algorithms did their thing. A few days later, an advertisement for a necklace popped up on Sally's feed. The ad featured a silver medallion with two dragonflies, one large and one small. Their wings sparkled with aquamarine jewels, and like a star in the sky, a peace symbol floated above them. The smaller dragonfly appeared to be flying away, into the far distance, while the larger one stayed behind. Encircling this scene was an inscription: *My mind still talks to you. And my heart still looks for you. But my soul knows you are at peace.*

Zuckerberg cynics, be damned. Sally's heart told her the necklace was a sign. One that came to her through Facebook. And so, Sally bought it.

Today, a similar solace reaches her through the scenic shots and smiling selfies that she views in the hiker Facebook groups. "Washington Hikers and Climbers" is her favorite. "I love this group!" she posted in 2019. "Your photos are so amazing, and it gives me so much peace knowing my son is surrounded by so much beauty, and I know he is loving it all!"

In her own way, Sally has given Kris up to the mountains, but that doesn't mean she's let go of her desire to find him. She still wants to know what happened. She still wants to bring her son home, to Ohio, where he can rest in peace near his friends and family.

In Pam Coronado's reading on the Kris Fowler case, there were "no trees, just rocks, gray rocks, everywhere." These rocks weren't like the massive identifiable boulders the clairvoyant saw in her mind's eye when she watched David O'Sullivan tumble. And there was no hint of "human intervention" like she'd envisioned with Chris Sylvia. With Kris Fowler, Pam saw the hiker "slide down really fast… a force of speed pulling him down and earth, or snow, going with him, and he was covered up." With most cases, the psychic's visions left her optimistic the missing subject can be found. But Kris's case reminded Pam of a reading she did on a diver lost in the Pacific

Ocean. With Kris and the diver, her visions told her that "the odds of finding his remains are really, really miniscule."

But that's not how she put it to Sally Fowler.

Pam spent an hour on the phone detailing her vision to Sally, but in describing the sensation that we may never find Kris, the psychic minced her words. "I'm so careful what I say to the families, so careful," Pam explained. "I don't want the responsibility of telling somebody we're never going to find their loved one. Nobody wants to do that." Besides, "what if I'm wrong?"

Back in 1995, I'd worried that I was wrong to tell the parent of a missing hiker that he had been a good father, that his son would have been proud of how hard he worked to find him, and that now it was okay for us to stop searching. I remember how awkward, useless, and guilty I had felt in the moment. Who was *I* to give a grieving man permission to stop looking for his son?

This is always a delicate subject for loved ones of the missing. "Not saying you should" is how one friend brought this up to Sally after her second trip to Washington, "but will you ever be able to stop looking for Kris?"

"It's probably going to kill me if I don't," Sally replied, "but the people in that [Facebook] group don't let you stop. And my heart. My heart won't let me stop."

Like Sally, Carmel O'Sullivan still prays for answers. In her dreams, she shouts and shouts for David, waiting for a response that never comes. "I can't plan anything or go on any long trips," she said recently, "because I never know when I might get the call." And yet, as much as she and Con yearn for the day when they'll get that horrible call, the one that means they can bring their son back to Ireland, they also can't stand the thought of anyone else getting hurt while looking for him. That would only multiply their heartbreak.

"It's *our* cross" is how Con explained their burden—and the responsibility that comes with it—to his wife.

After three years of working with these mothers and listening to their stories, I'm more at peace with my failure to locate Gabriel Parker so many years ago. I did my best to find that missing hiker, and considering all of the critical duties my younger self was juggling back then, my colleagues and I did a decent job of helping his father navigate the crisis. I knew better than to tell Parker's dad he should give up, move on, and get over it. That's impossible. But when a loved one has been missing for a long time, and the fatigue and the uncertainty become too much to bear, it *is* okay for us to stop searching. Or at the very least, it is okay to take a break from it.

And, for the record, if I disappear while hiking, I don't want my family to work so hard to find me. I don't want them to suffer so much for so long if something bad happens to me while I'm in the mountains. A request like this is profound and personal, not unlike the advance directives we prepare for doctors and our next of kin to guide them while they make tough medical decisions during our last days on earth.

"If I ever go missing in the wilderness," is what I instructed my husband after I fractured my ankle, "take a year, if you must, to get it out of your system, but after that, for the love of God, stop looking for me."

For me, I can't imagine a better final resting place than a shaded nook in the forest or a granite ledge under a star-filled universe.

In 2019, the intelligent blonde woman with a soft heart who needed therapy after being gaslighted by Dr. Vass and his believers called me with a proposition. Was I interested in creating a nonprofit to help families of missing hikers? Even though this woman was serious, and she had the means to provide logistical support and financial backing, I balked at her offer. Since 2007, I'd worked full-time as a nurse. And, in all honesty, my twenty-five years in health care and public service had depleted all the idealistic fuel one needs to spend her off-duty hours establishing, promoting, and managing a nonprofit.

Sally had expressed interest in creating a foundation in honor of Kris, but, after some initial conversations with a grant writer, she decided that her day job, combined with her ongoing search for Kris, demanded too much of her time. I also suspected that, like me, she didn't want to take on any new group project hassles. When I brought the idea up to Cathy, she demurred until her tax guy told her she was operating as a one-woman nonprofit anyway. Why not make it official? After mulling it over for several months, Cathy agreed to an introduction.

The intelligent blonde woman connected Cathy to grant writer Susi Banes, and the two women initiated the legal process of obtaining 503(c) status for the Fowler-O'Sullivan Foundation (FOF). The founding board members (Cathy, Morgan Clements, Pam Coronado, Mackenzie Pollard, Gloria Boyd, Theresa Sturkie, and I) came up with the following mission statement:

> With safety and compassion as our core principles, the Fowler-O'Sullivan Foundation provides assistance to families of missing hikers, connects them to vetted resources, facilitates searches on their behalf once official efforts have been suspended, and supports initiatives to prevent future missing hiker cases.

When Cathy told Sally that she had named her nonprofit in honor of David O'Sullivan and Kris Fowler, it gave Sally "a mental lift." She believed that wherever he was now, Kris would be embarrassed by all the drama displayed in the Facebook group his stepmother administers to find him, but "he would love the Fowler-O'Sullivan Foundation and its mission to help families of missing hikers. He would think that was cool."

In early January 2021, Cathy's foundation received a grant that allowed her to pay any travel expenses associated with her first case. We found Rosario Garcia, the missing grandmother, two weeks later—on January 24, 2021.

Later that same year, Cathy organized a drone search for Chris Sylvia in collaboration with Western States Aerial Search. I participated in the image squinting and followed up on the leads we saw in the photographs. The image quality was excellent and covered an approximately three-mile radius of Mike's Place and the gear site. I found a small green box and Morgan spotted something weird under a boulder. I hiked into the coordinates and discovered the green box was an ammunition can geocache and the mysterious object under the boulder was a trekking pole. Alas, neither item led us to Chris Sylvia.

Not long after I first met Cathy in 2017, she told me explicitly that "I'm not here to make friends" while outlining her priorities for helping the families of missing hikers. But, years later, when she asked me what I planned to do after I wrangled our stories together and wrote this book, I heard a tenderness in her voice. Was the writer she spent three years pouring her heart out to going to abandon her and her cause once I had what I needed?

"Oh, don't worry." I smiled. "You can't get rid of me that easily."

I meant this. I had grown to love Cathy and all that she represented. But a moment later, I ran my palms down my face and let out a weary breath.

"I want to help, but..." I hesitated.

My long search for the PCT Missing had exhausted me to the bone. Tasks associated with being a founding board member of Cathy's nonprofit had become a constant chore. The seven-inch scar on my ankle was a harsh reminder of the sacrifices that I, and many others, had made. Slowly but surely, discontent had crept in, and I was pining for the more pleasant activities I did in my spare time before I had taken on all these missing hiker cases.

"I've got to finish this damn book," I explained. "I'm a nurse in a pandemic who wants to retire and enjoy life a little before I die."

Cathy completely understood. *Life's too short to spend it in an office with no windows.* The woman with breast cancer, the pharmacy manager who left a corporate job to attempt a thru-hike of the PCT at fifty-two, knew *exactly* where I was coming from. But "intentionally give up" wasn't on Cathy's to-do list, and she's still out there looking for new clues.

"Here's another possible David O'Sullivan area to search," she recently posted in our private Facebook group. "I want to get this droned."

According to Dr. Pauline Boss, to be resilient in the face of ambiguous loss, we must "learn how to hold two opposing ideas in [our] minds at the same time." In the end, Pam's intuition could be right. No matter how hard we search, we may never find Kris Fowler. And we may never learn what happened to David O'Sullivan or Chris Sylvia. Or maybe someone like Cathy Tarr or Morgan Clements has found one of them by the time you read this. Or maybe, decades from now, a random hiker or hunter stumbles upon a body in the forest, by chance. Or maybe one of the PCT Missing resurfaces in society to tell us he's alive.

Any day, a new lead—the one that breaks the case—may drop from the sky, but I've come to accept the harsh reality. There's a good chance that despite all our best efforts, all of the time we spent searching by land and by screen, I may never learn what happened to the PCT Missing.

But I do find comfort in one thing—the trail. Those 2,653 magnificent miles are solid, constant, enduring. Whatever fate befell those men, when they saw an opportunity to escape the incessant buzz of civilization and immerse themselves in the magic and splendor of the natural world, they took it. I, too, have responded to the call of the wild, and I hope they were able to experience the same joy I did as they embarked on their own respective journeys.

Most of all, I take heart in knowing this same call—the one that drummed so fiercely within the hearts of Chris Sylvia, Kris Fowler, and David O'Sullivan—lives on, especially every spring, when a new batch of hopefuls set out to walk the long path of the Pacific Crest Trail, plunging, climbing, and twisting its way through the mountains.

# *Acknowledgments*

First and foremost, I'm overwhelmed by the generosity, selflessness, and courage I observed during the years I worked on this book. More than a hundred people have searched for one or more of the PCT Missing. I, alongside their families, appreciate every single person (volunteer and professional) who participated in a search for these missing hikers and/or investigated their cases. We are also grateful to everyone who donated funds to pay for gear, meals, and travel expenses to support air and ground searches. In a continuation of this charitable spirit, I am donating at least 10 percent of my advance and any royalties I receive from *Trail of the Lost* to the Fowler-O'Sullivan Foundation.

Among the many who volunteered their time to search, I'd like to acknowledge the following for their contributions: My August 2019 squad of line searchers: Laura Kosten Blatt, Tyler Meyerhoff, Laura Hausen, Jessie Palacious, Benjamin Palma, David Sloothoff. The five backpackers who spent five days in the backcountry, searching around the ditty bag site: Colin Hurley, David Wolfe, Katie Howe, Tim Crocker, and Scott Graves. The hunters who organized the search that inspired Cathy to come to Washington, Andrea and Josh Kirkman. Searchers for David O'Sullivan: "Hiker Jim," Kristina Mohos, Jessica Knoelk, Amy Wulf Johns, Martin Carew, Tim Riley, Jeanette and Johannah Ragland, John Powers, Jill Hileman Tavolazzi, and all the volunteers with the Irish Outreach

Center, San Diego. Western States Aerial Search pilots: Greg Nuck-olls, James Badham, Justin Holm, Brad Larson, David Reid, Fiona Rose Carmichael, Samuel Carmichael, and David Harolde. And last but not least, our desktop heroes, the image squinters: Mary Kaufman, Karen Frauson, Jennifer Mengel, Jill Ferdinand Rickett, Avaline Jewell, Judy Spowart, Laurencia Bourget, Tasha Van Der Meer, Sandra Oostlander, Aaron Samuel Wheeler, Mackenzie Pol-lard, Gloria Boyd, and Sarah Kelly.

Excerpts from early drafts of this manuscript benefited from the advice of professional editors Mary Kole and Audie Alcorn. The acumen I gained from Lisa Cooper Ellison's "Camp Struc-ture" course helped me tackle those dreaded chapter summaries, and my screenwriting friend, Diah Wymont, propped me up with invigorating discussions about inciting incidents, pinch points, and dark nights of the soul. My mother, Patricia Lankford, kept me well supplied with high-quality notebooks, my father, Ted Lankford Jr., instilled in me a joy for hiking. If it weren't for my longtime hik-ing buddy, Nicole "Hurricane Red" Vanoni, and her partner, Byron Freney, I may have never met the keen-eyed literary agent Andrea Blatt. Andrea immediately grasped what was special about this story and shepherded it into capable hands at Hachette.

I owe a round of watermelon mojitos to my badass editor, Carrie Napolitano, who kept her red pen well aimed while covering my back and shouting for me to "dig deeper!" This book is a tidier one thanks to project editor Amber Morris and copyeditor Christina Palaia. I appreciate all the hard work the design team put into this project, the photographers for sharing their work, and professional illustrator Joe David who created the maps under a tight deadline.

I'm grateful to the following experts and sources for sharing their insights, experiences, and/or their expertise: Paul Crawford, Kristy Slaven, Rosie Peragine, Chris Kounkel, "Strange Bird," "Jet Fighter," "Stork," "Man Bear Pig," Steven "Big DogCruxen"

Sheppard, Jeffery "Hatchet" Lewis, Randy "Redo" Berton, Daniel Bardwell, John Reece, Eric Trockman, Jordan Babb, Ryan Goebels, Randy "Sage" Welch, Paul Lockney, Mary "Pilsbury" Scudder, Pat "Kushy" Tyche, Mary "Trail Mary" Litch, Marilyn and David Linder, Don Line, Patrice Mallory, Mike Herrera, Deputy Paige Kneeland, Detective Ron Garverick, Detective Jackie Nichols, Nic Sandberg, Seth Derish, Melissa "T-Rex" Rexillius, Wayne Frudd, Marion Matthews, Kory Knox, Liz Fritz, Keven Bachard, Shawn Delaney, Cora Lee Cooper, Doug Newton, Jon Lines, Maria Mathison Prentice, Amy Mundorff, William Whittaker, Barbie Bigelow, Edward Newland, William T. Weldon, Shelton Brown, David Pike, Ann Japenga, Ilya Koshkin, Marcia O'Rourke, Ingrid Tanner, and Dr. Monte Miller.

Raj Panchal, the proprietor of the Idyllwild Bunkhouse, brought Cathy and me champagne when we needed it most. Josh McCoy gave me hospitality and homemade pizza. Dr. Bharat Desai bolted my bones back together and Dr. David Kipper took time out of his busy schedule to peer at pictures of "bones" on my iPad.

The following friends and family of the missing should be commended for going out of their way to help me tell this story with authenticity: Bob Giauque, Min Kim, Elizabeth Henle, Ron and Patty Sperl, Tory Strader, Brandi Valenza, Nancy Warman, and the unflappable Theresa Sturkie, who continues to pay it forward to other families of the missing. I'm also in awe of Con and Carmel O'Sullivan, who have shown an extraordinary amount of grace and generosity while facing a parent's worst nightmare. And I want you to know that Joshua Sylvia is a talented artist who remained patient, supportive, and forthcoming with me throughout the years I investigated his brother's case.

I'm indebted to Jon King. In addition to assisting me off that cursed mountain, the intrepid Englishman shared his immense knowledge on all things related to the San Jacintos. Meanwhile, the positive outlook, intuitive wisdom, and on-the-ground dedication displayed by the psychic Pam Coronado has melted the heart of this die-hard skeptic.

To Morgan Clements—one of the most dedicated and clever investigative partners I have ever worked with and who I trust implicitly although we've yet to meet face-to-face—I say, "Thanks for everything, and I'm looking forward to those beers we'll have by the firepit."

I'm also looking forward to a poolside rum and coke in Ohio with Sally Fowler. Her strength, forthrightness, and unbreakable sense of humor have been a wellspring of inspiration. I wish we had met under different circumstances, but I'm deeply honored that she entrusted me to write the story about her search for Kris. During my fact-checking process, when I called Sally to read parts of the manuscript to her over the phone, we both sobbed.

"I'm so sorry," I said, wiping away tears and apologizing for the plaintive storyline, "but maybe it's good that the writing makes us cry."

"Thank you," Sally replied, "for feeling it."

During my decades as a park ranger and a nurse, I've worked with scores of courageous and compassionate people, but I have never met anyone like Cathy Tarr. She invited me into her heart and her life and was always game to chase a lead. Cathy's dogged dedication to help the families of missing hikers—for nothing in return and despite all the setbacks she's faced—restores this cynic's faith in humanity, and our harrowing journey together keeps us connected. One evening, at sunset, we were enjoying a drink in Idyllwild when I looked out the window and saw Tahquitz Rock looming above the town.

"I'm afraid my book might scare people," I said, anxious to see how the optimistic realist would react to my somber revelation.

Undaunted, Cathy took a swig from her hard cider and said, "Maybe it should."

During the many times this endeavor rattled me, I was lucky to be married to retired Special Agent in Charge Kent Delbon, who must be sore from all the leads and theories I've bounced off him—not to mention the scratches and bruises he received while bush-whacking to drone coordinates. He kept this writer going through many periods of angst, frustration, and fatigue with an oft-repeated mandate: "Lankford, just get in there and file your report."

# Selected Bibliography

## Books

Asars, Tami. *Hiking the Pacific Crest Trail: Washington*. Seattle: Mountaineers Books, 2016.

Billman, Jon. *The Cold Vanish: Seeking the Missing in North America's Wilderness*. New York: Grand Central Publishing, 2020.

Boss, Pauline. *Loss, Trauma, and Resilience: Therapeutic Work with Ambiguous Loss*. New York: W. W. Norton, 2006.

Geiger, John. *The Third Man Factor: Surviving the Impossible*. New York: Hachette Books, 2009.

Go, Benedict. *Pacific Crest Trail Data Book*. Birmingham: Wilderness Press, 2013.

Hazard, Joseph T. *Pacific Crest Trails*. Seattle: Superior Publishing Company, 1946.

Hesse, Hermann. *Siddhartha*. Translated by Hilda Rosner. London: Bantam, 1982.

Hill, Kenneth, ed. *Managing the Lost Person Incident*. San Bernardino: NASAR, 1997.

Kelley, Dennis. *Mountain Search for the Lost Victim*. Montrose, CA: Dennis Kelley, 1973.

Kessler, David. *Finding Meaning: The Sixth Stage of Grief*. New York: Scribner, 2019.

Koester, Robert J. *Lost Person Behavior: A Search and Rescue Guide on Where to Look— for Land, Air, and Water*. Charlottesville, VA: dbS Productions, 2008.

Larabee, Mark, and Barney "Scout" Mann. *The Pacific Crest Trail: Exploring America's Wilderness Trail*. New York: Rizzoli International Publications, 2016.

Powell, Joshua M. *The Pacific Crest Trail: A Visual Compendium*. Seattle: Sasquatch Books, 2021.

Ryback, Eric. *The High Adventure of Eric Ryback*. San Francisco: Chronicle Books, 1971.

Salabert, Shawnte. *Hiking the Pacific Crest Trail: Southern California.* Seattle: Mountaineers Books, 2017.

Stoffel, Brett C., and Robert C. Stoffel. *Managing the Inland Search Function.* Centre-
ville, VA: NASAR, 1985

Strayed, Cheryl. *Wild: From Lost to Found on the Pacific Crest Trail.* New York: Vin-
tage, 2012.

Syrotuck, William G. *Analysis of Lost Person Behavior: An Aid to Search Planning.*
Mechanicsburg, PA: Barkleigh Productions, 1976.


**Articles, Papers, Presentations, and Theses**

Abdollah, Tami. "How a Suspected Killer Eluded Police on the Pacific Crest Trail."
Associated Press, August 18, 2015.

Associated Press. "Rescuers Trying to Aid Hiker Robbed at Gunpoint." Associated Press, July 10, 2017.

Barnes, George. "Sex Assault Suspect Is Spotted." *Telegram & Gazette* (Worcester,
MA). August 7, 2008.

Donahue, Bill. "Kidnapped on the Pacific Crest Trail." *Backpacker.* December 12, 2019.

Ebersole, Rene. "He Teaches Police 'Witching' to Find Corpses. Experts Are
Alarmed." Marshall Project. March 17, 2022.

Federal Bureau of Investigation. "Open Investigation Based on Allegations That
Children Are Being Sexually Exploited." Case ID# 31C-CE-2799059 (2013).

Japenga, Ann. "Lost & Found: The Mystery of Louise Teagarden." *Sierra Magazine,*
January/February 2009.

KESQ News Team. "Cold Case Follow Up: Father Returns to Where Son Was
Killed." KESQ News (Palm Springs, CA), February 27, 2015.

Kotowski, Jason. "Clerk Who Reported Manhunt Suspect Says He's to Receive
Reward." *Bakersfield Californian,* August 17, 2015.

Kwak-Hefferan, Elisabeth. "Why Women Shouldn't Worry About Hiking Alone."
*Backpacker,* September 14, 2015.

Livermore, Jenn. "The Pacific Crest Trail: A History of America's Relationship
with Western Wilderness." Scripps Senior Thesis, 2014.

Taylor, Michelle. "Adding Scat to the Missing Persons Identification Forensic Tool-
box." Forensicmag.com, February 16, 2022.

Tompkins, Fred D., et al. "Matter Detector, Sensor and Locator Device and Methods of Operation." Patent #US10001577B2, publication date June 19, 2019.

Twelve Tribes. "Our Child Training Manual." 2000. http://question12tribes.com
/wp-content/uploads/2014/07/OUR-CHILD-TRAINING-MANUAL.pdf.

Vass, Arpad. "Forensics: Dr. Arpad Vass at TEDxYYC." YouTube video, 15:31. TEDx Talks, July 5, 2012. https://www.youtube.com/watch?v=l0Qd2nxMC2Y.

Weldon, William T., and Joseph Hupy. 2020. "Investigating Methods for Integrating Unmanned Aerial Systems in Search and Rescue Operations." *Drone* 4, no. 3: 38.

## Websites

Anonymous: http://searchandrescuescams.com/fraud/andrea-lankford/

Clements, Morgan: www.globalincidentmap.com

Coronado, Pam: www.pamcoronado.com

Forensic Recovery Services: www.forensicrecoveryservices.org

Fowler-O'Sullivan Foundation: www.fofound.org

King, Jon: www.sanjacjon.com

Lankford, Andrea: www.pctmissing.org

Pacific Crest Trail Association: www.pcta.org

Riverside Mountain Rescue Unit: www.rmru.org

Twelve Tribes: www.hikershostel.org

Valenza, Brandi: "Kira and 'Jim' on PCT Timeline." www.timetoast.com/timelines/kira-moon-pct

Winsor, Daniel: www.hikerbeta.com